Using Internet Primary Sources to Teach Critical Thinking Skills in History

Recent Titles in
Greenwood Professional Guides in School Librarianship

Using Internet Primary Sources to Teach Critical Thinking Skills in History

KATHLEEN W. CRAVER

Greenwood Professional Guides in School Librarianship
Harriet Selverstone, Series Adviser

GREENWOOD PRESS
Westport, Connecticut
London

Library of Congress Cataloging-in-Publication Data

Craver, Kathleen W.
　　Using Internet primary sources to teach critical thinking skills
　in history / Kathleen W. Craver.
　　　　p.　cm.—(Greenwood professional guides in school
　librarianship, ISSN 1074–150X)
　　Includes bibliographical references (p.) and index.
　　ISBN 0–313–30749–0 (alk. paper)
　　1. History—Study and teaching (Secondary)—United States.
　2. Critical thinking—Study and teaching (Secondary)—United States.
　3. Electronic information resource literacy—Study and teaching
　(Secondary)—United States.　4. History—Sources—Study and teaching
　(Secondary)—United States.　5. High school libraries—Activity
　programs—United States.　6. Junior high school libraries—Activity
　programs—United States.　I. Title.　II. Series.
　D16.2.C79　1999
　907.1'273—dc21　　　　99–17841

British Library Cataloguing in Publication Data is available.

Library of Congress Catalog Card Number: 99–17841
ISBN: 0–313–30749–0
ISSN: 1074–150X

First published in 1999

Greenwood Press, 88 Post Road West, Westport, CT 06881
An imprint of Greenwood Publishing Group, Inc.
www.greenwood.com

Printed in the United States of America

∞

The paper used in this book complies with the
Permanent Paper Standard issued by the National
Information Standards Organization (Z39.48–1984).

10 9 8 7 6 5 4 3 2 1

Contents

Acknowledgments xi

Introduction xiii

Part I   Using Critical Thinking Skills in History 1

Part II   Using Primary Sources 15

Part III   The Primary Source Sites 31

Ancient Civilizations

Diotima (3900 BCE–476 CE) 33

Vanished Kingdoms of the Nile: The Rediscovery of Ancient
Nubia (ca. 3800 BCE–300 CE) 34

Duke Papyrus Archive (ca. 2600 BCE) 35

The Egyptian Book of the Dead (2500 BCE) 36

Mystery of the Maya (2500 BCE–950 CE) 38

Exploring Ancient World Cultures: China (2205–479 BCE) 39

Law Code of Hammurabi (1750 BCE) 40

Perseus Project (1200–323 BCE) 42

Rome Resources Project (753 BCE–476 CE) 43

The Dead Sea Scrolls (200 BCE) 45

The Silk Road (ca. 202 BCE) 46

Early Christian Era 48

The Ecole Initiative (ca. 30–1500 CE) 48

Pompeii and Mt. Vesuvius (79 CE) 49

Lepers (ca. 300 CE) 51

Byzantium: Byzantine Studies on the Internet
(330–1453 CE) 52

Zen Buddhist Texts (ca. 500–1200 CE) 53

The Camelot Project (ca. 537 CE) 55

Eleventh–Fourteenth Centuries 57

Peter Abelard: Historia Calamitatum, "The Story of My
Misfortunes" (1079–1142) 57

The Crusades (1096–1270) 58

Robin Hood Project (ca. 1180–1210) 59

Statutes of Biella (1248 and 1348) 61

Extracts of Travels of Marco Polo (ca. 1300) 62

Plague and Public Health in Renaissance Europe (1347–1351) 63

The Forbidden City (1368–Present) 65

Fifteenth–Sixteenth Centuries 67

Tres Riches Heures (ca. 1412) 67

Leonardo da Vinci Museum (1452–1519) 68

Witchcraft: Joan's Witch Directory (1484–1692) 70

1492: An Ongoing Voyage (1492) 71

Extracts from Christopher Columbus' Journal (1492) 72

Vasco da Gama: Round Africa to India (1497–1498) 74

Public Executions in Early Modern England (ca. 1500–1600) 75

Missionaries and Mandarins: The Jesuits in China
(ca. 1500–1600) 76

Utopia by Sir Thomas More (1516) 78

Martin Luther's 95 Theses (1517) 79

The Works of Elizabeth I (1533–1603) 80

The History of Costume (1500–1800) 82

Letter from Lope de Aguirre, Rebel, to King Philip of Spain
(1561) 83

Seventeenth–Eighteenth Centuries 85

The Galileo Project (1564–1642) 85

United States Gazettes, Newspapers (1600–1900) 86

Account of the Great Fire of London (1666) 87

Accounts of Louis XIV (1671) 88

Essay on East-India Trade (1697) 90

Liberalism (1700s–1800s) 91

Native American History Archive (1700s–1980s) 92

Slavery Resources On-line (1700s–1800s) 94

Third Person, First Person: Slave Voices from the Rare Book, Manuscripts, and Special Collections Library (1700s–1800s) 95

The Age of Enlightenment in the Paintings of France's National Museums (1715–1799) 96

Colonial Lima (1748) 97

Reveries on the Art of War (1757) 99

The Industrial Revolution (1760–1848) 100

Lord Jeffrey Amherst's Letters Discussing Germ Warfare Against American Indians (1763) 101

Arctic Dawn Report (1768) 102

Documents from the Continental Congress and the Constitutional Convention (1774–1789) 104

Convicts to Australia (1788–1868) 105

Portraits of the Presidents and First Ladies (1789–1992) 106

The French Revolution (1789–1799) 108

United States Historical Census Data Browser (1790–1970) 109

A Vindication of the Rights of Woman with Strictures on Political and Moral Subjects (1792) 111

T. Robert Malthus Home Page (1798) 112

Nineteenth Century 114

Nationalism (1800s) 114

African American Perspectives (1818–1907) 115

Confessions of an English Opium Eater (1822) 116

The Confessions of Nat Turner (1831) 118

The Victorian Web (1837–1901) 119

The Marx/Engels Archive (1843–1888) 120

Views of the Famine (1845–1851) 121

Scientific American of the 19th Century (1845–1859) 123

Votes for Women: Selections from the National American Woman Suffrage Association Collection (1848–1921) 124

California As I Saw It: First-Person Narratives of California's
Early Years (1849–1900)   126

Valley of the Shadow (1850–1865)   128

Sectional Conflict (1850–1877)   129

Sectional Conflict, African-American Women (1850–1877)   130

Evolution of the Conservation Movement (1850–1920)   132

Origin of Species by Charles Darwin (1859)   133

London Low-Life: Beggars and Cheats (1860)   134

Letters from an Iowa Soldier in the Civil War (1862–1865)   135

Native American Documents Project (1870s)   137

Temperance and Prohibition (1873–1928)   138

Jack London (1876–1916)   140

The Northern Great Plains (1880–1920)   141

Jack the Ripper (1888)   142

How the Other Half Lives (1890)   144

The Georgetown Audio-visual Electronic Library Project for
the Study of Emile Zola and the Dreyfus Case (1894–1899)   145

Gold in the Klondike (1896)   147

Emma Goldman (1869–1940)   148

Anti-Imperialism in the United States (1898–1935)   149

"The White Man's Burden" and Its Critics (1899)   151

Twentieth Century   152

Life Automobile Page (1901–1995)   152

San Francisco Great Earthquake and the Fire of 1906 (1906)   153

The Middle East: Documents (1907–Present)   154

Mexican Revolution (1910)   156

Eyewitness: A North Korean Remembers (1911–1955)   157

Encyclopedia Titanic (1912)   158

Trenches on the Web (1914–1918)   160

Bolshevik "Coup d'Etat" (1917)   161

Library of Congress Soviet Archives Exhibit (1917–1991)   163

Treaty of Versailles (1919)   165

The Wolf Lewkowicz Collection (1922–1939)   166

Howard Carter Personal Diaries (1923)   167

California Gold Northern California Folk Music from the
Thirties (1930s)   168

The 1930s in Print (1930s)   170

The FDR Cartoon Archive (1932–1943)   171

Appeal to the League of Nations by Haile Selassie (1936)   172

American Life Histories (1936–1940)   174

The Nanjing Massacre (1937)   175

U-Boat War (1939–1945)   176

Primary Source Documents on the Holocaust (1939–1945)   178

Cybrary of the Holocaust (1939–1945)   179

Powers of Persuasion Posters from World War II (1939–1945)   180

Japanese Internment (1942)   181

World War II (1939–1945)   183

What Did You Do in the War Grandma? Women and World
War II (1939–1945)   185

Voices from the Dust Bowl (1940–1941)   186

Venona Project (1943–1980)   187

A-Bomb WWW Museum (1945)   189

The Japanese Surrender Documents of World War II (1945)   190

Nuremberg War Crimes Trials (1945–1946)   191

Crime, Justice & Race in South Africa (1948–Present)   193

Tibet: Tradition and Change (1950s)   194

The United States, China, and the Bomb (1950s–Present)   195

Korean War Project (1950–1953)   197

Senator Joe McCarthy—A Multimedia Celebration
(1950–1954)   198

Everest '97 (1953–1997)   199

CIA and Assassinations: The Guatemala 1954 Documents
(1954)   200

U.S. Nuclear History Documentation Project (1955–1982)   202

European Union (1957–Present)   203

The U-2 Incident (1960)   205

The Sixties Project (1960–1969)   206

Documents from the Women's Liberation Movement
(1960s–1970s)   208

The Berlin Crisis (1961)   209

The Cuban Missile Crisis: Fourteen Days in October (1962)   211

John F. Kennedy Assassination Homepage (1963)   212

Free Speech Movement (1964)   214

Black Panther Party Information (1966)   215

Sayings of Chairman Mao (The Little Red Book) (1967)   216

When Nixon Met Elvis (1970)   217

The Wars for Vietnam (1970s)   219

The India-Pakistan War (1971)   220

The Pentagon Papers (1971)   221

Watergate (1972)   222

The Contras and Cocaine (1985–1987)   224

The Chernobyl Disaster (1986)   225

Reactions to the Tiananmen Square Massacre (1989)   227

Computer History (1990s)   228

The Gulf War (1991)   230

Yugoslavia University of Minnesota Human Rights Library
(1991–Present)   231

NAFTA (North American Free Trade Agreement) (1994)   233

Quebec Separatism (1995)   234

Widnet—Statistics—Africa: Women in Development
Network (1995)   235

Coalition Against Slavery in Mauritania and Sudan
(1998–Present)   237

Selected Primary Source Databases   239

Index   247

Acknowledgments

I wish to thank my husband Charlie for his enthusiasm and encouragement while I worked on this book. I gratefully acknowledge the advice, interest, and support that my editors, Barbara Rader and Harriet Selverstone, gave me throughout this exciting project. I would also like to express my appreciation to copy editor Barbara Goodhouse whose attention to detail and knowledge of history greatly improved the book and David Palmer, production editor, for his highly professional assistance. Finally, I would like to thank NCS Librarian Sue Gail Spring for her tireless checking of Internet sites.

Introduction

THE NEED FOR INSTRUCTIONAL CHANGE

The instructional role of history educators and school library media specialists is being influenced not only by advances in technology but also by economic, educational, and employment changes. Faced with expanded access and increased storage and retrieval capabilities in an electronic environment, we are fast discovering how obsolete our former methods of instruction have become and how particularly limiting the textbook-lecture-classroom approach is to learning in this new electronic age (Craver 1994, 148).

With improvements in telecommunications, cable and satellite resources, computer hardware and software, scanners, CD-ROMs, and the Internet, school library media specialists and history educators have the ability to provide information to students on a scale never before imagined. The major thrust of these electronic changes is being generated by the nationwide installation of fiber-optic cabling. This telecommunications backbone, which currently supplies access to the Internet, serves as the engine that drives every type of information, whether it be book, recording, or video, to become digitized. Once digitized, information is no longer bound by time or place. It can be quickly and inexpensively transmitted through fiber-optic cabling not only to school library media centers (SLMCs) but also to history classrooms and to students' homes. As this telepower revolution renders the walls of schools superfluous, it is simultaneously providing students and faculty with a wealth of information never before thought possible. With one Internet-connected computer, even the smallest school in the remotest location can provide its students and faculty with information that should satisfy many of their research needs. But this increased access in a timeless and wall-less environment will also have negative aspects if students are not able to apply critical thinking skills to the materials they electronically retrieve.

MONITORING THE WORKPLACE

It is imperative that school library media specialists and history educators require students to use critical thinking skills to meet their educational and future employment needs. By 2010, 90 percent of all jobs will be computer dependent, a forecast confirmed daily by the proliferation of computers and modems in homes and businesses. In 1981 there were only 750,000 computers in U.S. homes. Today, more than 45 percent of American homes have personal computers ("Over 45%," B8).

Employers are indicating that the level of employee higher order thinking skills is too low to satisfy workplace demands. A survey of business executives, for example, indicates that they expect more than routine production-services work that involves repetitive tasks usually performed by clerks and data processors. They also want workers to have analytic reasoning, logic, and communication skills to enable them to adjust to increased workplace demands. These are the same skills that characterize symbolic-analytic service workers or employees who must think critically in their occupations. Their jobs entail identifying, problem solving, and strategic brokering functions. Their products are not tangible; they deal with the manipulation of data, words, and graphic representations. Occupations representing symbolic-information services comprise software designers, engineers, lawyers, tax consultants, management information specialists, systems analysts, writers, and musicians. Workers who are engaged in symbolic-analytic services account for only about 20 percent of American jobs, and this percentage is not predicted to grow appreciably (Reich, 173–203).

WHAT'S THE CONNECTION?

Most employment specialists note that a much larger percentage of workers will need these same skills just to survive as more occupations become increasingly technologically advanced. The level of education workers attain is strongly related to their income level. In the next five to ten years, this equation will have a distressing impact upon those who are unable or unwilling to heed it. In the years ahead, more than 50 percent of new jobs will require some education beyond high school, and almost one-third of these jobs will be filled by college graduates.

Only 22 percent of today's occupations require a college degree (Person, 477).

Employment statistics show that the absence of a college degree may preclude workers from achieving a decent standard of living. In 1980, male college graduates earned about 80 percent more than their high school counterparts. By 1990 the gap had nearly doubled (Murnane and Levy, 1–9). The main reason given for this growing divergence between male high school graduate and male college graduate earnings is a lack of education.

During the 1980s, when employers could have filled positions vacated by high school graduates with other high school graduates, many chose instead to hire college graduates. Economists believe that they were responding to increased competition and to changes in the way work was being performed. Some companies, for example, contracted high school level work out to workers in lower-wage countries and hired college graduates for marketing and financing tasks. Other companies introduced advanced technologies that required better-educated workers to operate machines.

WHAT SKILLS ARE NEEDED?

What are the skills that high school graduates need to increase their wages? Many studies suggest that reading and math skills and a facility to use these skills to solve problems matter more in today's workplace than they did in the workplaces of the 1970s (Murnane and Levy, 8). The correlation between reading, mathematics, and reasoning skills and the fastest growing jobs is direct. Natural scientists and lawyers, for example, whose skills requirements in these areas were rated highest by the U.S. Department of Labor, are among the two fastest growing occupations (Person, 472). Yet many labor economists are not confident that improving literacy and mathematics skills in a standardized back-to-basics fashion is the answer to diminished employment opportunities. Reich, for example, in *The Work of Nations* (1991), advocates centering education around "a lifetime of symbolic-analytic work." A symbolic analyst combines four critical thinking skills: "abstraction, system thinking, experimentation, and collaboration" (Reich, 227). To think abstractly means to be able to discern patterns and meanings in information so that it can be equated, formulated, analyzed, or categorized. The abstract process of construing information into usable patterns is characteristic of occupations such as scientist, attorney, engineer, designer, and systems consultant. These are the positions that, although susceptible to global competition, will be growth occupations accompanied by decent standards of living.

System thinking, a more advanced stage of abstraction, requires that individuals be able to recognize patterns and meanings and how they relate to something as a complete process or cycle. Problems are identified and then linked to other problems. The use of DDT and its deleterious concatenated connection to an entire ecosystem of animals and plants is illustrative of system thinking. Experimentation, rarely used as a teaching method in most disciplines with the exception of science, is needed to establish cause and effect, similarities and differences, and possibilities and outcomes. It provides opportunities for students to use tools to structure their own learning situation.

Last is the ability to collaborate, to work in teams and to share information and solutions. The means to do this can be provided through oral reports, designs, scripts, discussion groups, debates, symposia, or focus groups. The emphasis on this form of learning—using critical thinking skills instead of mere acquisition of unrelated facts—is to stimulate the type of thinking that will be needed to achieve success in a technologically globally advanced marketplace (Craver 1994, 67–68).

Although critical thinking skills will be essential to meet the educational, employment, and technological demands of the twenty-first century, they do not come easily and naturally to the untrained mind. In his book *Critical Thinking: What Every Person Needs to Survive in a Rapidly Changing World*, Richard Paul states that the mind is "instinctively designed for habit, associating 'peace of mind' with routine" (v). According to Paul, the mind is naturally inclined to simplify the complex and to make things recognizable in familiar, well-ordered patterns. His thoughts on this subject are reinforced in several national educational assessments. All of them show that in every subject, American students can perform basic tasks successfully, but they do not score well on parts of the tests that measure thinking and reasoning skills. In mathematics, they can compute, but they cannot reason. They can complete and correct sentences in English, but they cannot draft an argument (Paul, 19). In addition, American students are falling behind other nations on standardized tests that require critical thinking skills (Craver, 1994, 75–76).

RETHINKING THE TEXTBOOK APPROACH

One factor that may contribute to these poor test results is the textbooks that students are using to obtain their information. While the materials in it are usually factually correct, a textbook is designed to cover large amounts of material superficially. To achieve this goal and reach a broad market in different states, authors must avoid analysis and resist the desire to pose questions or suggest activities that would require critical thinking skills. History texts need to include as much material about as many historical periods as possible. For years, history educators had to be content with the textbook approach because school library media centers lacked the funds and storage space to stock large amounts of primary and even secondary source materials. With the advent of the Internet, however, this is no longer the case. Now, history educators and school library media specialists have a wealth of primary historical sources electronically available at the click of a mouse.

PURPOSE

The purpose of this book is to discuss and demonstrate how primary sources found on the Internet can be used to teach critical thinking skills in history. It also aims to provide history educators and school library media specialists with practical guidelines and sample suggestions and questions for using primary sources in a variety of formats to stimulate critical thinking skills.

One of the wonderful aspects of my profession is that it enables me to work collaboratively with faculty members in every academic discipline. A good deal of the time I spend in the library is dedicated to developing resource-based units for faculty in various subjects. With the arrival of the Internet, that part of my job has become even more exciting. By using the Internet, I am no longer in the position where I must inform faculty members that they cannot bring their classes to the school library media center because I lack sufficient resources. Now I can accommodate classes for subjects that in the past were too esoteric or obscure. Nowhere has this become more apparent than with history and its required evidentiary materials—primary sources. Because so many primary sources are no longer protected by copyright, libraries, archives, and other educational institutions have been digitizing them and posting them on the Internet. Even more important is the search software that accompanies them. Students who years ago had to sit at library desks and wade through documents looking for mention of a public figure or historical event can simply perform a keyword search and the database will produce the exact passages where their search terms appear.

The implications for teaching history and using critical thinking skills are vast. History educators are no longer bound to the classroom-textbook-lecture method. School library media specialists are no longer confined to poring over history books looking for that elusive primary source excerpt that each student is required to have in her term paper. Instead, we can provide our students with learning experiences and resources that may rival even colleges in their approach to the study of history.

USER POPULATION

In addition to aiding history educators and school library media specialists who wish to collaborate on units involving the use of primary sources and the teaching of critical thinking, this book is also designed to encourage the continued use of school library media centers for the secondary sources that are also essential to historical research. The school library media center remains the best site for the integration of print and electronically accessible materials. Both are equal sources for teaching critical thinking skills. In a SLMC, students can also easily work in small groups without the history teacher having to change the classroom setup for perhaps only one or two classes. The questions included for each primary source Internet site are designed for students in grades 7–12. Their use and application, however, are probably dependent upon a particular grade's course of study.

REQUIRED ELECTRONIC EQUIPMENT

While it would be preferable to have more than one computer terminal and printer to teach the concepts in this book, it requires only one Windows-compatible computer and the installation of either Netscape's Navigator or Microsoft's Internet Explorer as an Internet browser. School library media centers or history classrooms must have a connection to the Internet from a network provider. If there is an insufficient number of computers, some of the primary sources can be printed and photocopied before the class meets. For some primary Internet source sites, users will need to download specific software to permit audio and video formats to be heard and seen. Instructions are given for this specialized software by the site's sponsor(s).

BOOK ARRANGEMENT

The book is arranged in three parts. Part I presents an overview of critical thinking. It discusses the definitional problems that have occurred over the years, provides a brief summary of critical thinking research findings, and discusses how they can be applied to the study of history. In addition, it features examples of how to teach critical thinking skills using either the process or content approach. Part II defines primary and secondary sources and outlines their characteristics. It lists primary source formats and the types of questions to which each format is predisposed. The limitations of primary sources are discussed, and instructional strategies are provided for using document-based lessons in the classroom or school library media center. Part III contains 150 primary source Internet sites arranged chronologically. A summary supplies appropriate background material and highlights of each site's contents. The summary is followed by six critical thinking questions that relate to the primary sources. One or two annotated, subject-related Internet sites follow the questions. These supplemental sites contain either subject-related background or overview material. In some cases, they also include additional primary sources on the same subject. The book concludes with subject and title indices and a list of primary source Internet sites for future reference.

SITE SELECTION CRITERIA

Several criteria were used for site selection. The first was to include sites that were related to most standard history curricula. This meant searching for sites from a broad range of history ranging from ancient times to the last years of the twentieth century. Sometimes it was easy to find primary sources about a particular event or period of history, and sometimes, despite long search efforts, the result was a disappointing zero. The second criterion was to include sites that students would find stimulating, exciting, and interesting, to make it even easier to teach critical thinking skills. Thus you will find sites on the *Titanic*, Jack the Ripper, the Great Fire of London, the San Francisco earthquake and fire of 1906, and the U-2 spy plane affair in addition to the scholarly U.S. Civil War site, Valley of the Shadow, the FDR Cartoon Archive, and The Victorian Web. I also deliberately searched for sites that were posted by universities, academic libraries, or other reputable educational institutions. I relied upon the accuracy of their sources. I also thought that they might withstand the vicissitudes of moving, changing their addresses, disappearing, or commercialization in the future. A significant number of sites are from the Library of Congress. I selected many sites from their databases because of the stability they represented and the excellent quality and quantity of resources that each site contained. The final criterion was to have a selection of primary sources that reflected the diversity in the world. Unfortunately, this objective was not so easily achieved. Because of language barriers, many sites from Asia, for example, are not available in English. While I found many sites about Africa, few contained primary sources. Despite these setbacks, the Internet represents a treasure trove of primary sources for future history educators and school library media specialists to use in the course of their daily instruction.

INTERNET IDIOSYNCRACIES

Although I have tried to select resources that will remain on the Internet, there is no way to guarantee that they will. The Internet, as wonderful as it is, is not a stable electronic information resource. It is possible that some Internet addresses will be unresponsive for a variety of technical, personal, financial, or commercial reasons. I have endeavored to verify their availability as this book went to press. If an Internet address is inaccessible, refer to the site title and enter the keywords in a search engine such as Alta Vista. Perhaps the site may still be retrieved even though it may have moved to a new address. Another solution may be to wait a month and try again. Some authors or institutions may remove the site entirely from the Internet when they wish to repair parts of it or make changes. As a last resort, try removing the last part(s) of the URL address and try to connect to the main sponsoring institution. Once there, search for the title of the database if the site has a search engine or browse their set of hyperlinks to see if it is listed.

A second area for possible problems rests with the directions for using a specific site. The instructions given for selecting a particular page and hyperlink may have become obsolete if a site has been moved or redesigned since this book was published. Again, the best solution is to identify the keywords or subject matter of the question and re-explore where or how the site sponsors are allowing one to access it.

REFERENCES

Craver, Kathleen W. *School Library Media Centers in the 21st Century Changes and Challenges*. Westport, CT: Greenwood Press, 1994.

Johnson, William B., and Arnold E. Packer. *Workforce 2000*. Indianapolis: Hudson Institute, 1987.

Murnane, Richard J., and Frank Levy. "Why Today's High School–Educated Males Earn Less than Their Fathers Did: The Problem and Assessment of Responses." *Harvard Educational Review* 63 (Spring 1993): 1–9. The absence of women in the Murnane-Levy study was due to the difficulty in interpreting earnings of women over a period of time (1973–1987) because of differences in census reporting of full-time and part-time employment.

"Over 45% of U.S. Homes Had Computers Last Year." *Wall Street Journal* March 10, 1998, B8.

Paul, Richard. *Critical Thinking: What Every Person Needs to Survive in a Rapidly Changing World*. Santa Rosa, CA: Foundation for Critical Thinking, 1993.

Person, James E., ed. *Statistical Forecasts of the United States*. Detroit: Gale Publications, 1993.

Reich, Robert. *The Work of Nations*. New York: Alfred A. Knopf, 1991.

USING CRITICAL THINKING
SKILLS IN HISTORY

I

AN OVERVIEW OF CRITICAL THINKING

There is considerable disagreement among scholars and researchers regarding critical thinking terminology, definitions, and characteristics. Terms such as higher order thinking, logical thinking, associative thinking, creative thinking, and scientific method have been used as synonymous concepts. There are also major differences as to how one characterizes critical thinking. Some researchers describe critical thinking as the pursuit of knowledge, the generation of explanations, the judging of ideas, or the construction of relationships between similar unassociated concepts. Others characterize critical thinking as a set of skills that encompass observation, classification, summarization, and interpretation.

Researchers differ concerning their respective pedagogical approaches to critical thinking. Some contend that critical thinking does not occur in isolation and therefore cannot be taught as a separate subject. It must be integrated into specific subjects, because critical thinking in science, for example, is essentially different from critical thinking in history. These same proponents of critical thinking also believe that one must possess substantive knowledge of the particular subject before one can engage in critical thinking. Scholars espousing the opposite view, termed the process approach, assert that critical thinking is a sequential process engaged in rather independently of the subject content. This means that students can be instructed in (1) identifying problems, (2) formulating hypotheses, (3) collecting relevant data, (4) evaluating hypotheses, and

(5) deriving conclusions regardless of previous subject expertise (Craver 1989, 13–14).

Definitional Problems

Since critical thinking comprises a complex set of concepts and can be taught independently or integrated into various academic subjects, it has numerous well-constructed definitions. Each of these definitions features an aspect of a researcher's philosophy and instructional methods for applying critical thinking to education. Harvey Siegal, for example, defines critical thinking as "thinking appropriately moved by reasons." Siegal believes that thought processes are influenced by phenomena rather than by reasons such as fears, reinforcement, and consequences (97). Robert Ennis, on the other hand, defines critical thinking as "rational reflective thinking concerned with what to do or believe" (11). Ennis's definition is universal in that it can readily be applied to all disciplines and the day-to-day conduct of personal affairs.

Matthew Lippman's definition of critical thinking is "skillful, responsible thinking that is conducive to judgment because it relies on criteria, is self-correcting and is sensitive to context" (1). Lippman's definition is predicated upon students understanding the differences between responsible and irresponsible thinking and the application of criteria indigenous to a specific discipline.

All of these definitions were formulated by researchers to suit the design of their respective studies and philosophical frameworks. While they shed light on the somewhat amorphous concept of critical thinking, they also tend to confuse educators who wish to employ the concepts in their respective disciplines (Paul, 135–136).

In *Critical Thinking: What Every Person Needs to Survive in a Rapidly Changing World*, Richard Paul recommends an eclectic approach to defining critical thinking. Rather than choosing one definition, why not employ a list of definitions that indeed reflect several views of critical thinking? His definition, which does assimilate different dimensions of critical thinking, is an attempt to do just that. To Paul, critical thinking is a "systematic way to form and shape thinking. It functions purposefully and exactingly. It is thought that is disciplined, comprehensive, based on intellectual standards, and as a result, well-reasoned" (20). Paul believes that critical thinking can be distinguished from other forms of thinking because the student is cognizant of the systematic nature of a higher order thought process. As with any system, critical thinking is not an isolated set of characteristics and components. All of its aspects combine to form an integrated network that can be applied to all academic subjects.

CRITICAL THINKING CHARACTERISTICS

Multiple definitions of critical thinking are useful only to an extent. Educators also need a set of criteria by which they can measure the degree to which an assignment is characterized by critical thinking. Lauren Resnick believes that critical thinking or higher order thinking contains the following dimensions:

- Critical thinking is nonlinear. It does not follow a prescribed path of action.
- Critical thinking tends to be multifaceted. The thought process is not comprehensible from a single perspective.
- Critical thinking often results in more than one solution. Each solution may have advantages and disadvantages.
- Critical thinking entails subtle interpretation and evaluation. Answers do not exist in colors of black and white, but rather shades of gray.
- Critical thinking requires the employment of multiple criteria, which may conflict with other perspectives.
- Critical thinking contains elements of uncertainty. Often, certain pieces of the problem will be unknown.
- Critical thinking reflects self-regulation of the thought process. While educators may teach thinking criteria, the student must be able to apply the process to a specific problem or task, independently of the instructor.
- Critical thinking attempts to impose meaning, finding patterns and structure among diverse concepts and ideas.
- Critical thinking demands effort. Since there are numerous ambiguities in this type of thought process, it requires hard work and a strong commitment on the part of educators and students. (Resnick, 3)

With these general characteristics in mind, it is important to know what types of learning activities are conducive to producing critical thinkers. Most empirical research suggests that critical thinking is related to reading, writing, group interaction, and speaking. All of these activities are constantly employed in the study of history.

CRITICAL THINKING RESEARCH RESULTS

Critical thinking studies can be divided into four areas of study: those employing reading, writing, group activities, and speaking. Reading studies involved students at various educational levels, ranging from elementary school to college, receiving instruction in either logic, critical thinking concepts, or different types of reasoning in control group settings. Afterward, either the Watson-Glaser Critical Thinking Appraisal, the Cornell Critical Thinking Test, the Wagmis Test, the PSAT, or the SAT were used to measure the differences between experimental and control groups. Results showed that students who had received some sort of instruction in how to think critically about either a specific subject or specific material scored significantly higher on these types of tests than did students who did not receive similar instruction.

While it is essential to recognize the relationship between reading and critical thinking, it is also important to recognize the relevance of writing and reasoning skills to critical thinking. Studies on the relationship between writing and critical thinking are based on two schools of thought. First, writing improves reading comprehension. Improved reading and comprehension thus enhance critical thinking. Second, writing by itself can cause or stimulate critical thinking because of the mental processes involved in generating ideas and organizing and evaluating them.

The majority of research that employed writing activities to improve reading comprehension also reported significant gains on standardized critical thinking tests. In addition, the most effective writing activities consisted of summation, abstract writing, outlining, paraphrasing, note-taking, and writing paragraph headings rather than reading or underlining important passages (Stosky, 627–638).

A third area researchers have studied concerns the relationship between group activity and critical thinking. Group interaction is thought to serve as a stimulus to critical thinking. Some studies have found, for example, that student interaction and faculty-student interchange correlated positively with achievement on the Watson-Glaser Critical Thinking Appraisal and the Chickering Critical Behaviors Test. Researchers such as Bloom and Maier found that if classroom participation was increased, class achievement increased. Other researchers reported that students working in groups of two to four members generally solved more problems than did students working alone (Suydam and Warner, 40–42).

A final research domain relates to speaking studies. Since speaking assists in creating and modeling thought, researchers have hypothesized that speaking may also act as a stimulus to critical thinking. Gall, for example, found that students who participated in class discussions scored significantly higher on tests of fact and demonstrated higher cognitive learning than did nondiscussion, control group students (Gall, 40–47). Researchers have also discovered that the deliberate use of wait time by teachers conveys to students that they are expected to respond intelligently rather than expeditiously. When, for example, faculty members waited at least three seconds, additional students gave longer and more complex responses, frequently commented on a peer's response, and supported more inferences with evidence and logical argument. Researchers also noted an increase in speculative thinking, the number of questions posed, and the number of proposed experiments (Craver, 13–18).

APPLYING CRITICAL THINKING RESEARCH TO THE STUDY OF HISTORY

The implications of these findings for school library media specialists and history educators are exciting. A school library media center offers a natural setting in which to employ critical thinking skills with history students. It also serves as an excellent laboratory for applying various methods and techniques of critical thinking instruction. Librarians and history educators are fortunate in that this subject lends itself to reading, writing, speaking, and group interaction. The study of history is also predisposed to either the process or content critical thinking skills approach.

History can be studied three ways. The narrative school of history looks at what specific people have done, said, and thought in the past. Historians who approach the discipline from a biographical perspective attempt to reconstruct the life, thoughts, and time of individuals who actually lived in the past. The sociological school of history analyzes human beings in their social aspects both past and present (Cantor and Schneider, 17). Narrative history can take one of four approaches: political-institutional, intellectual, economic, or cultural. Political-institutional history focuses on what people have said, thought, and done in government and law. Intellectual history, or the history of ideas, considers the development of higher thought and feeling in philosophy, art, literature, science, and other subjects to be the main domain of the historian. Economic historians research how people have made a living and maintained their surroundings. Some historians believe that this form of historical research is the main vehicle for revealing human thought and action. Cultural historians are often thought of as generalists. A cultural historian explores the development of ideas in their social, political, and economic context (Cantor and Schneider, 17–21).

The study of history as the biography of important women and men is also dimensional in scope. One school of history holds that the actions and motivations of men and women in the past can and should be examined in terms of modern psychological theories and concepts. A second school of thought believes that men and women of the past can only be studied in light of the prevailing psychological concepts, beliefs, and theories of their era.

The sociological school of history studies human beings in their past and present social aspects. This school is associated with sociology and is also divided into historical schools of thought. It explores the characteristics and actions of a distinct society, group, or community, or compares similar patterns found in all or several societies.

Despite the complexity of schools of historical thought, the history student still needs to find evidence about the past and evaluate its significance, meaning, and importance to a particular area of study. History is no longer thought of as the business of fact collection. It is also about amassing appropriate historical evidence to enable one to establish causal relationships and patterns that will shed light on the hows and whys of history (Cantor and Schneider, 17–22). How and why, for example, did the Roman Empire thrive or fall? How and why did Adolf Hitler come to power in Germany? How did the Mayan society function? To be able to provide historical evidence on the hows and whys of history requires two elements: (1) the application of critical thinking skills, and (2) the judicious use of historical evidence in the form of primary sources.

When students rely on a secondary source, usually a history textbook, as their basic source, they do not have to employ critical thinking skills. Almost all of the work of making assumptions, identifying causes and relationships, and arriving at judgments has been done for them. They are not called on to find systematic patterns and to create order out of disorder, to make inferences, or to examine and evaluate evidence. It is only through the use of primary historical sources that students can apply critical thinking history skills that involve reading, writing, speaking, and group interaction. These are also the main areas in which the employment of critical thinking skills correlates with increased achievement on standardized tests.

In constructing a list of these skills, the author selected pertinent information from the California English Language Arts Assessment, David Kobrin's book *Beyond the Textbook: Teaching History Using Documents and Primary Sources*, and the National History Standards. The skills, mindset, and competencies that a student should bring to bear on the study of history are formidable. Students must be able to do the following:

Critical Thinking Skills for History

- Explore different ideas, think divergently, take risks, and express opinions. These generalities include the ability to speculate, infer, hypothesize, entertain alternative scenarios, pose questions, make predictions, and think metaphorically.

- Examine multiple possibilities of meaning and determine the cultural and psychological nuances and complexities in a text.

- Recognize and comprehend ambiguities in a text and understand archaic vocabulary.
- Understand the importance of context and perspective in a source and be able to examine internal and external evidence to determine its validity.
- Discern the main ideas in a historical source.
- Make connections between the source and one's own ideas, experiences, and knowledge.
- Make generalizations that are supported by historical evidence.
- Discern themes and patterns in a set of primary sources.
- Communicate one's ideas clearly and persuasively in oral and written communication.
- Collaborate with peers in group interaction assignments.

Critical thinking skills in history cannot be taught all at once. Devising assignments, however, that highlight or reinforce a specific skill—such as the ability to discern patterns or themes in a diverse collection of primary sources—can. What is also important is to create assignments that repetitively foster these skills so that students eventually internalize them for all types of future work.

TEACHING CRITICAL THINKING SKILLS USING INTERNET PRIMARY SOURCES

Unfortunately, the study of history is still undertaken by students reading the distilled textbooks of professional historians rather than the undiluted evidence of history itself. It is difficult to teach critical thinking history skills when students' primary sources of history are, in reality, secondary sources. Reliance on a history textbook as the primary source should become a thing of the past as more primary sources become available on the Internet. In the future, a history textbook should be used for overview and background material or for factual information about a specific person, event, place, or time period.

History textbooks also introduce bias at a time when students lack the knowledge, experience, and even political savvy to recognize it. The majority of history textbooks, because of length and scope considerations, cannot include conflicting accounts of events. Some, depending on the geographical area for which they were published, are precluded from raising important ethical and moral questions relating to specific historical occurrences or time periods. How many U.S. history textbooks, for example, fully describe the systematic exploitation of Native American lands and resources under various presidential administrations? How many textbooks discuss the view that the United States may also have shared some of the responsibility for the Cold War?

As is the case with all history, textbooks are written from a point of view. The only way to avoid exposing students to built-in bias, whether subconscious or conscious, is to provide them with the evidence of history—primary sources—and have them apply critical thinking skills to the materials.

THE INSTRUCTIONAL VALUE OF PRIMARY SOURCES

Primary sources are the fundamental materials that furnish the raw data and information for the historian. They enable history students to establish facts, make inferences, and formulate opinions. These three elements constitute the critical study of history. In general, primary sources have the following advantages over secondary sources.

They provide an instantaneous representation of events. Primary sources possess a wonderful "you are there" quality that makes reading them exciting even after the fact. They represent the words of the first on the scene and are usually devoid of omnipresent criticism and analysis. Neil Armstrong's conversations back to earth about his first walk on the moon riveted millions of people to television and radio stations to see and hear his first impressions. His words establish the facts about the first landing on the moon by human beings, enable inferences to be made from the historic event, and allow students to form judgments, opinions, and conclusions about the event.

Looking at the correspondence between Premier Nikita Khrushchev and President John F. Kennedy during the Cuban missile crisis is not only fascinating but an absolute necessity if we are to attempt to learn how to avoid coming to the brink of nuclear war in the future.

They furnish information not found in other sources. Primary sources are the best pieces of evidence to aid in the search for the truth. When the United States was embroiled in the Vietnam War, the issuance of "The Pentagon Papers" by Daniel Ellsberg revealed the extent to which the United States government had been less than candid with the American public about the number of casualties and bombings. Its publication had a significant impact on government policy toward Southeast Asia and the presidency of Lyndon B. Johnson. Students who read sections of "The Pentagon Papers" will have to apply critical thinking history skills to establish the facts, make appropriate inferences, and arrive at their own conclusions regarding some aspect of the Vietnam War.

They do not interpret evidence after the fact. Although primary sources may have been written, created, or designed from a certain perspective, they are generally devoid of hindsight. As such, they have not been colored by the critic's palette or the editor's pencil. They are alive with their own interpretations of particular tragedies and triumphs. They remain the closest records of what really happened before others had a chance to analyze, critique, or put their spin on it.

Pliny the Younger's vivid description of the eruption of the volcano Vesuvius in 79 CE, which buried the cities of Herculaneum and Pompeii and many of their inhabitants in molten ash, provides a much more accurate account than one by archaeologists who reconstructed the same event from excavated ruins. Students reading Pliny the Younger's version have the opportunity to speculate, infer, hypothesize, entertain alternative scenarios, and derive their own opinions about this cataclysmic environmental event.

They assist in the discovery of truth about persons, events, and issues. Primary sources are the basic tools to help discover the truth about persons, events, and issues. Just as "the truth is the first casualty of war," primary sources are the first casualty of secondary sources. Each time another person writes about a person, event, or issue, he or she can wittingly or unwittingly add another layer of personal bias that can prevent the discovery of the truth. When students rely solely on secondary sources to study history, they are deprived of the chance to make connections between the source and their own ideas, experience, and knowledge. Many times secondary sources supply students with not only a historical bias toward a particular historical event but also a singular interpretation of it. Primary sources enable students to construe multiple interpretations of meaning and to determine what they believe are the cultural and psychological nuances and complexities in a document.

Primary sources may be the only sources we can rely on to discover the causes of a war, decisions by government officials, or the nature and implications of the computer revolution. *The Diary of a Young Girl* by Anne Frank, for example, sheds enormous light on the nature and extent of the Nazi Holocaust, which the Germans tried to cover up during and after World War II (Craver 1997, 152–153). The testimony of Japanese Americans concerning their unjust internment in United States concentration camps provides a record of the climate of fear that was generated as a result of Japan's bombing of Pearl Harbor in 1941.

Documents like these can also be used to discern historical themes and patterns and perhaps make historical generalizations. The pattern of a climate of fear can be established in numerous documents concerning the Salem Witch Trials, the McCarthy era, and the Cold War as well as the previous two examples. How and why does this pattern occur throughout history? What conditions make a country or group of people susceptible to it? What danger does it present to a country now and in the future?

When students work with primary sources it gives them the opportunity to recognize the historical dimensions of problems they face in everyday life. The study of history becomes a vehicle to ingrain critical thinking skills which they will need to apply to choosing a future president or to supporting or not supporting government decisions and policies on a war, the environment, health care, or education. While critical thinking skills are applicable to all learning domains, they are especially relevant to history.

CRITICAL THINKING GUIDELINES FOR USING INTERNET PRIMARY SOURCES

Research studies about critical thinking do not favor either a process or a content approach. In some process experiments, students who received instruction in defining problems and making deductive and inductive inferences prior to an assignment showed significant improvement on various standardized critical thinking skills tests. Other studies that integrated critical thinking skills into the assignment by posing questions designed to stimulate critical thinking also showed significant student achievement on various tests. All critical thinking skills research, however, did find a statistically significant correlation with reading, writing, group interaction, and speaking activities. With these results in mind, it is up to history educators and school library media specialists (SLMSs) to decide whether to employ a process or content approach to inculcating critical thinking skills.

THE CRITICAL THINKING SKILLS PROCESS APPROACH

The process approach entails giving students a definition of critical thinking and a rationale for its use. This explanation can be followed by the distribution of the "Critical Thinking Skills for History" list to each student. Review each item on the list with students and give examples from selected primary source questions in Part III of the text. You may wish to select ones that are related to a current subject under study. Divide the class into groups of five to six students and ask them to complete the following questions about the document(s) you have assigned.

Document Identification Form

1. Identify this document. Who wrote it? What kind is it? When was it written? Where?

2. Is it a primary or secondary source?

3. What is the point of view of the author(s) of the source?

4. Why or for what purpose was this document written? How reliable and trustworthy is it?

5. To what extent does the document reflect its historical context (the values and experiences of the time period)?

6. What is it about (subject matter)?

7. How is the document organized or structured?

8. What does it assume?

9. What does the document omit? What is missing? What are the document's silences?

10. What tentative conclusion can you make based on this document?

11. What other documents support or augment this one?

12. What questions do you wish to ask based on this document?

Once the group has completed the worksheet, ask them to choose a format to present all of this information to the class. The presentation must, however, incorporate reading, writing, group interaction, and speaking activities. You may suggest the following types of activities formats. Explain how certain types of presentation formats may lend themselves to their particular assigned primary source(s).

Television or videotaped interview	Construction of a model
Play	Puzzle
News report	Panel discussion
Debate	Case study
Travel agent package	Book reviewer/critic
Diaries, personal letters	Law enforcement report
Legislative committee report	Archaeological discovery
Visual depiction (charts, graphs, tables)	Drawing, portrait
Psychological profile	Poster
Web page	Mock trial

As students observe and listen to the presentations, ask them to identify the set(s) of critical thinking skills that were employed by each group. Use the "Critical Thinking Skills for History" list as part of the evaluation criteria for each group's presentation and ask students who are not presenting to complete the evaluation form (Figure 1) for each group.

Figure 1
Critical Thinking Skills in History Evaluation

On a scale of 1 to 5, please characterize the critical thinking skills of the group presentation that you just observed.

Clear	1	2	3	4	5	Unclear
Precise	1	2	3	4	5	Imprecise
Specific	1	2	3	4	5	Vague
Accurate	1	2	3	4	5	Inaccurate
Relevant	1	2	3	4	5	Irrelevant
Plausible	1	2	3	4	5	Implausible
Consistent	1	2	3	4	5	Inconsistent
Logical	1	2	3	4	5	Illogical
Deep	1	2	3	4	5	Superficial
Broad	1	2	3	4	5	Narrow
Complete	1	2	3	4	5	Incomplete
Significant	1	2	3	4	5	Trivial
Adequate	1	2	3	4	5	Inadequate
Fair	1	2	3	4	5	Biased

Source: This questionnaire was adapted from "Intellectual Standards that Apply to Critical Thinking in Every Subject," in Richard Paul, *Critical Thinking: What Every Person Needs to Survive in a Rapidly Changing World* (Santa Rosa, CA: Foundation for Critical Thinking, 1993), p. 63.

Evaluation Criteria

To evaluate the effectiveness of the process approach, you may wish to assign a score or scores to the following critical thinking skills requirements: (1) completed Document Identification Form; (2) individual's contribution to the group presentation; and (3) tabulated peer results of the Critical Thinking in History Evaluation Form.

The Content Approach

Because none of the critical thinking research points to a specific pedagogy for integrating critical thinking skills into a discipline, history educators and SLMSs can also choose the content approach. The content approach simply means that history educators and school library media specialists integrate primary sources into various class activities and assignments to stimulate critical thinking skills in all history curriculum areas. The content method can be employed in either of two ways. History educators and school library media specialists can select curriculum-related primary sources and their accompanying critical thinking questions from Part III of the text and employ them in various types of assignments. The second way requires identifying other primary sources and creating similar types of questions and group activities that stimulate critical thinking. To find additional primary Internet source databases, consult the list of databases at the end of this volume.

After selecting relevant primary sources, create questions that are designed to employ critical thinking skills for history. Write questions that cause students to do the following:

1. Compare	Have them note the similarities and dissimilarities between or among historical periods, events, policies, wars, and the like.
2. Classify	Group sets of documents into definable categories based on their common characteristics, intent, purpose, etc.
3. Induce	Infer unknown generalizations, themes, or patterns from analyzing a primary source or sources.
4. Deduce	Infer unstated conditions and consequences from a primary source or sources.
5. Analyze Errors	Find fallacies and flaws in a primary source or in the reasoning behind it.
6. Build Support	Discover and build support for an argument or debate about a primary source or sources.
7. Think Abstractly	Discern significant underlying patterns or themes in a primary source or sources.
8. Analyze Perspectives	Identify and articulate the point of view or perspective in a primary source or sources.

Source: Adapted from R. J. Marzano, *A Different Kind of Classroom: Teaching with Dimensions of Learning* (Alexandria, VA: Association for Supervision and Curriculum Development, 1992), p. 3.

After identifying and writing questions for each primary source, provide opportunities for students to present their information in such a manner that they incorporate speaking, writing, reading, and group interaction skills in their presentations. To inspire their presentation creativity, suggest some of the possible activities formats listed in the critical thinking skills process approach section.

Evaluation Criteria

To evaluate the effectiveness of the content approach, you may wish to use the Critical Thinking in History Evaluation form and also assign a score that reflects your evaluation of the student's or group's ability to demonstrate critical thinking skills in response to instructor-generated questions.

REFERENCES

Bloom, Benjamin S. "The 2 Sigma Problem: The Search for Methods of Group Instruction as Effective as One to One Teaching." *Educational Researcher* 13 (June 1984): 4–16.

Cantor, Norman, and Richard I. Schneider. *How to Study History.* New York: Thomas Y. Crowell, 1968.

Craver, Kathleen W. "Critical Thinking: Implications for Research." *School Library Media Quarterly* 18 (Fall 1989): 13–18.

———. *Teaching Electronic Literacy: A Concepts-Based Approach for School Library Media Specialists.* Westport, CT: Greenwood Press, 1997.

Ennis, Robert H. *Goals for a Critical-Thinking/Reasoning Curriculum.* Illinois Critical Thinking Project. Champaign: University of Illinois Press, 1985.

Gall, Meredith. "Synthesis of Research on Teachers' Questioning." *Educational Leadership* 42 (November 1984): 40–47.

Kobrin, David. *Beyond the Textbook: Teaching History Using Documents and Primary Sources.* Portsmouth, NH: Heinemann, 1996.

Lippman, Matthew. "Critical Thinking and the Use of Criteria." *Inquiry,* March 1988. Newsletter of the Institute for Critical Thinking, Upper Montclair, NJ: Montclair State College.

Maier, Norman R. *Problem Solving and Creativity in Individuals and Groups.* New York: Brooks/Cole, 1970.

Marzano, Robert J. *A Different Kind of Classroom: Teaching with Dimensions of Learning.* Alexandria, VA: Association for Supervision and Curriculum Development, 1992.

National Cathedral School History Department. *Readings in American History.* Washington, DC: National Cathedral School, 1995.

National History Standards Task Force. *National History Standards.* Los Angeles: National Center for History in the Schools, 1994.

Paul, Richard. *Critical Thinking: What Every Person Needs to Survive in a Rapidly Changing World.* Santa Rosa, CA: Foundation for Critical Thinking, 1993.

Resnick, Lauren. *Education and Learning to Think.* Washington, DC: National Academy Press, 1987.

Samplers for English Language Arts Assessment for Elementary and High School. Sacramento: California Department of Education, 1993.

Siegal, Harvey. *Educating Reason: Rationality, Critical Thinking and Education.* New York: Routledge, 1988.

Stosky, Sandra A. "Research on Reading/Writing Relationships: A Synthesis." *Language Arts* 60 (May 1983): 627–642.

Suydam, Marilyn N., and J. Fred Warner. "Research on Problem Solving: Implications for Elementary Schools." *Arithmetic Teacher* 25 (November 1977): 40–42.

USING PRIMARY SOURCES

II

WHAT ARE PRIMARY SOURCES?

Just as there are multiple definitions of critical thinking, so there are multiple answers to the question, What constitutes a primary source? Students usually think of primary sources as old, yellowed letters or documents that were found in someone's attic and eventually placed in a large library or a place called the archives. Accessing an Internet database containing primary sources and printing an excerpt from the 1492 ship's log of Christopher Columbus on a laser printer can quickly disabuse students of this notion (Craver, 152–153). Still, however, multiple meanings abound concerning the definition of a primary source. It may be helpful for some students to compare primary sources to some secondary sources with which they are more familiar. Here are some definitions that have been used at the Yale University Library Primary Sources Research Colloquium: "A primary source is firsthand testimony or direct evidence concerning a topic under investigation. The nature and value of a source cannot be determined without reference to the topic and questions it is meant to answer. The same document or other piece of evidence may be a primary source in one investigation and secondary in another. The search for primary sources does not, therefore, automatically include or exclude any category of records or documents" (Yale University Library Primary Sources Research Colloquium, 1997, 1).

From this explanation, it is readily apparent that the definitional problems concerning primary sources lie in their context. Students must be able to discern that a source may be primary only in relation to its connection to their topic or assignment. The use of a source in its correct context is what determines its designation as a primary or secondary source. In *How to Study History,* Cantor and Schneider use the element of time to help history students understand the difference between the two types of sources. They consider a primary source a "work that was written at a time that is contemporary or nearly contemporary with the period or subject being studied" (2). Passages from Adolf Hitler's *Mein Kampf,* for example, would be a primary source for the study of Hitler's influence on the German people in the 1930s and 1940s. Samuel Pepys's account of the Great Fire of London in 1666 would be a primary source for the study of the architecture, life, and businesses of sixteenth century London.

Cantor and Schneider further clarify the contextual problem by defining a secondary source as "one that discusses the subject but is written after the time contemporary with it" (23). Thus Bruce Catton's Centennial History Civil War series published in the 1960s is a secondary source for the study of the Civil War, and Barbara Tuchman's *A Distant Mirror: The Calamitous Fourteenth Century,* published in 1978, is a secondary source for the study of the Middle Ages. Although most secondary sources are based on primary sources or derived from them, they are after the fact and considered a second set of judgments or perspectives.

There remains only one distinction between the two types of sources about which students could become confused. Occasionally a source or document may serve as a secondary source for one subject and as a primary source for another altogether different subject. Niccolo Machiavelli's *The Prince,* published in 1513, is an important secondary source for any study of the various Renaissance princes in the Medici family; but the same book is also a primary source for the political thought that was characteristic of the sixteenth century because it reflects the attitudes of a person living in the 1500s.

PRIMARY SOURCES CONTEXT REVIEW

As a review of this section, it may be helpful to provide students with a set of contextual examples that are subject-related, if possible, and that reinforce the definitions of primary and secondary sources. Refer to the following examples and use them as a learning activity, or create new ones. Do not supply students with the italicized explanations before they attempt to answer the questions. After students have had an opportunity to complete the questionnaire, review the answers and give additional examples for questions the majority of the class had difficulty answering.

Contextual Internet Primary Source Examples

I am writing a biographical sketch about the 1991 Nobel Peace Prize winner Aung San Suu Kyi from Myanmar (formerly known as Burma) and have found an interview on the Internet in which she discusses her political views. Is this a primary source?

Yes. The interview directly relates to an important aspect of Aung San Suu Kyi's life.

I am researching Charles Lindbergh's solo flight across the Atlantic Ocean and have found a microfilm article from the *New York Times* dated May 22, 1927, that describes his trip. Is this a primary source?

Yes. Since Charles Lindbergh and many witnesses to this event are no longer living, this article describing his flight within the time it happened would constitute a primary source.

I am writing a report about medieval illuminated manuscripts and have found examples of them at the Internet Vatican Library exhibit site. If I print them on a color printer and discuss them in my report, are these considered to be primary sources?

Yes. The Vatican Library exhibit on the Internet features pages and examples of illuminated manuscripts that were physically on display at the Library of Congress several years ago.

I am researching the origin and development of the middle class in Europe and have found an article titled "The Middle Classes in Europe" in the December 1995 issue of the *Journal of Modern History*. Is this a primary source?

No. The Journal of Modern History is a scholarly journal that publishes articles based on primary sources. You would need to find these sources and examine them yourself.

I am researching the slave population by gender of several Maryland counties in the year 1800 and have found census data on the Internet that give the total slave population, but no gender breakdown. Is this a primary source?

Yes. You have found a primary source, but it does not provide a breakdown of Maryland census data containing slaves by gender. You must look elsewhere for the information.

I am writing a report about the conviction and execution of Julius and Ethel Rosenberg for espionage in 1953. I have just finished reading Louis Nizer's *The Implosion Conspiracy*, which was published in 1973. Is this a primary source?

No. While the book was published more than twenty years ago, it was not written at a time contemporary with the 1950s.

I am researching the social life and customs of the United States from 1947 to 1953. I have found two reports about Americans' sexual behavior by Alfred Charles Kinsey, published in 1948 and 1953, respectively. Are these reports primary sources?

Yes. The Kinsey Reports were the first major comprehensive survey of sexual behavior in the United States. Their findings can be considered indicative of some aspects of the social life and customs of the United States during this period.

PRIMARY SOURCE FORMATS AND CHARACTERISTICS

Primary historical sources span a vast amount of material and are highly diversified in character. They can include written records, oral traditions, shards from a prehistoric settlement, petroglyphs on the side of a cliff, and electronic mail. In summary, they are any indication of human activity. Some historians look upon primary sources as the "traces left behind by past events" (Garraghan and Delanglez, 103). Their purpose, sometimes accidentally, is to provide evidence of the events of countless people "who have disappeared into the remorseless silence of the past" (Cantor and Schneider, 91).

The range of primary sources is so broad that classifying them is the only way to impose order on such a chaotic assortment of historical materials. For the sake of organization, a modified and modernized version of historical materials classification from John Martin Vincent's *Historical Research* (13–18) has been used.

Primary sources can be classified into groups depending upon how the materials are transmitted. For example, some primary sources are transmitted orally in the form of legends, sagas, and songs. Visually transmitted materials may include paintings, photographs, and sculptures, for example. Within each group, some of the transmissions may possess characteristics that cause them to overlap with another major grouping. For teaching purposes, however, they have been assigned to the group that reflects their major means of transmission. Primary sources can be classified into four groups: (1) written, (2) oral, (3) visual, and (4) electronic transmissions. The list that follows under each group is meant to be suggestive of the types of sources that may be found within a category. They are by no means comprehensive. There are many more types of materials that could probably fall under one of the four rubrics.

- Written transmissions consist of historical materials whose principal transmission mode is writing. Examples include:

books	newspapers
journals	diaries
letters	chronicles
annals	government documents
dissertations	personal or institutional papers
public records	genealogies
census data	manuscripts
eyewitness accounts	laws

| scripture | scrolls |
| inscriptions | period literature and poetry |

- Oral transmissions include historical materials whose principal mode of transmission is word of mouth. Examples include:

speeches	ballads
anecdotes	legends
sagas	telephone conversations
oral histories	recordings (tape and records)
music	myths
interviews (not videotaped)	

- Visually transmitted sources are those whose principal means of conveyance is through sight. Examples include:

sculpture	historical paintings
photographs	engravings
portraits	models and dioramas
maps	woodcuts
cartoons	architecture
coins	etchings
videotapes	relics
films	artifacts
posters	computer-generated graphics

- Electronically transmitted sources comprise materials whose main mode of transmission is by electronic means. Examples include:

| faxes | machine-readable databases |
| electronic mail | |

Written Transmissions

There are two types of written transmissions: public and private. Public correspondence predisposes itself to the following guidelines:

1. *Examine public correspondence to determine the purpose for which the government or institution published the document and the means by which it amassed power and wealth or institutionalized social order and welfare.* A study of the Code of Hammurabi, for example, reveals a wealth of information about the purpose of a Babylonian king and his govern-

ment. The laws that he promulgated were an attempt to regulate and standardize the social and economic behavior of citizens.

2. *Try to find out the objectives of the government or organization, whether they are stated explicitly or not.* A further exploration of the Code of Hammurabi shows that the king may have attempted to codify information from previously existing laws with the idea of establishing a state-sponsored system of justice.

3. *Search for values and assumptions that reflect the political and social point of view held by the document's author(s).* Hammurabi, for example, prescribed retribution in kind, such as "an eye for an eye." Before this law, a personal crime was handled privately, with cash payments rendered to the persons who had been wronged. Under Hammurabic law, as barbaric as it seems to us, the government was beginning to take jurisdictional control of crimes against people rather than just those against the state. These laws show a more advanced form of legal thinking by Babylonian society.

4. *Look for indications of social change with which the organization, government, or institution has had to deal.* In looking at the Code of Hammurabi, it is interesting to pose questions concerning the social conditions that may have caused their inscription on a Babylonian stele. In addition to the laws, there is a prologue that celebrates the justice of the king and his care for the citizens of Babylon. One might infer that perhaps Hammurabi felt the need to establish a public record of justice to enhance his political stature.

Private correspondence predisposes itself to the following guidelines:

1. *Examine private documents for the societal position of the author(s).* Some private documents, for example, contain private letters and diaries of statesmen, politicians, famous artists, musicians, physicians, writers, scientists, and the like. They are people who may have formulated the major triumphs and tragedies of their age or who actively participated in them. Another group of authors are people in semi-public positions. While they did not make history per se, they were close to those in power and had an insider's view of it. The last group of authors are totally private people who have left their commentary on some aspect of history or whose descriptions of their own lives furnish useful information about the period in which they lived.

2. *Read private documents to confirm general historical events.* Private documents make history personal. They can help establish empathy with and understanding for a period of history that seems unusually complacent, violent, or fearful to us. Boccaccio's introduction to *The Decameron* contains a horrifying description of the outbreak of bubonic

plague in Florence, Italy, in 1353. It not only assists in confirming the existence of this terrible disease but also evokes compassion in us for the preposterous superstitions that were generated as a result of it.

3. *Search private documents to find new and different perspectives about history.* Private diaries, letters, and journals, for example, can show social behavior and conduct that may be totally at odds with the official public documents of a given period of history. Letters from literate plantation slaves paint an altogether different picture of life in antebellum America than the sometimes idealized version depicted in official histories of the early 1800s. The letters show the dark underbelly of America during a time when there were two societies, a free one and an imprisoned one.

4. *Use private documents to confirm, deny, or explicate the accomplishments and reputations of famous people.* The private correspondence of semi-public people is extremely useful in shedding light on the daily lives and personal characteristics and traits of the makers of history. Many times public figures such as former President Richard M. Nixon leave voluminous writings behind that cast themselves in a more positive light. It is this material that is sometimes reproduced in history textbooks. Reading the journal entries of John Dean, one of President Nixon's aides, in *Blind Ambition: The White House Years* (1976), gives another perspective on President Nixon's personality that helps balance his autobiographical portrait. Without Dean's and other presidential aides' documents, this view of President Nixon might be lost to history.

5. *Examine private documents of public figures to juxtapose their public personas and proposals with their privately held beliefs.* Private papers of public figures can be employed to show the conflict—or confirm that there is none—between a public figure's openly espoused policies, decisions, and assertions and the opinions expressed to his or her friends, aides, and colleagues in private. President Lyndon B. Johnson, for example, supported the war in Vietnam with additional American troops, military supplies, and bombings. He even questioned the patriotism of his critics, denouncing them as doves and people who were encouraging the Viet Cong to persist in the hope that they would obtain a victory. Yet memoranda to various advisors and aides reflect his ambivalent attitude to the war, and remarks to his wife, Lady Bird, indicate his uncertainty about what course to pursue (Dallek, 255).

6. *Use literary works and poetry as contemporary, formal accounts that illustrate general societal norms.* The poem "The White Man's Burden," written in 1899 by Rudyard Kipling, for example, rationalized colonial imperialism. It ignited a storm of pro and con cartoons and essays at the turn of the century. Imperialists in the United States used the

poem to help justify the acquisition of Puerto Rico, Guam, and the Philippines, whereas their critics used it as another reason to form the Anti-Imperialist League in 1899. Selections from literature can evoke the climate of the times or reflect a period's values and beliefs much more powerfully than a mere recitation of the historical facts.

Oral Transmissions

Since many speeches, ballads, anecdotes, and legends are in printed form, many of the guidelines suggested in the written transmissions section apply here as well. There are, however, some specific guidelines that may help students who are working with orally transmitted materials.

1. *Examine myths, legends, tales, sagas, and the like for their origin, versions, or anachronisms in selected historical periods.* Although facts may be passed on orally for long periods of time, there is a great potential for the distortion of truth as details are either dropped from or added to an orally transmitted story to appeal to listeners. An obvious example is the legend of Robin Hood, which changes character descriptions and deeds over several historical periods. In some cases, legends and myths that are attributed to a particular nation originated in another. The legend of William Tell and the liberation of Switzerland in 1291, for example, cannot be verified in any authentic Swiss records. Yet the apple-shooting event appears in the poetry and legends of other nations (Vincent, 152).

2. *Examine myths, legends, sagas, and the like for a unifying theme or motif and compare or contrast it to others from different countries or historical periods.* The "wandering saga" motif can be found in Homer's *Odyssey* as well as Virgil's *Aeneid*. The "quest theme" is central to the King Arthur legend as well as to those associated with the Crusades.

3. *Listen to speeches, tape recordings, and telephone conversations not only for their content but also for the speaker's ability to evoke an emotional response in the listener.* Listening to audio excerpts of Senator Joseph McCarthy as he rants about the infiltration of communists into every branch of government reveals another dimension of his power to bully and scare people.

Visual Transmissions

Visually transmitted source guidelines also overlap with orally transmitted guidelines because some of the sources in this section, such as videotapes and films, possess an aural component.

1. *Examine artwork such as historical paintings, portraits, photographs, wood-cuts, cartoons, and the like for their expressive content and subject matter.* If one is looking at an illumination from the medieval book of hours, *Tres Riches Heures* (ca. 1412), for example, only the Bishop and the Duc de Berry in the January illumination are pictured as seated at a feast. What, for example, might this seating arrangement tell us about who are the wealthiest people in the room? What does it tell us about the customs of the Middle Ages? Which two people might have the money to pay for the services of an illuminator in the future?

    Jacques Louis David, also known as the Master of Propaganda for the French Revolution, painted *The Death of Marat*, picturing the French revolutionary Jean Paul Marat, who was killed by Royalist Charlotte Corday while in his bath in 1793, as a martyr similar to Christ. David painted him at the moment of his death, lying in his bath, scrawling "for the good of the people" on a piece of paper. The expressive content of this painting and the subject matter were skillfully used by the revolutionists to help foment a reign of terror against members of the French aristocracy and other people suspected of loyalty to the Bourbon monarchy (Wilson, 86).

2. *Examine castles, monuments, sculptures, temples, tombs, churches, and other architectural forms for their shape, size, construction materials, and function.* The existence of stained glass, for example, is an indication that a church was built in the medieval period, when glass was used for both decorative and educational purposes. During the Middle Ages, many people were illiterate, and the Bible stories portrayed in the stained glass were used to provide religious and ethical instruction. The construction of castles with their moats and drawbridges leads one to conclude that the people living in that age and area were possibly subject to frequent attacks by other people. The size and shape of the pyramids in Egypt are, for example, indicative of an ancient civilization that possessed skilled artisans, engineers, and builders.

3. *Research artifacts such as coins, relics, clothing, jewelry, frescoes, mosaics, and weapons for their purpose, construction materials, and artistry.* Artifacts are visually transmitted primary sources that can aid in establishing the existence of a group of people or a civilization in a certain area and time period. An examination of the materials of which a weapon was constructed—for example, wood versus iron—can provide evidence of the age in which a group of people may have lived. The type of clothing they wore, the material of which it is made (e.g., silk, cotton or an animal's skin), and its decoration or the absence of decoration are additional pieces of historical evidence by which the level of a society and its values and beliefs can be determined. Relics or human remains can be examined to discover if a society may have

practiced human sacrifice, believed in an afterlife, suffered from specific diseases, or deified certain individuals. Jewelry can help establish
how advanced a society was. Questions should be asked about how
finished the jewelry is and what parts of the body it was meant to
adorn.

4. *Look at videotapes, computer-generated graphics, and films to determine the
   purpose, goals, message, values, and action of the person(s), event, place, or
   object under study.* Audiovisual materials in the form of films and vid-
   eos are primary sources for many events that have taken place in the
   past forty years. Footage of the film showing the assassination of President John F. Kennedy is historical evidence of this tragic event. A
   film clip of Dr. Martin Luther King, Jr., delivering his "I Have a
   Dream" speech to thousands of people at the Lincoln Memorial in
   Washington, D.C., is historical evidence of his persuasive oratory. The
   response of the crowd is also historical evidence of the need for civil
   rights for African Americans in the 1960s. Video and films are also
   historical evidence of the tenor of the times. They provide documentation of the language, phrases, slang, and idioms that characterized
   a certain historical period. This form of media shows evidence of the
   clothing that was worn and the artifacts and objects that a society
   valued and consumed. Nonprint media are evidence of an age's
   hopes, dreams, and fears.

Electronically Transmitted Sources

The guidelines for electronically transmitted sources are somewhat
similar to those for written sources since electronic transmissions are
read by the researcher. For purposes of historical evidence, faxes,
machine-readable data files, and electronic mail may be stored in some
type of electronic form where they can be read on a computer screen or
printed in hard copy.

• *Apply the public and private correspondence written sources guidelines to all electronically transmitted documents.* With all electronic transmissions take special
  care to verify the author's, corporation's, or government's credentials, and the
  validity and accuracy of the document's contents. Electronic mail, faxes, and
  machine-readable data files, although electronically mutable, are potential primary sources. For example, electronic mail among employees of Microsoft is
  being used by the United States Justice Department as evidence that Microsoft
  violated antitrust laws (Wilke, B20). In the future, it may provide historic evidence of Bill Gates's intention to monopolize the Internet aspect of the computer industry.

PRIMARY SOURCE CAVEATS

Since most students in high school and college classes are not studying to become historians, there is an assumption that they will not need to learn how to externally evaluate a source for authenticity. If, for example, they are asked to examine the Japanese Surrender Documents of World War II, it is a foregone conclusion that the documents are not fraudulent and that the words in the documents have been translated as they were originally intended. While students do not have to study the arts of external criticism, such as verifying signatures, seals, monograms, and so on, they need to bring critical thinking skills to bear on the content of the primary source.

Primary sources may be subjective, polemical, and illustrative of one opinion or have a limited perspective. Suppose that in the year 2500 historians find documents published by the National Rifle Association, a right to life group committee, or the Hemlock Society. It is likely that the documents would reflect the point of view of the group that published them. Without having sufficient background material about these documents, the student must apply critical thinking skills to every primary source.

PLANNING TO USE PRIMARY SOURCES

After all the emphasis on primary sources, it is ironic indeed to recommend that students consult secondary sources as well. Yet even though secondary sources diminish the need for critical thinking skills, they are a necessary component of historical research.

Students do not arrive in a classroom with an innate sense of history. With the exception of some awareness of current events and having seen some historically based films, many will have little prior information on primary sources in any area of history. They need to consult collateral sources such as historical encyclopedias, online history databases, subject-specific history books, the Internet, and their history textbook. Each primary source summarized in Part III, for example, includes at least one Internet-related site where either background or overview information relating to the cited primary source can be found.

Secondary source materials will provide students with several kinds of necessary information. In addition to citations, excerpts, and quotations from primary sources, they may find statistical compilations concerning, for example, the number of immigrants to the United States from Ireland in the 1800s. These facts can be further employed to make critical inferences about the impact of the potato famine in Ireland during the middle of the nineteenth century. Students may correctly summarize that this devastating famine was one of the major causes of Irish emigration during this period (Cantor and Schneider, 92–94).

A second reason for using secondary sources is that students need to realize that there may be several different interpretations of a particular historical event. Reading secondary sources about the United States Civil War demonstrates very quickly that historians do not agree on what caused it. Some historians believe that slavery was a primary cause, while others believe that an impasse in political compromise was a major cause (O'Reilly, 111). Exposing students to multiple interpretations stimulates critical thinking. It requires them to look at a primary source from different viewpoints and to suggest generalizations and conclusions that draw on adequate facts and historical evidence.

INSTRUCTIONAL STRATEGIES

Primary sources can be used in a variety of ways in the classroom. Document-based education creates a classroom atmosphere where critical thinking skills can easily be integrated into the curriculum and where the instructor serves as a guide rather than as the sole source of information and knowledge. Documents can be analyzed on several levels, and differences in students' abilities, competencies, and interests can be channeled to stimulate class discussions and other activities. Here are some suggested approaches for using primary sources found in Part III or for using ones that you have found either on the Internet or in books and area archives. You will encounter examples of all of these approaches when you peruse the questions in Part III.

• Thematic Approach	This approach traces a pattern or theme in a primary source that may appear in a different period of history. Students learn to compare and contrast, for example, a particular event in history with other similar incidents. This type of approach helps develop historical perspective.
• Database Approach	Some primary source Internet sites serve as individual or group activity databases. They contain sufficient numbers of primary sources to allow students to select a category of sources and formulate their own thesis statements. Census data and other statistically oriented primary sources lend themselves to this approach.

- Role-Playing Approach

Role-playing activities create a "you are there" atmosphere that can help students realize the relevancy of primary sources. Having to put themselves in the place of someone who lived long ago enlivens the study of history.

- Class Involvement Approach

Using primary sources to conduct debates or host mock trials can involve the entire class in using primary sources. It also gives history educators the opportunity to design activities for students that are commensurate with their abilities.

- Counter-Factual Approach

This approach requires students to ask themselves, "What if?" with primary sources and then research and think critically in accord with that historical assumption. Asking the question, "What if President Saddam Hussein of Iraq had invaded Kuwait and Saudi Arabia in 1991 and not one country took military action to stop it?" is an example of a counter-factual approach.

- Assignment Approach

Many primary sources predispose themselves to individual questions that can be assigned to a designated student or group. They provide opportunities for students to use the critical thinking skills process approach or can help students who are searching for ideas for a research paper.

- Simulation Approach

Employing primary sources to re-create past historical events such as military encounters creates a dynamic approach that enlivens the study of the past and enables students to see the immediate consequences of their chosen course of action.

PRIMARY SOURCE PREPARATIONS

Employing primary sources in a history curriculum that is already highly content-structured and prescheduled requires some classroom planning and management skills. Here are some suggestions for ensuring a successful document-based unit. Take into account (1) the type of activity, (2) the site where you are going to hold the activity, (3) the time allotted for completing it, and (4) how you plan to evaluate it.

1. Type of Activity: Decide on the approach you are going to take for using primary sources. Will you have individual, group, or entire class participation? This decision will help determine the site selection.

2. Site Selection: Select a site that is conducive to your pedagogical ap-

proach. Confirm that it has a sufficient number of Internet-accessible computers. The school library media center might be the best location because it also contains secondary historical sources.

3. Time: Ask yourself how much time you can afford for small group discussion or oral presentations. Frequently this part of the assignment consumes more time than you planned for.

4. Evaluation: Determine the product and/or presentation that students will complete as a result of their work with primary sources and formulate a grading plan for the unit.

PLANNING FOR FUTURE DOCUMENT-BASED ACTIVITIES

The Internet abounds in primary sources in a variety of formats. In some cases, Internet databases such as the Avalon Project at Yale Law School have classified documents by century and chronological order to make it easier to access them. Many of these primary sources can be found only at the Library of Congress, for example, and could never be used off-site.

Primary Internet sources can be found in almost every field of history. Unlike years ago, when a student had to drive to a library archive and wade through pages of materials looking for mention of a public figure, they are easily accessed. Many of these documents include search software. A quick search on a historical phrase, person, or event will produce the exact passage that matches one's search terms. With this historical bounty only a click away, history educators and school library media specialists have an unprecedented opportunity to infuse history units with the real voices and deeds of those who lived it. The Internet is a tremendous democratizing agent for the study of history. Even the most geographically isolated school can have access to all these primary sources with just one Internet-connected computer. The Internet also opens the electronic doors to others with similar historical interests. Students and history educators can join or monitor history-related discussion groups such as H-Net: The Humanities Network, and discourse with academicians and other historians about specific topics. Students can also e-mail experts in a particular field of history and receive advice and assistance.

So what can history educators and school library media specialists do to take advantage of this electronic primary source banquet? First, search for primary sources related to every area of the history curriculum. Second, begin incorporating them into daily lesson plans and classroom activities. Make them second nature for students to use. Third, be creative in employing them. Design questions that (1) present a puzzle, (2) challenge a stereotype or conventional wisdom, (3) present a contradiction, (4) offer an insight or an aha! experience, (5) promote empathy through a human-interest story, or (6) present a generalization or explanation against which different generalizations or explanations can be compared later ("Library of Congress," 2). Choose activities that get students role-playing, experiencing simulations, and thinking, "what if?" Foster a learning environment that demands that students employ critical thinking skills not just some of the time but all of the time. Finally, render a history textbook obsolete or something that will be consulted only as a reference book.

REFERENCES

"Age of Enlightenment in the Paintings of France's National Museums." http:// www.culture.fr/luminiere/documents/files/imaginary-exhibition.html (July 18, 1998). Contains an image of *The Death of Marat* by Jacques Louis David.

"American Life Histories." http://rs6.loc.gov/amhome/html (August 17, 1998). Contains oral histories of approximately 2,900 Americans from every walk of life during the Great Depression.

Boccaccio, Giovanni. *The Decameron*. New York: Modern Library, 1930.

Cantor, Norman, and Richard I. Schneider. *How to Study History*. New York: Thomas Y. Crowell, 1968.

Craver, Kathleen W. *Teaching Electronic Literacy: A Concepts-Based Approach for School Library Media Specialists*. Westport, CT: Greenwood Press, 1997.

Dallek, Robert. *Flawed Giant: Lyndon Johnson and His Times, 1961–1973*. New York: Oxford University Press, 1998.

Garraghan, Gilbert, and Jean Delanglez. *A Guide to Historical Method*. New York: Fordham University Press, 1946.

"H-Net: The Humanities Network." http://www.h-net.msu.edu/ (September 2, 1998). Serves as a clearinghouse for materials supplied by a variety of subject-oriented electronic discussion groups.

Kipling, Rudyard. "The White Man's Burden and Its Critics." http://www. boondocksnet.com/kipling/kipling.html (July 12, 1998). Contains a copy of the poem and the criticism that was generated when it was published.

"Law Code of Hammurabi." http://www.humanitas.ccny.cuny.edu/history/ reader/hammurabi.htm (May 19, 1998). This site contains the prologue and selected laws from Hammurabi's code, including the retributive laws.

"Library of Congress Learning Page: Framework for Using Primary Sources." http://memory.loc.gov/ammem/ndlpedu/lessons/fw.html (July 11, 1998). Includes suggestions for using primary sources in the classroom.

Lorimer, Susan, et al. "What Is a Primary Source?" Yale University Primary Sources Research Colloquium. http://www.library.yale.edu/ref/err/ primsrcs.htm (March 18, 1998).

O'Reilly, Kevin. *Teachers Guide Book Two New Republic to Civil War*. Pacific Grove, CA: Critical Thinking Books and Software, 1993.

"Senator Joseph McCarthy—A Multimedia Celebration." http://webcorp.com/
mccarthy/ (August 18, 1998). Contains audio excerpts of Senator Joseph
McCarthy's fiery speeches warning of communist infiltration in various
U.S. government branches.

Taylor, Joshua C. *Learning to Look: A Handbook for the Visual Arts*. 2nd ed. Chicago:
University of Chicago Press, 1981.

Tetlock, Philip E., and Aaron Belkin. *Counterfactual Thought Experiments in World
Politics*. Princeton, NJ: Princeton University Press, 1996.

"Tres Riches Heures." http://humanities.uchicago.edu/images/heures/heures.
html (July 25, 1998). Contains illuminations for the months of January and
May from the Duc de Berry's book of hours.

Trinkle, Dennis A., ed. *Writing, Teaching and Researching History in the Electronic
Age*. Armonk, NY: M. E. Sharpe, 1998.

Vincent, John Martin. *Historical Research: An Outline of Theory and Practice*. New
York: Peter Smith, 1929.

Wilke, John R. "Microsoft Internal E-Mail Bolsters Case Against Software Maker,
U.S. Contends." *Wall Street Journal*, November 21, 1997, B20.

Wilson, Elizabeth Barkley. "Jacques-Louis David." *Smithsonian* 29 (August 1998):
81–91.

THE PRIMARY SOURCE SITES

ANCIENT CIVILIZATIONS

DIOTIMA (3900 BCE–476 CE)

URL ADDRESS: www.uky.edu/ArtsSciences/Classics/gender.html

SITE SUMMARY: Diotima was a woman who, according to Socrates, taught him something about the god Eros. This site serves as an inter-disciplinary resource for users who are interested in gender issues in various ancient Mediterranean countries and territories. Started in 1995, it includes course materials for women's studies courses as well as links to many online articles, book reviews, databases, and images. It also provides additional links to extensive women's studies sites based at Yahoo and at the National Women's History Project. Students can move quickly among categories by clicking on links such as courses, images, essays, biblical studies, and bibliographies. Diotima has a search engine that supports keyword searching of selected parts of the database.

DISCUSSION QUESTIONS AND ACTIVITIES

1. Select *Search* and enter the name *Cleopatra*. Select *Public Life*****. Cleopatra was many things to many different people. To some men, she was a dangerous mixture of decadence and corruption. To others, she was a highly educated, multilingual, astute politician. Using quotations and evidence from Virgil, Horace, and Plutarch, present a dramatic dialogue in the persona of Cleopatra that portrays some aspect of her multifaceted character.

2. Select *Search* and enter the name *Pandora* in the search box. Select *Rebecca Resinski*****. In Greek mythology, Pandora was the first woman. Created by Zeus, she was sent to earth with a vessel containing all the ills of the world, and in a final command, Zeus forbade her to open it. But, of course, she did. Read Hesiod's account of Pandora in this paper and write an angry letter to Hesiod expressing your opinion that he is perpetuating a negative stereotype that women are always deceitful.

3. Select *Images* and click on *Gender and Power*. Select *Go to Images of Artifacts*. What symbols of power are the women associated with in these artifacts?

4. Select *Images* and click on *Daily Life*. Based on the descriptions and

images, design a fifth or sixth century BCE Greek house for five persons. If you have drawing software, design it on a computer. Otherwise, you can construct the house from paper or render blueprint-style drawings.

5. Select *Images* and click on *Men's Life*. How were men depicted compared to women in these Greek images? Look for signs of power, gender role, active versus passive living, and other comparative clues.

6. Select *Images* and scroll down to *Vergil's Dido: A Multimedia Path*. Choose *Dido and Aeneas*. Dido founded the city of Carthage, which ruled the Mediterranean for centuries. She fell in love with Aeneas, who was fleeing the flaming Troy. When he left her to continue his travels to Italy, she killed herself with his sword. At this site there are several depictions of Dido in paintings. How do you think she is portrayed as a woman?

RELATED INTERNET SITE(S)

Classics and Mediterranean Archaeology
http://rome.classics.lsa.umich.edu/welcome.html
This is an excellent gateway site to other Internet links dedicated to ancient history. Users can search within a variety of subjects.

VANISHED KINGDOMS OF THE NILE: THE REDISCOVERY OF ANCIENT NUBIA (ca. 3800 BCE–300 CE)

URL ADDRESS: http://www-oi.uchicago.edu/OI/PROJ/NUB/NUBX92/NUBX92_brochure.html

SITE SUMMARY: Nubia was a country of mystery, legend, and great wealth. It occupied a large amount of territory south of Egypt. This exhibit, mounted by the University of Chicago's Oriental Institute Museum, features a brochure with selected images from various Nubian archaeological sites, a map, photographs, a bibliography, and, more important, a hypertext article about the ancient kingdom of Nubia. A second related site provides information about a museum exhibit mounted in 1987.

DISCUSSION QUESTIONS AND ACTIVITIES

1. You are an archaeologist with a specialty in hieroglyphic, hieratic, and demotic forms of writing. You have been asked to certify that the sample of Meroitic script is from the first–second centuries CE. What

clues does the sample give you that will permit you to date it with a fair degree of accuracy?

2. Nubia was dominated by Egypt for several centuries. Examine the drawing of Apedemak, the lion-headed warrior god of Nubia. Compare it with pictures of Egyptian gods. Write a short paper, complete with your own drawings, showing the possible origin of this Nubian god.

3. What can you tell about Nubian economic life from the picture of a Nubian princess in her ox-chariot from the Egyptian tomb of Huy, ca. 1320 BCE, and the decorated pot from the first–second centuries CE?

4. Nubia thrived as a homeland to one of the world's first black cultures. It was known for its gold, ivory, and trade with Egypt and other African countries. What social, environmental, and economic factors may have been responsible for its demise?

5. At times in its history, Nubia dominated or was dominated by Egypt. Discuss the possible social, geographic, economic, and military reasons for this cultural reversal.

6. The Romans copied much from the Greeks. Why did the Nubians adopt many aspects of Egyptian culture?

RELATED INTERNET SITE(S)

Excursis IV: Nubia the Land Upriver
http://www.library.nwu.edu/class/history/B94/B94nubia.html
   Includes a hyperlinked outline of the geography and history of Nubia.

Nubia: Its Glory and Its People
http://www-oi.uchicago.edu/OI/PROJ/NUB/NUBX/
NUBX_brochure.html
   Features an introduction and images of various Nubian archaeological sites.

DUKE PAPYRUS ARCHIVE (ca. 2600 BCE)

URL ADDRESS: http://odyssey.lib.duke.edu/papyrus

SITE SUMMARY: Duke University's papyrus archives furnish electronic access to 1,373 papyrus images and selected texts from ancient Egypt. Students can read introductory sections about Egypt during the time papyrus was in use and about Egyptian papyrus writing under Greek and Roman rule. The site features a search engine for keywords and subsequent access to 72 links and 150 electronic images. Brief translations of various papyri are grouped under categories such as family papers, women and children, slaves, scripts, and religious and cultural aspects.

DISCUSSION QUESTIONS AND ACTIVITIES

1. Browse through the papyri texts relating to slaves. How are slaves viewed in the various pieces of papyri correspondence? Are there any human considerations evidenced?

2. Compare the Egyptian view of slaves to those held by slaveholders in the United States. What are the similarities and dissimilarities?

3. Browse through the papyri texts by *material aspects*. What can you tell about the level of Egyptian commerce from the translations of various papyri?

4. Many ancient Egyptians were illiterate and relied on scribes to write their correspondence. What kind of power would a scribe have in a mainly illiterate society?

5. Browse through the texts about women and children. What kinds of problems were they dealing with that are similar to ones in today's society? Find several articles from current periodicals that could have been written by the ancient Egyptians.

6. Browse through the *cultural aspects* of papyri that describe clothing, flowers, and food. What inferences can you make about how sophisticated Egyptian society was at various times in its civilization?

RELATED INTERNET SITE(S)

American Society of Papyrologists
http://scholar.cc.emory.edu/scripts/ASP/ASP-MENU.html
Includes links to educational institutions with papyrology collections, images, other papyrological resources, and related Web resources.

Egyptology Resources
http://www.newton.cam.ac.uk/egypt/
Provides links to Egyptian tombs, museums, organizations, and societies and other Egyptian Web resources.

THE EGYPTIAN BOOK OF THE DEAD (2500 BCE)

URL ADDRESS: http://eawc.evansville.edu/anthology/ani.htm

SITE SUMMARY: The exact title of the best known book of the ancient Egyptians is *The Book of Coming Forth by Day*. It consists of guidelines for living an ethical, moral, and religious life. Inscribed on the sarcophagi of Egyptian kings in 2500 BCE, it was later transcribed onto sheets of papyrus and buried with the dead so that they could refer to it. While there are various versions of the book, all of them are characterized by instructions to the soul (the "ka") after the death of the body and during the ka's journey to Anenti, the region of the dead. Students may draw many parallels from this book to tenets from the Bible, the Torah, and other liturgical texts.

DISCUSSION QUESTIONS AND ACTIVITIES

1. There are many references to Osiris, the god of death and resurrection. What other religions have a similar god? Compare their beliefs about death to what happens to the souls of ancient Egyptians.

2. During your passage through the underworld, your heart will be weighed by Anubis, the soul leader. The ultimate fate of your "ka" or soul is dependent upon his judgment. Describe the sins or bad deeds that you are accused of committing.

3. From reading various passages of *The Book of the Dead*, what do you think is the Egyptians' attitude toward death?

4. *The Book of the Dead* is an erroneous title for *The Book of Coming Forth by Day*. Why did the Egyptians use this title for a book about death? What does the title imply about their religious beliefs?

5. Spells or incantations comprise much of this ancient text. What is the intent of these spells? Were they to be followed only in the afterlife?

6. In this ancient text, there is an ambivalence in the dead Egyptians' wish to accompany Re, the sun god, on trips throughout the sky or to travel with Osiris, the god of the underworld who is also associated with life-giving earth. Why were the ancient Egyptians so hesitant to accompany a single god?

RELATED INTERNET SITE(S)

Egypt
http://ancienthistory.miningco.com/
Provides a series of related links to Egyptian art, architecture, archaeological sites, and museums.

History of Egypt
http://interoz.com/egypt/ehistory.htm
Includes biographies of pharaohs and descriptions of their gods.

MYSTERY OF THE MAYA (2500 BCE–950 CE)

URL ADDRESS: http://www.civilization.ca/membrs/civiliz/maya/mminteng.html

SITE SUMMARY: The Mayan civilization encompassed the present-day countries of Mexico, Guatemala, and Belize and parts of El Salvador and Honduras. These creative people were astronomers, evolved a writing system, and were considered fine mathematicians and calendar developers. They constructed, without metal tools or the wheel, entire cities whose architectural qualities are copied in modern office buildings and even entire towns. The ruins of their highly developed civilization can be found in Palenque, Tikal, Tulum, Chichen Itza, Copan, and Uxmal. This site contains links to images of ruins, writing and hieroglyphics, mathematics, the Mayan calendar, astronomy, cosmology, and religion.

DISCUSSION QUESTIONS AND ACTIVITIES

1. The Mayans practiced human sacrifice in their religion. We consider this evidence of barbarism. Why do you think the Mayans indulged in this practice? Are there any aspects of our society—for example, certain types of sports, capital punishment, or the use of weapons—that they would have considered uncivilized?

2. Typology is a classification system that archaeologists use to group objects according to what they look like, their construction, and their use. Seriation is a classification system that is employed to see if objects of one type reflect sufficient similarities so that they can be called a style. Mayan civilization has been divided into Early, Classic, and Mexican periods. Choose specific Mayan images and artifacts and prepare a museum catalogue brochure for an upcoming exhibit of these periods.

3. How sophisticated a civilization's calendar was is an indication of how developed its civilization was. Read the site information about the Mayan calendar. What did it allow the Mayans to do? How did the Mayans construct it so that it was one ten-thousandth of a day more exact than our present-day calendar?

4. Archaeologists consider the Mayan writing system evidence of a highly developed civilization. Read the site information about writing and hieroglyphics. Use this information to construct a hand shield that reflects your own family's name, ethnic origins, type of employment, interests, or hobbies.

5. The design of buildings usually takes into account the local climate, topography, and regional flora and fauna. Select images of various Mayan ruins and analyze how they suited their environment. Use your analysis to recommend a similar design for a new Guatemalan resort.

6. The Maya have been termed mysterious because of the disappearance of their civilization. Look at different aspects of this site. What are some possible reasons for their collapse and demise?

RELATED INTERNET SITE(S)

Maya Links
http://indy4.fdl.cc.mn.us/~isk/maya/maya1.html
Includes a series of annotated links to Mayan history, culture, and learning activities.

Maya Civilization—Past and Present
http://indy4.fdl.cc.mn.us/~isk/maya/maya.html
Provides a series of links about past and present Mayan civilization and culture and an interview with Rigoberta Menchu Tum, 1992 Nobel Peace Prize laureate and Mayan refugee.

Maya Culture
http://indy4.fdl.cc.mn.us/~isk/maya/mayastor.html
Features traditional Mayan storytellers' tales and information about Mayan village life and language.

EXPLORING ANCIENT WORLD CULTURES: CHINA (2205–479 BCE)

URL ADDRESS: http://eawc.evansville.edu/chpage.htm

SITE SUMMARY: China is just one of the cultures at this extensive site. Within the section about China is a search engine that supports either a global or regional search of Chinese chronologies, essays, images, sites, and ancient texts. A text search produces primary translated works written by Confucius, Lao Tzu, and Sun Tzu. The best part of the search engine is a global search function by date that yields related sites, essays, texts, or images in other parts of the world so that students can make appropriate developmental comparisons.

DISCUSSION QUESTIONS AND ACTIVITIES

1. Sun Tzu's classic military text, *The Art of War*, is still being studied by today's generals, business executives, sociologists, and others be-

cause the ancient truths proposed in it are eternal laws that operate even in contemporary society. You are a four-star general who has been asked to lecture at the United States War College about Chapter 3, "Attack by Stratagem." Why have you titled your lecture "Fighting Is the Last Option of the Soldier"?

2. You are a former Vietnamese general who has been asked to speak to West Point students about some of the principles in Chapter 7 of Sun Tzu's *The Art of War* and how it applied to maneuvers during the Vietnam War. What ancient Chinese military advice did you use either during specific battles or as a general military strategy?

3. At the beginning of the text, Sun Tzu says that "all warfare is based on deception." Provide victorious examples from the American Revolutionary War or other wars that support Sun Tzu's statement.

4. *The Tao Te Ching* is a collection of ancient Chinese poems that contain relevant philosophical and historical truths. Read #3, *If you esteem great men, people become powerless*. What lessons can you draw from this adage and the leadership of men such as Mao Tse-tung, Joseph Stalin, and Adolf Hitler? How did people become powerless under these rulers?

5. Read #17 of *The Tao Te Ching*, about governance. Describe three rulers from any historical period who, in your opinion, have practiced the recommendations concerning how to rule.

6. Read #29 of *The Tao Te Ching*, about the world. What are the pros and cons of this belief? Provide examples from environmental history, geography, and former civilizations to illustrate both sides of this poem.

RELATED INTERNET SITE(S)

Voice of the Shuttle
http://humanitas.ucsb.edu/shuttle/history.html
   This is a gateway site to excellent secondary sources about China and other countries.

LAW CODE OF HAMMURABI (1750 BCE)

URL ADDRESS: http://eawc.evansville.edu/anthology/hammurabi.htm

SUMMARY: Hammurabi was the sixth ruler of the first dynasty of Babylon and the leader chiefly responsible for creating the world's first metropolitan area. His code of laws was drawn up to regulate economic, social, and political relations in the new kingdom. The laws were carved on a monument and placed in public view. While the punishment for many crimes was death, issues dealing with contracts, employment, marriage, property, taxes, military service, and the status of women were also strictly regulated. The uniform aspects of Hammurabi's law code ensured that tribal customs involving blood feuds and marriage by capture were abolished.

DISCUSSION QUESTIONS AND ACTIVITIES

1. Read the prologue by Hammurabi. In it, Hammurabi explains the purpose of his legal code. What are his reasons for creating the code?
2. You have deliberately knocked out your neighbor's tooth. What will happen to you under Hammurabi's legal code? What would happen if you were in an American court? Which system of justice do you prefer? What if your neighbor had knocked your tooth out?
3. What are the rights of women under Hammurabi's law code? Do they have the same rights as men? What is the purpose of marriage in Babylonian society? Would you have liked to be a woman in Babylonian times?
4. Read through selected laws. Do you see any relationship to Islamic laws, particularly those called Sharia?
5. Law 195 makes a stern reference to one's filial duties. How does this law compare to Chapter 20 of Exodus? What does this law tell you about these two civilizations?
6. What are the similarities and dissimilarities between Mosiac law and Hammurabi's code?

RELATED INTERNET SITE(S)

Hammurabi's Code of Laws
http://wwwlia.org/hamm1.htm#1
Contains an excellent scholarly description and interpretation of Hammurabi's code of laws (1–282) and includes the Formal Preamble and Epilogue.

Law Code of Hammurabi
http://mistral.culture.fr/louvre/louvrea.htm
Select *Collections* and click on *Oriental Antiquities Islamic Art*. Choose *Major Works*. Select *Mesopotamia and Anatolia*. Scroll down to *Law-Codex of Hammurabi Susa* to retrieve an expandable image of the monument containing Hammurabi's code of laws.

PERSEUS PROJECT (1200–323 BCE)

URL ADDRESS: http://www.perseus.tufts.edu/

SITE SUMMARY: This vast primary and secondary electronic database illustrating the archaic and classical Greek world continues to evolve as more materials are added. It contains more than 24,000 images, 179 sites, and 524 coin images. Perseus also includes two-thirds of the surviving literature up to the death of Alexander the Great in Greek with English translations. It features a color atlas of the Greek world, student papers, articles about ancient authors and archaeology, an overview of Greek history from Homer to the death of Alexander, and a 2,600-entry bibliography. All sites are extensively hyperlinked, and a search engine provides easy keyword, subject, and known-item access. The database is especially suited to group questions. Refer to Thomas Martin's site within Perseus entitled *Overview of Archaic and Classical Greek History* for appropriate question sites.

DISCUSSION QUESTIONS AND ACTIVITIES

1. Why is geography a country's destiny? Use the Perseus Atlas to prepare a series of maps that shows the gradual development of Greek civilization as towns and eventually city-states expanded along the shores of the Mediterranean and Black Seas and included southern Italy and Sicily. With each map, provide geographic, topographical, agricultural, and socioeconomic reasons for growth in a particular direction. How did this pattern of growth help unify or separate the Greeks into city-states?

2. In 1200 BCE, Mycenaean Greece experienced a violent conflict that threatened the entire civilization. Read the primary sources that describe the poverty, loss of writing skills, and invasions. Why was this period known as the Dark Ages?

3. By 900 BCE, Greek civilization was thriving again. Read the primary sources associated with this period and outline and analyze the various economic, social, agricultural, and political factors that are thought responsible for this transformation.

4. After the Dark Ages, Greece developed an aristocracy. Read the primary sources that describe its social structure and value system. Form a debate team to discuss the pros and cons of this form of society and its implications for government.

5. Men and women were viewed differently from one another during

the aristocratic Greek period. Read the primary sources that support this statement. If you were living during that period, which gender would you choose to be, and why?

6. Democracy as a form of government was one of the most important legacies of Greek civilization. Read the primary sources that cite how the poor and women contributed to its development. Can you find incidents of hypocrisy in Greek democracy? What were the franchise rights of slaves?

RELATED INTERNET SITE(S)

The Ancient Greek World Tour
http://www.museum.upenn.edu/Greek_World/Intro.html
Contains images of artifacts relating to ancient Greek daily life, religion, death, the land, and history.

Ancient World Web
http://www.julen.net/aw/
This is a gateway site containing excellent links to all aspects of ancient Greece.

The Ancient City of Athens
http://www.indiana.edu/~kglowack/athens/
Provides a photographic archive of the archaeological ruins of ancient Athens.

ROME RESOURCES PROJECT (753 BCE–476 CE)

URL ADDRESS: http://www.dalton.org/groups/rome/

SITE SUMMARY: Winner of several awards for excellence in site design and presentation, the Rome Resources Project is a large database of primary and secondary sources about the Roman Republic and Empire. It is divided into nine sections: (1) Literature, (2) Military, (3) Archaeology, (4) Political, (5) General, (6) Philosophy, (7) Drama, (8) Religion, and (9) Search Engines. Students will find thousands of links to materials such as law codes, online Latin texts, images of archaeological sites, and translations of plays. The site also contains timelines and chronologies, religious and mythological information, resources on military equipment, and maps of the Roman Empire.

DISCUSSION QUESTIONS AND ACTIVITIES

1. Under the political section, click on *The Law of the Twelve Tablets*. Compare these tablets to Hammurabi's Code of Laws. Are the Roman laws

as harsh? Do people have more rights under the Roman laws? Do Hammurabi's laws prohibit people of different classes from marrying? Why is the Roman law forbidding marriage between patricians and plebeians deleterious to a country or empire? Compare this attempt at Roman apartheid to South Africa's twentieth century apartheid.

2. In this same section, examine the Julian marriage laws. They were passed to encourage people to marry and have children. Who had more rights under these laws, men or women? Suppose that our population is dropping and more people are choosing either not to marry or to have children outside of marriage. You are a United States senator who has drafted a similar set of laws. Make a speech about them to your constituents (your classmates) and take note of their reactions, criticisms, or acceptance.

3. Under the military section, click on *Catapults in Greek and Roman Antiquity* and *The Catapult Museum Online*. Based on images of ancient drawings, construct a working Roman catapult. Demonstrate it in class.

4. Under *Archaeology*, click on *The Palace of Diocletian at Split*. You and a team of architects have been chosen by the United Nations to restore the palace to its former glory. You must provide plans based on the images, drawings, and descriptions at this site. Why would the United Nations be involved in this restoration process?

5. Under *Literature*, click on *Pliny: Letters 10.96–97*. Read Pliny's correspondence with the Emperor Trajan. What is Pliny's attitude toward Christians? What is the Emperor's? Do you think that Trajan is fair-minded? Why do you think the Christians were a threat to the Roman government?

6. Under *General*, click on *Roman Board Games*. Read through the descriptions of various Roman board games and design a similar one for four players. Identify which games or variations of specific games are still being played today.

RELATED INTERNET SITE(S)

Rome
http://www.taisei.co.jp/cg_e/ancient_world/rome/arome.html

Sponsored by a Japanese architecture firm, this site contains reconstructed, expandable images of the ancient city of Rome.

Rome-History Resource Center
www.ucr.edu/h-gig/horuslinks.html

This is an excellent gateway site to resources about the people and events of the Roman Empire. One link provides access to 15,000 photographs, images, diagrams, and maps of Roman and Greek sites and artifacts.

THE DEAD SEA SCROLLS (200 BCE)

URL ADDRESS: http://lcweb.loc.gov/exhibits/scrolls/toc.html

SITE SUMMARY: Found in caves near the northwestern shore of the Dead Sea in 1947, the Dead Sea Scrolls consist of papyrus and letter fragments dating to 200 BCE. They include all of the books of the Old Testament except Esther, fragments of the Septuagint, which is the first known Greek translation of the Old Testament, and parts of the Aramaic version of the Book of Job. They also contain writings of the Qumran community that flourished in the area where the scrolls were found. They provide a rare glimpse of one group of Palestinian Jews who lived 2,000 years ago and how Qumrans conducted their daily affairs. This site features twelve scroll fragments accompanied by detailed translations and interpretations. It also provides background information about the Qumran community.

DISCUSSION QUESTIONS AND ACTIVITIES

1. What are the climatic conditions around the Dead Sea area? What role does humidity play in the decomposition process? Why were the scrolls so well preserved?

2. Scholars are still wondering why the scrolls were hidden in a cave. Some refer to evidence in Genesis 19 of an earthquake during the time of Abraham as a possible factor. Others refer the destruction of the Temple in Jerusalem in 70 CE as a reason. Why do you think the scrolls were hidden?

3. Look at the artifacts recovered from the Qumran site. What evidence do they provide that the scrolls were hidden by a people living in the area around 200 BCE and not a group from the outside area?

4. The Qumran site was excavated by Roland de Vaux, a French Dominican priest, in an attempt to discern who had hidden the scrolls. He believed that a Judean sect called the Essenes were the ones responsible. Others believe that the Sadducees, another Judean group, were responsible. Formulate arguments that support both sides based on the primary source excerpts at this site.

5. The Dead Sea Scrolls are considered the greatest manuscript find of the twentieth century, but their authenticity is still being debated. De-

scribe the process that archaeologists used to confirm the age and authenticity of the scrolls. Using this evidence as support, give your opinion on the origin of the scrolls.

6. What is the religious significance of the Dead Sea Scrolls? How do they enrich the religious and historical heritage of Christians and Jews?

RELATED INTERNET SITE(S)

Qumran Library Related Library of Congress Materials
http://lcweb.loc.gov/exhibits/scrolls/lc3.html
Provides an annotated bibliography of related Dead Sea Scroll materials.

Scrolls from the Dead Sea: The Ancient Library of Qumran and Modern Scholarship
http://lcweb.loc.gov/exhibits/scrolls/article.html
Contains a short article on the creation of the Dead Sea Scrolls exhibit at the Library of Congress.

THE SILK ROAD (ca. 202 BCE)

URL ADDRESS: http://www.china.trav.net/china/attractions/silkrd3.html

SITE SUMMARY: The Silk Road was not only an extremely important historic trade route but also a cultural one. The first Buddhist monasteries came to China along the Silk Road, spreading a religion that dominates many contemporary Asian countries. This site contains eight recent images that illustrate contemporary and historic aspects of the Silk Road. The textual part of the site, while not a primary source, is so rich in geographic, cultural, and historical detail that it is extremely useful from many different perspectives. It covers the early history of the route in the time of the Roman Empire and discusses the influence of the Mongols, its greatest years, and present-day foreign influences.

DISCUSSION QUESTIONS AND ACTIVITIES

1. The Silk Road was a tortuous route of 7,000 miles through more than a half-dozen kingdoms. You are a Chinese trader from Xian who wants to sell your goods to a business person in Rome. Trace your

itinerary on a map, indicating the shortest route and the kingdoms that you must pass through.

2. You are a caravan leader who has to negotiate the price you will charge to transport some precious metals, ivory, and jewels to China. As a basis for bargaining, you must compile a list of human, weather, and natural hazards you will face, taxes and tributes you must pay, the food, clothing, and upkeep for your animals and workers, and other essential items necessary for a successful journey. Refer to some of the site's images for ideas relating to geographical and weather hazards.

3. The Chinese government has put you in charge of policing the Central Asian trade route. You must build fortifications and caravansaries at which travelers can stay while they transport their goods. Draw up a plan to protect this part of the route from bandits. Refer to some of the site images and descriptions. Where do you think the weakest areas of the route are? Where are bandits most likely to attack?

4. The Silk Road was also a cultural route. Discuss the major religions that were also transported and their central ideas. How did they come to influence other parts of Asia, India, Arabia, and Europe?

5. When hostilities erupted between the Christian and Moslem worlds, the Mongols from the East under various khans unified the area and kept the route open. Discuss the role of Genghis Khan in reestablishing this important trade route. Why was it important to him, and what was the cultural significance of his achievement?

6. Analyze the cultural, geographic, political, and technological factors that may have contributed to the decline of the Silk Road.

RELATED INTERNET SITE(S)

In Celebration of the Silk Road
http://goldoak.edcoe.k12.ca.us/plv/silkroad.htm
   Contains a map of the Silk Road and ideas for lesson plans.

The Silk Road
http://www.mfa.gov.tr/GRUPE/silkroad.htm
   Includes textual information about the Silk Road and several maps showing different parts of the route.

THE ECOLE INITIATIVE (ca. 30–1500 CE)

URL ADDRESS: http://cedar.evansville.edu/~ecoleweb/

SITE SUMMARY: This vast ecumenical religious history site is a hypertext encyclopedia of pre-Reformation church history. It features a glossary of hundreds of entries and an articles index with lengthy essays about major religious history topics and figures. An images index also provides pictures of Judaeo-Christian iconography and religious art. The chronology and geographical cross index search engine are useful additions. However, the Ecole Initiative's greatest treasure is its documents section. Translated works by Maimonides, the great Jewish philosopher and physician, Muhammad, prophet of Islam, Thomas Aquinas, and Zoroaster are examples of some of the hundreds of entries. All the Councils of the Church before 1054 are also present. This site is especially useful for group projects.

DISCUSSION QUESTIONS AND ACTIVITIES

1. Click on the letter *A* and scroll down to *Augustine, Bishop of Hippo, "De Bono Conjugali."* According to St. Augustine, what place does friendship have in marriage? What role does sex play in marriage? What place do children have in marriage? How do you view St. Augustine's position on these matters? Do you see him as an enlightened person or a reactionary on the subject?

2. Click on the letter *B* and scroll down to *Boniface, VIII, Pope of Rome* and read his papal bull, *Unam Sanctam*. Why did this assertion of papal authority over secular rulers and all Christians lay the foundation for a future anti-Catholic movement?

3. Click on the letter *C* and scroll down to *Charlemagne*, Frankish Roman Emperor of the West (VIII/IX Centuries) and select *Letter to Bagnulf on Education*. From your reading of the letter, what was the position of Charlemagne, the Frankish Roman Emperor, toward education? Discuss the pros and cons of educating people. What dangers might it pose to an emperor? If you were an emperor, what would be your position on public education?

4. Click on the letter *C* and scroll down to *Constantine I* (the Great),

Emperor of Rome, (III/IV Centuries) and select *The Edict of Milan*. Read the Edict of Toleration by Galerius and the Edict of Milan by Constantine Augustus. Both men had persecuted Christians during the earlier part of their rule. What made them change their minds? When a group of people is being persecuted, do you think that statements and speeches by public officials denouncing it are sufficient, or do you think that laws should be passed making it a crime to persecute or discriminate against groups of people?

5. Click on the letter *J* and scroll down to *Joan of Arc*. Read *Letter to the King of England and his Generals, 1429*. In an age when women did not have a major role in politics, let alone the military, what would be your reaction as the king of England when you received this letter? Would you feel threatened by it? Would you take any military precautions?

6. Click on the letter *M* and scroll to *The Thirteen Principles of Judaism* by Maimonides. Using outline form, compare and contrast the thirteen principles of Judaism with the basic principles of Christianity and Islam. Where are there similarities and dissimilarities? Are the differences greater or less than you thought?

RELATED INTERNET SITE(S)

Guide to Early Christian Documents
http://www.iclnet.org/pub/resources/christian-history.html
   Includes copies of Christian texts, canons, creeds, and other relevant Web sites.

Islamic Scriptures and Prophetic Traditions
http://wings.buffalo.edu/hh/student-life/sa/muslim/isl/texts.html
   Provides copies of all the major texts and articles of faith relating to Islam.

Judaism and Jewish Resources
http://shamash.org/trb/whjr95.html
   Features text copies of the main tenets of Judaism.

POMPEII AND MT. VESUVIUS (79 CE)

URL ADDRESS: http://www.academyonline.com/academy/athens/latin/

SITE SUMMARY: On August 24, 79 CE, Mount Vesuvius, a volcano near the Bay of Naples, erupted, completely burying the ancient cities of Pompeii, Herculaneum, and Strabiae in cinders, ashes, and mud. Pliny the Elder, a Roman statesman, soldier, and author, was in charge of the Imperial fleet. He sailed to Vesuvius to aid the rescue attempt and either suffocated or had a heart attack from the noxious gases. Included in this site is the only eyewitness account of the disaster—a letter to Tacitus from Pliny the Younger. In it, he describes the terror of the inhabitants, the heat, and the subsequent death of his uncle. The site also includes many related links and an excellent set of discussion/writing exercises concerning the event.

DISCUSSION QUESTIONS AND ACTIVITIES

1. Mt. Vesuvius has erupted fifty times since it killed Pliny the Elder in 79 CE. Lately there have been physical signs that the mountain may erupt again. Using the risk analysis information at this site, calculate the chances of this occurring within the next fifty years. Based on your risk analysis, what general advice do you have for the current inhabitants?

2. Read the excerpted accounts by Pliny the Younger about his uncle's death. What mistakes do you think Pliny the Elder made? Would Pliny have died that day if he had made other decisions?

3. You are a Roman reporter who was on one of the ships that sailed to rescue the volcano victims. Write a story for the *Roman Daily News* describing the horrific events that you witnessed.

4. The Emperor Titus has put you in charge of a fact-finding commission to determine what could have been done to save more lives. Research the facts surrounding the eruption. Did the people have any previous warning? Read the eyewitness account. Could people have reacted differently if there had been evacuation drills, routes and signs to follow, and precautions to take? Write up your findings and present them to the Emperor.

5. From Pliny the Younger's account and other site information, design a timeline of events leading up to the eruption of Mt. Vesuvius and the burial of the cities of Pompeii and Herculaneum.

6. What is the archaeological legacy of these cities? Write an essay about the benefits that this geological disaster gave to the contemporary world.

RELATED INTERNET SITE(S)

Pompeii
http://jcccnet.johnco.cc.ks.us/~jjackson/pomp.html

This is an excellent site for background material about Pompeii and Rome in general.

Eyewitness to the Eruption of A.D. 79!
http://pompeii.Virginia.edu/pompeii/pliny.html
Contains translations of the two letters written by Pliny the Younger to the historian Tacitus on the death of Pliny the Elder.

LEPERS (ca. 300 CE)

URL ADDRESS: http://www.kenyon.edu/projects/margin/lepers.htm

SITE SUMMARY: Historians do not know the geographic or exact time origins of leprosy. The word does appear in the Bible, but it may not refer to the classic symptoms of the disease. The first accurate descriptions of the disease appeared before 300 CE in the writings of the Indian physician Sushruta. Leprosy did, however, reach epidemic proportions in Europe during the Middle Ages. This site focuses on the disease and how people dealt with it during the thirteenth and fourteenth centuries. It contains a copy of the *Mass of Separation*, the church's view toward the leper, illustrations depicting lepers in the Middle Ages, accounts of lepers, and links to other leprosy-related sites.

DISCUSSION QUESTIONS AND ACTIVITIES

1. Look at the images of lepers at this site. Why do you think they are always depicted with a bell or clapper?

2. Why do you think that the treatment of lepers was less harsh in Islamic countries than it was in Christian countries?

3. Click on *The Mass of Separation*. Describe how you would have felt if you had heard this mass being recited outside of your hut. Was this action better or worse than being sent to live on the island of Molokai in the 1800s if you were a Hawaiian leper?

4. Lepers were treated differently if they were rich. Click on *Alice the Leper*. Even though she suffers terribly from the disease, how is she depicted? Write a similar letter in this style describing a poor leper.

5. As leprosy became an epidemic in the Middle Ages, how did the status of lepers change? What role did the church play in their changing status?

6. Look up the definition of the word *leper*. Why do you think it changed to include social deviants, witches, and discriminated-against minority groups?

RELATED INTERNET SITE(S)

History of Leprosy
http://www.seattleu.edu/~blewis/Leprosy.htm
This site gives excellent background material on the history of leprosy, which was called the "Disease of the Damned."

Leprosy, a Medieval Diagnostic
http://www.millersv.edu/~english/homepage/duncan/medfem/lepers.html
This site contains a short description of leprosy from the book *Medieval Lore from Bartholomew Anglicus* by Robert Steele (1966).

Byzantium: Byzantine Studies on the Internet (330–1453 CE)

URL ADDRESS: http://www.bway.net/%7Ehalsall/byzantium.html

SITE SUMMARY: Byzantine Empire is more than just a site for accessing primary source documents. It also provides excellent background materials about the time period, events, significant people, and achievements of the empire. Consider it a gateway source for additional sites about studies syllabi, Byzantine reference documents, shareware, texts, images and sounds, book reviews, and discussion groups. Primary source documents include such items as *The Georgian Chronicle* and John Mamikonean's medieval romance, *History of Taron*. The Byzantine paleography site link contains a letter derivation chart that sheds light on how scholars go about translating historical manuscripts.

DISCUSSION QUESTIONS AND ACTIVITIES

1. Click on *Original Texts* and select *Full Text Sources*. Click on *Byzantium* and select *Procopius of Caesarea Secret History*. Read several sections about Theodora, the wife of the Emperor Justinian. Write a psychological profile of her. What are her strong and weak points? How would you treat her if you were a member of the government? How might you protect yourself from her wrath?

2. In the same site, read Procopius's assessment of the emperor in *The Character and Appearance of Justinian*. He portrays him as a wicked, corrupt leader. How do you account for his description and the ones you read in secondary sources such as encyclopedias and history books?

3. Click on *Liutprand of Cremona: Report on Mission to Constantinople, 963*. What do you learn from the bishop of Cremona about the living conditions under Otto?

4. This narrative also describes lavish exchanges of gifts between rulers. Why was this a practice among them? What underlying message was it meant to impart? Do leaders of countries still exchange gifts?

5. Click on *Links to Other Sites* and select *Miscellaneous*. Click on *Byzantine Chess*. Read the section about the game and look at the diagrams. Design a Byzantine chess game complete with instructions. Evaluate it by having two classmates play a game.

6. Return to the miscellaneous page and select *Byzantine Textiles*. Read the primary and secondary sections about Byzantine clothing. Based on your reading, design a silk caftan for a Byzantine evening bash. You must also design the pattern that will be imprinted on the material.

RELATED INTERNET SITE(S)

Byzantine & Medieval Links Index
http://www.fordham.edu/halsall/medweb
Features a gateway site whose objective is to amass all Byzantine links on the Internet.

The Glory of Byzantium
http://www.metmuseum.org/htmlfile/education/title.html
Contains the Metropolitan Museum of Art's online exploration of Byzantium in conjunction with their exhibit by the same title.

ZEN BUDDHIST TEXTS (ca. 500–1200 CE)

URL ADDRESS: http://www.io.com/~snewton/zen/index.html

SITE SUMMARY: This site is maintained by the Southwest Zen Academy in Houston, Texas. Although it features a random thoughts generator, information about the Houston Zen community, and other Buddhist sources, its value lies in the presentation and translation of seven primary Zen texts: (1) the Four Great Vows; (2) the Heart of the Prajna Paramita Sutra; (3) the Heart Sutra in Buddhist Sanskrit; (4) the Diamond Cutter Sutra; (5) Affirming Faith in Mind; (6) the Four Noble Truths; and (7) the Sound of One Hand Clapping. A dictionary of Zen and Buddhist terms and information about the traditional lineage of Zen are also included.

DISCUSSION QUESTIONS AND ACTIVITIES

1. Zen Buddhism is frequently referred to as a religious philosophy or way of life. It is practiced primarily in Japan, but also has many followers in the United States. Click on *The Four Noble Truths*. What do these truths say about life? If you believed in these truths, what would your actions be if you were ordered to go to war?

2. The Diamond Cutter Sutra is one of the main Zen Buddhist texts. You are a practicing Zen Buddhist who has been asked to speak to a class about the historical implications of your religion. Explain to your listeners what a sutra is. What is the significance of the Diamond Cutter Sutra? What purpose is served by answering questions with other questions?

3. Our society has been described by many sociologists as extremely materialistic. Why is our way of life so different from the precepts addressed by the Buddha in the index section to the Diamond Cutter Sutra? What style of life does the Buddha espouse?

4. You are a proselytizing Zen master who has gained a huge following in the United States by asking your followers to take the "four great vows." How are these vows a threat to the U.S. economy and society? If your followers were to number in the millions, how long do you think that you would be protected by the First Amendment? What arguments might the government make to deport you?

5. Read the text about *Affirming Faith in Mind*. Describe your lifestyle if you were to practice this life philosophy literally. What would you own? Who would be your friends? How would you converse? Would you still wish to have a career and achieve "success"?

6. It is easy to see the similarities among Christianity, Judaism, and Islam. Why is it so difficult to find any similarities among them and Zen Buddhism?

RELATED INTERNET SITE(S)

Zen Buddhism WWW Virtual Library
http://www.ciolek.com/WWWVL-Zen.html
   Contains an excellent set of links about practitioners of Zen Buddhism, its teachings, organizations, institutions, and much more.

Buddhist WWW Virtual Library
http://www.ciolek.com/WWWVL-Buddhism.html
   This is an excellent gateway site for information about Buddhism in general and Buddhist art.

THE CAMELOT PROJECT (ca. 537 CE)

URL ADDRESS: http://www.lib.rochester.edu/camelot/cphome.stm

SITE SUMMARY: King Arthur was a semi-legendary sixth century king of Britain. He fought successfully in several wars against invading Saxons and armies of the Roman Empire. He was killed at the Battle of Camlan in England by his nephew (sometimes the son of King Arthur), Mordred. This site serves as the main Internet access point for Arthurian history students. It contains the full text of many Arthurian tales, a collection of related images, a bibliography, a searchable character index, and links to related sites. A list of publishers specializing in Arthuriana is also included.

DISCUSSION QUESTIONS AND ACTIVITIES

1. Geoffrey of Monmouth's *British History* was in essence the chronicle of the adventures of King Arthur and his court, an ancient British heroic legend. It is equivalent to Britain's national epic and is viewed as serious history. What historical value does a national epic have to a country? Compare the King Arthur legend to Spain's *El Cid*, Babylonia's *The Epic of Gilgamesh*, or *The Odyssey* by Homer. Where do you find similarities?

2. Click on the Artists Menu and select the letter *M*. Select various artists' renderings of "Morte d'Arthur." How is King Arthur depicted in death by various artists? Is he always painted as a hero who has fallen in battle? How would you describe the artists' compositions? What type of setting is King Arthur shown in? What general themes are the artists trying to convey?

3. Merlin was Arthur's advisor, seer, and magician. Click on *Search the Camelot Project* and type in the search terms *Merlin* and *prophecies*. Search through the various matches and compare the prophecies attributed to Merlin. What is the purpose of having prophecies in a national epic? How are they instrumental in giving a country its feeling of destiny?

4. Under *Symbols and Motifs*, click on *Excalibur and the Sword in the Stone*. Read through some of the sections and look at some of the images that refer to Arthur's sword. Discuss its symbolism and King Arthur's right to rule as a royal person. What symbols do present-day leaders use as evidence of their right to rule?

5. Compare King Arthur's values to those of another real ruler of your

choosing. Would this ruler have accepted King Arthur's model of kingship? If not, why?

6. What qualities make King Arthur a hero? What is his attitude toward violence and the waging of war? Does he try other means to solve his differences with others?

RELATED INTERNET SITE(S)

The Labyrinth
http://www.georgetown.edu/labyrinth
Use the search engine and type in "King Arthur" to retrieve a set of excellent Web sites.

PETER ABELARD: HISTORIA CALAMITATUM, "THE STORY OF MY MISFORTUNES" (1079–1142)

URL ADDRESS: http://www.fordham.edu/halsall/basis/abelard-histcal.html

SITE SUMMARY: Reminiscent of the confessions of St. Augustine, this autobiographical letter not only relates Abelard's tragic love affair with eighteen-year-old Heloise, to whom he was serving as a tutor, but also describes his life as an intellectual. Peter Abelard became a philosophy teacher in 1079. He was hired by Canon Fulbert of Paris to tutor his niece, Heloise. They fell in love, were married secretly, and had a son named Astrolabe. Abelard was persecuted for this crime physically and politically. Both retreated to monastic life. Heloise became a well-known monastic administrator. Abelard continued to earn the dislike of the theologians and philosophers of his day by questioning religious history and practice. His contributions to the study of logic, however, are still thought to be significant.

DISCUSSION QUESTIONS AND ACTIVITIES

1. Today, Peter Abelard's affair with eighteen-year-old Heloise would be considered a case of obvious sexual harassment. Depending upon her parents and the institution that Abelard worked for, a lawsuit would be filed and perhaps a criminal and civil trial would follow. Based on the facts of this case, conduct either a criminal or civil trial of Abelard. Compare your decision and punishment to what he experienced in the eleventh century.

2. What attitude toward learning does Peter Abelard express in his autobiography? How might his views toward education clash with the church's view?

3. Why did Abelard keep changing teachers? What do you think he was looking for? He always seems to be complaining that his teachers are persecuting him. Does he bring some of this vitriol on himself?

4. What were the physical and intellectual characteristics of Heloise that attracted Abelard to her?

5. Why did Heloise object to marrying Abelard? Was she correct in her decision? Do you think that these reasons were expressive of her true feelings toward Abelard?

6. Discuss how Peter Abelard and Heloise were victims of the climate of their times. Would contemporary society view his violation of celibacy and his sin of adultery as harshly? Which countries might still persecute Abelard as harshly as he was treated in the eleventh century?

RELATED INTERNET SITE(S)

Internet Medieval Sourcebook
http://www.fordham.edu/halsall/sbook.html
    Contains a collection of hundreds of links to medieval history, full texts of medieval books, and biographies of the saints' lives.

THE CRUSADES (1096–1270)

URL ADDRESS: http://history.hanover.edu/medieval/crusades.htm

SITE SUMMARY: Arranged in chronological order, this easy-to-use site contains fourteen primary sources related to the Crusades. Beginning in 1074 with Gregory VII's "Call for a Crusade," it continues with some of the following documents: (1) "Livre du Roi," (2) "The King's Right of Confiscation," (3) Eugene III's "Summons to a Second Crusade," (4) The Achievements of Nur ad-Din, and (5) An Account of the Battle of Hattin (1187) as related by Ernoul, a local Frank. The site also features the Chronicle of the Fourth Crusade, a description of the sacking of Constantinople in 1204, and Innocent III's "Summons to a Crusade in 1215."

DISCUSSION QUESTIONS AND ACTIVITIES

1. The first crusade was called the Peasants' Crusade. Peter the Hermit, an itinerant preacher, and a knight known as Walter the Penniless led a group of peasants ahead of the official expedition. Select *According to Fulcher of Chartres*. You are an illiterate peasant whose village priest has just read Pope Urban II's call for a crusade. What does he promise in it that makes you want to abandon your work, family, and home for a crusade?

2. What parts of Urban II's appeal do you consider to be pure propaganda? Explain why.

3. Select *Anna Comnena: The Bad Manners of a Crusading Prince*. Anna is the daughter of a hosting eastern emperor. What does she think of the crusaders? After reading this selection, how do you think the crusaders were viewed by the local inhabitants? Explain how the crusading prince's bad manners might affect his dealings with local leaders.

4. Select *An Account of the Battle of Hattin (1187) by Ernoul, a Local Frank*. What rules of war did the crusaders violate to their detriment? Why was Saladin able to win so easily?

5. The Crusades were not just about winning back the Holy Land. They were also about plunder and destruction. Select *Nicetas Choniates: The Sack of Constantinople (1204)*. You are a reporter for the *Crusader Times* paper. Describe the looting of Constantinople for your readers. Do you think that it was justified?

6. You are a knight who survived two crusades and has finally come home to settle down. At a banquet, you are asked to speak about your participation in the Crusades. Describe some of your positive and negative experiences. Were your travails worth the sacrifice?

RELATED INTERNET SITE(S)

Internet Medieval Sourcebook
http://www.fordham.edu/halsall/sbook.html
This is a gateway site for additional information about the Crusades and the Middle Ages.

On-Line Text Materials for Medieval Studies
http://orb.rhodes.edu/
Contains many full texts relating to medieval studies, plus a host of related Internet sites.

ROBIN HOOD PROJECT (ca. 1180–1210)

URL ADDRESS:
http://www.lib.rochester.edu/camelot/rh/rhhome.stm

SITE SUMMARY: All of us respond to a superhero type of figure who helps the downtrodden against the powers that persecute and who is utterly fearless against any adversity. Robin Hood, "who robbed the rich and gave to the poor," was a supposed contemporary of King John of Britain (ca. 1167–1216) and his elder brother Richard I (the Lion-Hearted, ca. 1157–1199). Whether this man actually existed is a subject historians continually dispute. At this site are numerous full-text sources for the study of the Robin Hood legend, a comprehensive bibliography of Robin Hood literature, and a list of films. An excellent collection of artists' drawings relating to Robin Hood and his merry men is also included.

DISCUSSION QUESTIONS AND ACTIVITIES

1. Select the Artist Menu and analyze how three different illustrators from the nineteenth and the twentieth centuries have portrayed Robin Hood.

2. How does the legend of Robin appeal to people who are considered lower class? Do you know of any modern-day hero who might appeal to poor Americans?

3. If you were a ruler in the Middle Ages and witnessed how people responded to the Robin Hood legend with such approval, would you be afraid? Why might you be fearful?

4. Select a short version of the story of Robin Hood from several different historical periods. Compare and contrast the physical characteristics and deeds attributed to this engaging outlaw.

5. Select a period of American history when many people were without hope, such as the Great Depression. Invent a Robin Hood character and write a ballad about some of his exploits.

6. Discuss how the Robin Hood legend served as a psychological release for people who had little say in the government of their country. What were the economic and social conditions in Britain when the legend was first recorded?

RELATED INTERNET SITE(S)

Douglas Fairbanks in Robin Hood
http://www.mdle.com/ClassicFilms/Featured/Video/video7.htm

Although this is clearly a commercial site, it does contain three scenes from Douglas Fairbanks's portrayal of Robin Hood and a hyperlinked article about Douglas Fairbanks and other actors in the film.

In Search of Robin Hood
http://www.innotts.co.uk/~pansoft/local/robsites.htm

This is a noneducational site that features accurate descriptions and images of places and forests thought to have been frequented by Robin Hood and his band of outlaws.

STATUTES OF BIELLA (1248 AND 1348)

**URL ADDRESS: △ to http://www.ukans.edu/ftp/pub/history/Europe/
Medieval/latintexts/fiella-1.txt**

SITE SUMMARY: When merchants and craftsmen settled in medieval
towns they established organizations called guilds. A guild agreed upon
rules to protect its members against unfair business practices, guarantee
fair wages and prices for goods, and settle disputes between workers
and employees. Guilds are considered forerunners of present-day labor
unions. They also played a major role in town government and helped
people win the battle for self-governance over medieval lords who
owned the town and the land. The Commune of Biella's statutes show
how much the town's citizens, with the help of guilds, achieved in the
way of self-governance.

DISCUSSION QUESTIONS AND ACTIVITIES

1. Read the sections of the statutes dealing with the election of consuls.
   What do you think of the process? Is it democratic or autocratic? If
   you were a woman living in Biella, how might you feel about the
   consul election process and the gender-based language of the statutes?

2. The consuls have a great deal of power to regulate commerce, decide
   disputes, and collect taxes and fees. Read some of the statutes regarding the hearing of cases and rendering of judgments. Do you see any
   potential for corruption? Rewrite the statute sections in this area that
   pose a problem for you.

3. The town of Biella agrees to pay foreign workers on the first day
   rather than the usual eight-day payment for resident workers. Why
   do they seem to be so solicitous of foreigners? Do United States companies or businesses pay foreign workers before they do our own
   citizens?

4. Read the sections of the statutes dealing with overspending by the
   elected consuls and failure to execute some other tasks involving
   maintenance of open land. What do you think of the penalty? Do you
   think that the consuls should pay money out of their own pockets if
   they fail to balance the town budget? What are the benefits and drawbacks to this statute?

5. Biella has also enacted statutes against swearing, throwing stones over
   roofs, and climbing on churches. Do you think that the consuls have
   gone too far in trying to regulate social behavior? Draw up some

statutes for a condominium complex based on your observation of planned unit developments. What kinds of social problems do they have that might be similar to those in Biella, Italy?

6. Compare the commercial Biella statutes to those in Hammurabi's Code. Why do the statutes of Biella seem less Draconian?

RELATED INTERNET SITE(S)

Medieval Italy
http://www.georgetown.edu/labyrinth/subjects/italy/italy.html
This is an excellent gateway site to information about medieval Italian churches, manuscripts, castles, art, architecture, and much more.

EXTRACTS OF TRAVELS OF MARCO POLO (ca. 1300)

URL ADDRESS: http://www.fordham.edu/halsall/source/polo-kinsay.html

SITE SUMMARY: The city of Hanchow, China, served as a temporary capital for the great Kublai Khan in the 1300s. Marco Polo, the indefatigable explorer and trader, spent seventeen years in the great Khan's court. When he returned to Venice, he wrote an account of these years that is still, though less frequently, being disputed by historians today. In this full-text section of his book, he describes the great city of Kinsay (present-day Hanchow). Marco Polo discusses the customs, clothing, and daily life of its inhabitants. The related Internet site features pictures of various Asian cities and sights that Marco Polo describes in other parts of his book.

DISCUSSION QUESTIONS AND ACTIVITIES

1. Your name is Marco Polo. Your book, *The Travels of Marco Polo*, has become a best-seller and you have been asked to go on a book tour to various Italian towns. In one town, someone asks you if you wrote the book and if all of it was true. A buzz goes through the audience as they wait for your reply. What will you say to them?

2. Each person looks at a new place with their own eyes and brings their own cultural view of the world to bear when they assess it. What things does Marco Polo recall about Kinsay that reflect his cultural, economic, and societal values?

3. From Polo's description of guilds, architecture, clothing, and the arts,

which civilization seems further developed? Research the development of the maritime republic of Venice during this time period. Describe the similarities and dissimilarities.

4. You are a Venetian bureaucrat who is charged with collecting information about other parts of the world and organizing it into succinct memos for the city leaders. What parts of Marco Polo's observations would most interest the Venetians? Prepare several memos about various aspects of Kinsay, China.

5. You are Kublai Khan. Your empire is so large that you will never be able to revisit the cities and towns that you have conquered in your lifetime. You are curious, however, about where Marco Polo comes from. How would Marco Polo describe the city of Venice to you?

6. The people of Kinsay seem very prosperous. What conditions does a government have to maintain to permit the majority of the people to succeed economically? Be sure to include conditions such as freedom from war and political and religious toleration.

RELATED INTERNET SITE(S)

The Travels of Marco Polo
http://www.utexas.edu/depts/grg/ustudent/frontiers/fall95/tubb/marco_~1/travel.html
This site breaks Marco Polo's book into nine sections. Each one describes an area of the world to which he traveled in the Middle East, China, India, and the Arabian Sea. It provides linked images of many of the sights, monuments, and natural wonders as seen by tourists today.

PLAGUE AND PUBLIC HEALTH IN RENAISSANCE EUROPE (1347–1351)

URL ADDRESS: http://jefferson.village.virginia.edu/osheim/intro.html

SITE SUMMARY: The plague or Black Death was a terrifying epidemic that within two years killed one-third to one-half of Europe's population. Bubonic plague first appeared in 1348. After the initial onslaught, there wasn't a generation that did not suffer from either a local, regional, or continental epidemic for the next 200 years. The effect on the economy, demography, and general health of Europe was devastating. The documents in this collection focus on Tuscany, Italy, Avignon-Montpelier, France, and the Rhineland towns of Germany. They are extensive and provide information not only about the physical aspects of the disease but also about its cultural and social impact.

DISCUSSION QUESTIONS AND ACTIVITIES

1. Select *Florence, 1348*. Read the eyewitness account of the bubonic plague by Marchione di Coppo Stefani. Describe the physical symptoms of the disease. Consult a contemporary medical encyclopedia. Are the symptoms that Stefani writes about similar or dissimilar to the ones described in a current medical book?

2. Much of our knowledge of the plague or Black Death comes from people like Stefani who recorded his observations for others to read and learn from. The year is 3000 and you have been asked to write a story about a twentieth century disease called AIDS. What materials would you hope to find? What sources would you consider reliable?

3. The plague was so virulent in Florence that it was called the "Florentine disease." Read the Introduction to Boccaccio's *The Decameron*. Compare his description with Stefani's. Note the similarities. What seems to be the attitude of both men toward this terrible disease?

4. Select *Pistoia, 1348*. This small city is only a few miles from Florence, and by May 1348 it was still free of plague. Discuss the regulations that the town imposed on its citizens to prevent occurrence of the disease. Which ones strike you as either absurd or unrealistic? Research what happened to Pistoia, Italy. Did the inhabitants survive the plague?

5. In these accounts, there is evidence of large numbers of people dying. You are a demographer studying the effects of loss of population on the economy. Give a lecture to a group outlining the impact that the plague had on Europe's social structures and economy.

6. What were the emotional, social, and economic advantages and disadvantages of being a plague survivor?

RELATED INTERNET SITE(S)

Health and Disease in the Middle Ages
http://smsd.k12.ks.us/belinder/bebooks/plague.htm
   Although this site originates at a secondary school, the historically accurate description of plague symptoms makes it a worthwhile one.

Bubonic Plague Bibliography
http://www.geocities.com/Athens/2423/plague.html
   Provides an unannotated bibliography of books about the the plague.

THE FORBIDDEN CITY (1368–Present)

URL ADDRESS: http://www.chinavista.com/beijing/gugong/ !start.html

SITE SUMMARY: The Forbidden City in Beijing, China, includes the palaces of twenty-four former Chinese emperors. It is so named because only members of the emperor's household could enter it. It was the seat of power during the Ming and Qing dynasties (1368–1911). The site includes recent photographs of the Meridian Gate, the WatchTower, the Gate of Supreme Harmony, the Halls of Heavenly, Earthly, and Union Peace, the Imperial Gardens, and the North Gate. Each architectural site contains a brief annotation relating to the use of that part of the city for special ceremonies or to particular aspects of its construction.

DISCUSSION QUESTIONS AND ACTIVITIES

1. "Without seeing the magnificence of the royal palace, one can never sense the dignity of the emperor." How do you interpret this poetic line from a Tang dynasty poet? Do you think that leaders have to live in large houses, castles, or palaces to have dignity?

2. The year is 1468. You are a Chinese worker who is restoring part of a crumbling wall in the Forbidden City. You are impressed with the solid structure of the walls, gates, and watchtowers. What do they tell you that your emperor fears most—internal rebellion or invasion by a foreign force? Provide written and visual evidence in support of your theory.

3. Why was this part of Beijing called the Forbidden City? What were the benefits and risks to the emperors of being isolated from the rest of the population?

4. Many of the buildings use the color red as an adornment. What is the significance of this color in the Forbidden City?

5. The Forbidden City is a symbol of the opulence that characterized thousands of years of dynastic Chinese rule. When you look at the rooms, gates, and halls, how do you think this design helped contribute to the fall of the last emperors?

6. Leaders are sometimes prisoners of their administrators and advisors. How did the architecture of the Forbidden City contribute to the imprisonment of the Chinese rulers?

RELATED INTERNET SITE(S)

Beijing
http://www.chinavista.com/beijing/home.html
  Provides a history of Beijing and images of major historical sights.

Discover China
http://www.chinavista.com/discover.html
  Includes a virtual tour of the Yellow Mountains and the Great Wall.

TRES RICHES HEURES (ca. 1412)

URL ADDRESS: http://humanities.uchicago.edu/images/heures/heures.html

SITE SUMMARY: Between 1412 and 1416, the Limbourg brothers, Paul, Hermann, and Jean, painted the illuminations for a manuscript that is clearly equivalent in artistry and historic importance to the Mona Lisa in oil painting. *Tres Riches Heures* is a beautiful medieval book of hours. It contains a collection of text, calendars, prayers, psalms, and masses for holy days and for each liturgical hour of the day. The book was designed and painted for Jean, Duc de Berry, a wealthy French devotee of the arts. This site focuses on twelve color images of the calendar illustrations which are accompanied by helpful commentary.

DISCUSSION QUESTIONS AND ACTIVITIES

1. Illuminating manuscripts is one of the lost arts of the Middle Ages. It is writing made beautiful. Describe the process of illumination. Why did the materials used to decorate the pages, and the pages themselves, contribute to the preservation of these manuscripts?

2. Select the month of January. Look at the composition of the illumination. Who is at the center of it? What is the expression on his face? Why are only the Bishop and the Duc de Berry shown seated? What might the Limbourg brothers be trying to convey about this wealthy nobleman? Give an oral, artistic interpretation of this illumination to the class.

3. Select the month of May. Look at the colors in the illumination and the clothing worn by people seen riding. How do they look? Do the people appear to be having fun? Would you be happy if you had to get so dressed up just to go for a ride on a horse? Interpret this illumination in an oral presentation based on your responses to some of the questions posed.

4. Books of hours were owned by so many people during the Middle Ages that many still remain as evidence of a past way of life. What did these books mean to their owners, and how were they used?

5. What role did books of hours play in the democratization of religion in the Middle Ages?

6. Select various months from this site and look at the detail, color, composition, and actions of the people. Design and color a page for a modern-day book of hours that reflects the style of *Tres Riches Heures*, your favorite season, and the local flora and fauna of the state in which you live.

RELATED INTERNET SITE(S)

Images of Medieval Art and Architecture
http://info.pitt.edu/~medart/index.html
   Contains images of medieval cathedrals and focuses particularly on stained glass windows and decorations.

The Invention of Paper
http://www.ipst.edu/amp/inventn.html
   Presents a short history about the invention of papermaking.

Medieval Art
http://www.trinityvt.edu/hildegard/medart.htm
   Includes links to scriptoriums, illuminated manuscript pages from Oxford University's Bodleian Library, and the Vatican Library manuscript exhibit.

LEONARDO DA VINCI MUSEUM (1452–1519)

URL ADDRESS: http://museum.brandx.net/main.html#start

SITE SUMMARY: One of the most creative geniuses of the Renaissance, Leonardo da Vinci was trained as a painter. His inquisitiveness, however, about engineering, anatomy, botany, and geology led him to design and draw plans for many inventions. A flying machine and a parachute are just some of the designs with which he is credited. This site focuses on several aspects of Leonardo's world ranging from his paintings of the Mona Lisa and the Last Supper to engineering, futuristic designs, and anatomical drawings and sketches. The South Wing of the museum houses a biographical profile and information relating to the Italian Renaissance.

DISCUSSION QUESTIONS AND ACTIVITIES

1. Leonardo da Vinci is the personification of the Renaissance man. To us this means someone who is multitalented and who is able to prac-

tice and be recognized for these abilities. Describe Leonardo's talents as a painter, scientist, engineer, and inventor and provide examples of his work in each area. He believed that science and art were inseparable. Would Leonardo be able to have a dual career if he lived in the twenty-first century?

2. Select the East Wing and scroll down to the Mona Lisa. Leonardo used a technique called *sfumato*. It eliminates outlining by the artist and makes Mona Lisa look like she is emerging from the surface of the painting. Portions of her body are painted with gradations of light and dark that seemingly melt into one another. You are a Renaissance art critic who has been asked to review the Mona Lisa for a newspaper. Compare this new technique with the old outlining one used by other artists.

3. Select the West Wing and browse through the inventions of weaponry and flying machines. You are a psychologist whose specialty is giftedness. Look at the drawings and sketches as if you do not know their origin. Construct a psychological profile of Leonardo that includes his potential strengths and weaknesses.

4. Leonardo pioneered the anatomical techniques of four views of a subject and cross sectional representation of parts of the body such as arteries and nerves. What use did this have for the medical profession?

5. The Chinese have an expression that says, "May you live in interesting times." Argue that Leonardo was also a product of his environment. Describe how the period and place in which he lived fostered his creative genius.

6. Leonardo approached art as a science. Explain how his drawings, sketches, and inventions are evidence of this statement.

RELATED INTERNET SITE(S)

Leonardo: Drawings of da Vinci
http://banzai.msi.umn.edu/leonardo
   Provides screen-size images of da Vinci's drawings of the human form.

Leonardo da Vinci Scientist Inventor Artist
http://www.mos.org/leonardo
   This is a gateway site for information relating to Leonardo da Vinci and the Italian Renaissance.

WITCHCRAFT: JOAN'S WITCH DIRECTORY (1484–1692)

URL ADDRESS: http://www.rci.rutgers.edu/~jup/witches/

SITE SUMMARY: Witchcraft is thought of as the use of supernatural powers generally to harm people or their property. It has always been a fascinating aspect of history whether it involved the Salem Witch Trials or the concept of scapegoating someone by a charge of witchcraft. This site treats the subject from a European perspective. It begins with a chronology of witchcraft and a hyperlink to full-text classic primary sources such as *Malleus Maleficarum,* followed by *Canon Episcopi* and a list of accused witches in North America and individual European countries. It also features case studies and court transcripts of people tried as witches. The site concludes with an excellent set of witchcraft-related Internet connections.

DISCUSSION QUESTIONS AND ACTIVITIES

1. Select *Malleus Maleficarum* and click on *The First Part.* What evidence does this handbook on witchcraft use to support the statement that superstition is found chiefly in women? Explain how this evidence is or is not convincing.

2. Why do you think that women were thought to be witches more often than men?

3. Why did so many people confess to being witches? How did their confessions perpetuate the belief in witches?

4. Select *The Places.* Scroll down to *The Americas* and click on *Salem.* Read the information on this page and then click on *Salem Links.* After reading this material, how would you defend yourself if you were accused of being a witch?

5. How did the concept of witchcraft change through the centuries? Are there any diseases, catastrophes, or unusual events that you think could make people believe in witchcraft on a scale similar to that seen in earlier centuries?

6. What do people mean when they use the expression "witch hunt"? Describe three witch hunts from periods of modern European and or American history and explain why you consider them to be witch hunts.

RELATED INTERNET SITE(S)

Salem Witch Museum
http://www.salemwitchmuseum.com
Features a chronology, book reviews of witchcraft books, and links to a commercial site about the area of Salem, Massachusetts.

Salem Massachusetts What About Witches
http://www.salemweb.com/witches.htm
Gives a hyperlinked introduction about the Salem Witch Trials followed by specific links about witchcraft in general.

1492: AN ONGOING VOYAGE (1492)

URL ADDRESS: http://metalab.unc.edu/expo/1492.exhibit/Intro.html

SITE SUMMARY: This rich multicultural site contains significant background material in addition to a variety of primary sources. By weaving images and texts, the site designers explain and display what life was like in pre- and post-Columbus Europe, Africa, and the Americas. The site also examines the effect that the discovery of America had on each continent and the brutal aspects of colonization on indigenous cultures. Although primary sources are not indexed or listed separately, the site features original maps, facsimiles of ancient manuscripts, original photographs, and excerpts from diaries. Links showing a page from Columbus's *Book of Privileges*, drawings of Venetian sailing directions, Columbus's coat of arms, and ancient calendars are readily available.

DISCUSSION QUESTIONS AND ACTIVITIES

1. Look at all of the Americas sites and the primary source evidence of their civilization and cultures. Some civilizations, such as those of the Aztecs and Incas, were highly developed. Others, such as those of the Tainos and Caribs, were not. Draw a development chart that shows the diverse civilizations that existed before contact with Europeans.

2. Click on *Hammock* and read Fernandez de Oviedo y Valdes's description of the hammock and its use by the Caribbean Island societies. What conclusions can you draw about the indigenous people's society and lifestyle? Compare their way of life to de Oviedo's origins. Would he have slept in a bed? What type of house would he have lived in? What would his lifestyle have been like?

3. Even though some of the suppositions about the world and its continents were wrong, a significant number of improvements in nautical
   instrument design, shipbuilding, and cartography provided the
   framework for European exploration and expansion. Explore the sites
   under *Expanding Horizons*. Use these primary sources to support your
   argument that Europeans were predisposed to exploration before their
   American counterparts.

4. Click to enlarge the view of *The World Map in Germanus from 1482*. It
   reflects the Ptolemaic view of the world. Compare this map to a
   modern-day world map. Where do the major mistakes lie? Why did
   these mistakes exist until the late 1490s?

5. Between 1492 and 1600 there were continuous collisions and contacts
   among various American indigenous people and Europeans. Using
   the primary site sources, write a short retrospective history of the pros
   and cons of this period.

6. You are an anthropologist who has discovered a "lost people" living
   deep in the jungles of Peru. You wish to avoid the negative aspects
   of introducing them to a different way of life and simultaneously provide them with modern-day medicines, better shelter, and other
   amenities that will extend their lives. Describe how you would introduce them to our world in a way that would minimize their culture
   shock.

RELATED INTERNET SITE(S)

Christopher Columbus, Voyage of 1492 Exploration
http://marauder.millersv.edu/~columbus/
   Provides a database of scholarly publications about the significance of
the voyage of Christopher Columbus.

European Voyages of Exploration
http://www.ucalgary.ca/HIST/tutor/eurvoya
   Contains an overview of the rise of the Spanish Empire and the voyage
of Christopher Columbus.

EXTRACTS FROM CHRISTOPHER COLUMBUS' JOURNAL (1492)

URL ADDRESS: http://www.fordham.edu/halsall/source/ columbus1.html

SITE SUMMARY: This site contains the journal entries for several days
in August, and almost all of September and October 1492, when Chris-

topher Columbus was making his historic voyage of discovery to the New World. The extracts carefully record a journey that had no historic precedent and that forever changed the course of history. Historians refer to it not only as a bridge to the New World, but also as a historical link between the Middle Ages and the Renaissance. This voyage and subsequent ones also resulted in the fateful clash among cultures at different developmental stages. The indigenous peoples that Columbus met were no match militarily for a culture that had swords and armor.

DISCUSSION QUESTIONS AND ACTIVITIES

1. In the section entitled "In the name of our Lord Jesus Christ," Columbus writes to the King and Queen of Spain that he intends to meet the people of India and find the proper method of converting them to "our holy faith." In the same letter, he confirms that he will be called "perpetual Viceroy and Governor" in all the islands and continents that he discovers and acquires. Write an editorial for a paper pointing out the hypocrisy of Columbus's intentions. Is he going to convert or conquer?

2. Columbus knows that his voyage will be a long one, but he is determined to protect his men from fear of the unknown for as long as he can. In the first few days of the voyage, he notes that even though he has sailed many more leagues, he is "going to count less than the true number." Write an opinion paper on his decision from the viewpoint of either Columbus or a sailor.

3. On Thursday and Friday, October 11 and 12, the first contact is made with indigenous people. Read these sections and describe Columbus's attitude toward the people he meets. Base your opinion on Columbus's written impressions of all that he sees. What do you think of his decision to take six people home to Spain?

4. You are one of the first people to spot Columbus's ships and tell your neighbors that it looks like some people are going to come ashore. Everyone wants to know what they look like. Are they carrying weapons? Describe Columbus and his sailors to your neighbors.

5. Plot Columbus's daily journey, making allowances for the current's strength and direction, and hypothesize where his first landfall was. Do you agree or disagree with other scholars on the location of his first landfall?

6. With only a compass to guide a ship in 1492, what is the purpose of keeping a ship's log? Defend the absolute necessity of writing accurate descriptions regarding heading, speed, sea state, winds, leeway, and

any other factors that might affect the voyage. How might the log save the lives of those on board?

RELATED INTERNET SITE(S)

1492: An Ongoing Voyage
http://sunsite.unc.edu/expo/1492.exhibit/Intro.html
Provides additional primary source materials about Columbus from the Library of Congress exhibit.

VASCO DA GAMA: ROUND AFRICA TO INDIA (1497–1498)

URL ADDRESS: http://www.fordham.edu/halsall/mod/ 1497dagama.html

SITE SUMMARY: Vasco da Gama was a Portuguese sea captain and explorer. In 1497 he was given the command of four specially built expeditionary ships and sent to reach India from Europe. He sailed from Lisbon, Portugal, on July 8, 1497, rounded the Cape of Good Hope in Africa on November 22, and eventually reached India in May 1498. On the way he stopped at trading centers that are now Mocambique, Mozambique, and Mombasa and Mailindi, Kenya. In India, he encountered Muslim merchants who would not trade with him, and he insulted the Indian ruler by bestowing gifts thought to be of little value. Despite these setbacks, Vasco da Gama managed to bring back sufficient spices and evidence to verify the success of his mission. This site contains excerpts from the log of his voyage.

DISCUSSION QUESTIONS AND ACTIVITIES

1. On Sunday, November 12, da Gama reported that his emissary, Captain-Major Fernao Velloso, was attacked by Negroes running along the beach. He states that they looked "incapable of violence." Why did da Gama come to this conclusion? What do you think went wrong? Why were several of the Portuguese wounded?

2. From the ship's log and other secondary source descriptions, draw a map that traces Vasco da Gama's route from Lisbon to India.

3. Create drawings of the people that Vasco da Gama met based on his descriptions.

4. What gifts did Vasco da Gama present to King Camolim? Why was

the king insulted by them? What assumptions about the king and the people do you think da Gama made when he delivered such unpretentious gifts?

5. What is your opinion of how Vasco da Gama handled the negotiations between himself and King Camolim? Do you think that he relied unwisely on the Moors to translate his intentions?

6. What was the global significance of Vasco da Gama's voyage?

RELATED INTERNET SITE(S)

Treaty of Tordesillas
http://gate.ei.edu.ab.ca/sch/sht/Brazil-Early-Years.html
Provides background material about the early Portuguese explorers, including Pedro Cabral and Vasco da Gama. The site also contains other exploration-related links such as 1492: An Ongoing Voyage and Christopher Columbus.

PUBLIC EXECUTIONS IN EARLY MODERN ENGLAND (ca. 1500–1600)

URL ADDRESS: http://www.bouldernews.infi.net/~charliem/index.htm

SITE SUMMARY: Public executions had a ghoulish fascination for many people. The practice was thought to serve as a deterrent to future lawbreakers until many countries abandoned it because of its barbaric qualities. This site includes images of London executions from the 1500s and the 1600s, when the practice was also considered a tourist attraction. It was so commonplace that specific sites in London were allotted for specific types of crimes such as treason, piracy, and larceny. A collection of eyewitness accounts, speeches of the "about to be executed," background materials, and related English history links are also provided.

DISCUSSION QUESTIONS AND ACTIVITIES

1. Read the eighteenth century eyewitness accounts of public executions. Think of the meaning of the expression "their fires warm us." Why do you think people attended public executions? Do you think that people in the United States would attend them if they were made public again?

2. You are a lawyer whose client is about to be sentenced to death for

thievery. Make a plea before the court for his life based on the nature of his crime, the claim that the death penalty is not an effective deterrent, and your opinion that capital punishment is an act of barbarism.

3. You have been wrongfully accused of treason and have been sentenced to death. You are allowed to speak to the crowd and to your executioner before you die. Write a speech in the style of someone living in the 1500s declaring your innocence.

4. Public execution was the sentence for many crimes involving property, not loss of life. Do you think that a housebreaker or thief should have been executed? Draft a criminal law statute that includes all property and victim crimes and that defines their respective punishments.

5. Do people believe in the reality of their death? Do you think that capital punishment actually serves as a deterrent? Write a philosophical essay defending the position you decide to take.

6. Why do you think that Great Britain abolished public executions and the death penalty and the United States did not?

RELATED INTERNET SITE(S)

Lady Jane Grey
http://ladyjane.iinet.net.au

Contains information about the education, early life, and marriage of Lady Jane Grey, including correspondence dealing with her execution.

MISSIONARIES AND MANDARINS: THE JESUITS IN CHINA (ca. 1500–1600)

URL ADDRESS: http://metalab.unc.edu/expo/vatican.exhibit/exhibit/i-rome_to_china/Jesuits_in_China.html

SITE SUMMARY: As part of the Vatican Library exhibit mounted at the Library of Congress, this site provides interpreted images of the cartography, cosmology, and astronomy texts written in Chinese by Jesuit missionaries such as Matteo Ricci and Adam Schall von Bell in the 1600s. While the Jesuits' mission was to convert the Chinese, their eventual ability to read and speak Chinese broadened their minds and made them aware of the similar religious tenets they shared with their Asian counterparts. Their mission resulted in an extraordinary cultural exchange during a time when China was considered a closed country.

DISCUSSION QUESTIONS AND ACTIVITIES

1. How did the Jesuits' missionary policies help them to be successful in a country that had been traditionally closed to foreigners?

2. It is 1607 and you are a Buddhist missionary who wishes to establish a mission in the colony of Jamestown. Draw up a plan for your audience with the Jamestown governor that includes how you will dress, your reasons for wanting to have a Buddhist mission, and the compromises that you are willing to make to attain your objective.

3. You are the governor of the Jamestown settlement. A Buddhist missionary has just landed on your shore and in broken English asks for your permission to build a Buddhist monastery in the settlement and to try to convert the residents to Buddhism. If you agree to this arrangement, what rules would you create to ensure that problems are minimal? If you say no, state your reasons against the proposed arrangement.

4. Browse through the Vatican materials that are evidence of this remarkable cultural exchange. What did the Chinese receive from letting the missionaries into their country? What did the Jesuits learn about China?

5. You are a missionary who has been recalled to Rome. You are to give your superior a report on how the values and tenets of some of the Chinese classic texts reflect some of the classic beliefs of Christianity. Select the Chinese texts that you will refer to and provide a summary of each one's contents.

6. Write several days' worth of diary entries that describe what life may have been like for you as a Jesuit missionary in China during the 1500s. Do people stare at you? What customs do you find worthy of adoption, and which ones do you find repugnant?

RELATED INTERNET SITE(S)

Matteo Ricci The Art of Printing
http://acc6.its.brooklyn.cuny.edu/~phalsall/texts/ric-prt.html
  Matteo Ricci describes the uses and advantages of ancient Chinese printing methods.

Matteo Ricci on Chinese Government
http://acc6.its.brooklyn.cuny.edu/~phalsall/texts/ric-jour.html
  This site contains selections from Matteo Ricci's journals (1583–1610) that describe Chinese society and government at that time. It also includes a short biographical sketch of Ricci.

UTOPIA BY SIR THOMAS MORE (1516)

URL ADDRESS: http://library.tcu.edu/www/staff/dodom/fulltext.htm

SITE SUMMARY: Considered one of the greatest works of political theory, *Utopia* was written in 1516 by Sir Thomas More. The book is basically a satire that makes fun of sixteenth century beliefs about remote lands and peoples. Part I is essentially a satire on society and the political situation in England. It includes an extended conversation with Ralph Hythloday (Hythlodaye), whose name means "disperser of nonsense." Hythloday is an imaginary sailor who compares the social and economic conditions prevailing in Western Europe with those of the imaginary land Utopia. The site contains the entire text of the book.

DISCUSSION QUESTIONS AND ACTIVITIES

1. In Part I, Hythloday suggests abolishing the death penalty for property crimes, preventing gambling, making the economy less dependent on raising sheep for wool, and other economic and political reforms. Describe the conditions in Tudor England that caused More to recommend these reforms.

2. Who are some of the leaders or groups in sixteenth century Europe who would have criticized More's book? Why would they have been critical of it?

3. Refer to some of the reforms recommended in Part I. How would you have gone about making Tudor England more like More's *Utopia*?

4. Read Part II of *Utopia*. Why does More choose to place his kingdom on an island isolated and protected from encroachment by militaristic neighbors?

5. How is More's utopian government structured? What are the advantages and disadvantages of this system? Design your own utopian government based on your own ideas of an ideal society.

6. Sir Thomas More borrowed from Plato and other classic authors, just as Karl Marx and William Morris probably read and digested ideas from More. What would be Karl Marx's and William Morris's impressions of More's *Utopia*?

RELATED INTERNET SITE(S)

Utopia by Sir Thomas More
http://intech2000.miamisci.org/sss/la/utopia.html

Features well-conceived lesson plans for sections of *Utopia* and compares it to *The Once and Future King* by T. H. White.

MARTIN LUTHER'S 95 THESES (1517)

URL ADDRESS: http://library.byu.edu/~rdh/eurodocs/germany.html

SITE SUMMARY: This document, containing ninety-five paragraphs discussing the sale of indulgences and other practices of the Catholic Church, had vast implications for countries, kingdoms, and empires. The entire Protestant movement is attributed to Luther's document, which was divided into three parts. The first denounced papal venality, the second stated that the Pope had no jurisdiction over purgatory, and the third asserted that forgiveness is derived from God and cannot be purchased with money. This source also has several related sites that assist students with the study of Luther's ninety-five theses and the subsequent Protestant Reformation.

DISCUSSION QUESTIONS AND ACTIVITIES

1. Placing a disputation or statement of one's position in a public area was standard procedure at medieval universities. Martin Luther's, however, was so controversial that he was forced to flee into exile. What were the existing conditions with regard to the Catholic Church that made his disputation so threatening?

2. Does Luther criticize the underlying theory of indulgences, or is he critical only of the effects of selling indulgences?

3. To Martin Luther's surprise, three editions of his theses were printed within two months. Many historians attribute the widespread, almost instant, effect his statement had to the fast distribution of his writings. Write an essay linking the change Luther effected to the fast dissemination of his writings made possible by the invention of Gutenberg's printing press.

4. John Tetzel, a Dominican monk, was put in charge of selling indulgences in Germany. Half of the profits were to go to Rome and be used for building St. Peter's. You are John Tetzel and have just read Luther's disputation. Write a reply to him defending your position.

5. What is Martin Luther's attitude toward the poor? How does the selling of indulgences take advantage of them?

6. Compare Luther's theses to other historic documents that sparked

similar religious or political revolutions (e.g., Thomas Paine's *Common Sense*). What were the conditions that you think fueled their fire?

RELATED INTERNET SITE(S)

The Protestant Reformation
http://history.hanover.edu/early/prot.html
Furnishes excellent background material about the important people and events that influenced the Protestant Reformation.

Project Wittenberg
http://www.iclnet.org/pub/resources/text/wittenberg/wittenberg-home.html
Provides works by and about Martin Luther and other famous Lutherans.

THE WORKS OF ELIZABETH I (1533–1603)

URL ADDRESS: http://www.luminarium.org/renlit/elizabib.htm

SITE SUMMARY: Elizabeth I of Great Britain (1533–1603) reigned in a period called the Golden Age. It reflected a time of great achievement in the arts, exploration and discovery, and war. Elizabeth I's reign was successful in part because she was a well-educated, astute leader who employed all of her consummate skills to ensure religious toleration and economic prosperity for the majority of her subjects. Divided into five parts, this site includes poems attributed to Elizabeth, speeches concerning her proposed but never to be entered into marriages, exhortations to her troops, verse translations, and letters to various kings and queens.

DISCUSSION QUESTIONS AND ACTIVITIES

1. Read the accession speech and prayer of 1558. How does Elizabeth I use all the installation trappings of her office to impress the people that she is going to be a fit queen? What religious and political themes do you detect in her speech? You are an image consultant hired by the palace to plan the coronation events, including the parade. Your assignment is to make the new queen appear powerful, virtuous, and competent. Present your plan to her chief councilor.

2. Elizabeth I faced one of her greatest threats to national security when Spain decided to invade England. When Spanish ships were spotted

at the mouth of the English Channel, Elizabeth decided to address the army herself to exhort them to fight the Spanish if they landed. What were her words designed to appeal to? Why is there reference to the men being paid in her speech? If you had not been paid, would you have been moved by this speech? Explain why or why not.

3. Elizabeth I never married, but was urged to do so constantly by her advisors. Read the councilors' appeals to her to marry and her subsequent replies. What do you think Elizabeth was afraid of? Were her reasons for remaining single sound? You are her most trusted councilor. She confides in you that she will never marry. She asks your advice about how to keep the councilors from passing laws or taking other measures that would force her to marry. Proffer your advice in the form of a secret memo. The memo should also contain plans for preventing the councilors from knowing of her real intentions.

4. Mary, Queen of Scots was a true thorn in Elizabeth I's side. She threatened the political stability of England and was constantly consorting with other governments to overthrow her cousin. Finally she was caught in an attempt to have Elizabeth assassinated. Read *Elizabeth's Letter to Mary, Queen of Scots*. If you were Mary, how would you interpret Elizabeth's letter? Do you think that if you tell the truth, your life will be spared?

5. Read Elizabeth I's *Letter to James the Sixth, King of Scotland*. Why is Elizabeth reluctant to follow through on her execution of Mary, Queen of Scots? Did Elizabeth think that the death penalty was barbaric? Was she superstitious? Was the taking of another life a terrible sin to her?

6. Select one of the poems of *undoubted authorship*. Interpret it in relation to the circumstances, events, or issues surrounding the writing. From the words expressed, give your opinion on the education and thought processes of Elizabeth I.

RELATED INTERNET SITE(S)

Elizabeth I
http://www.encyclopedia.com/index.html
   Provides a hyperlink biography of Elizabeth I that includes all important events and people relating to her reign. The site, however, features a search box that requires the inputting of Elizabeth I's name.

Elizabeth I
http://www.royal.gov.uk/history/e1r.htm
   Includes a lengthy biographical sketch of Elizabeth I.

THE HISTORY OF COSTUME (1500–1800)

URL ADDRESS: http://www.siue.edu/COSTUMES/history.html

SITE SUMMARY: When a style of dress is about a decade old, it is often no longer considered daily attire and is termed a costume. Pictures of the clothes that people wore in different centuries and in different countries provide valuable clues about the economic prosperity of a nation and a society. This site includes numerous illustrations of costumes from the 1500s through the 1800s from France, England, Poland, Russia, Germany, Holland, and Switzerland. It features not only the dress of the nobility but also military uniforms and laboring-class attire.

DISCUSSION QUESTIONS AND ACTIVITIES

1. Compare the color plates of French, English, and Polish and Russian dress. How does the dress of the nobility of sixteenth century France compare with that of England and the other countries? The Western male of today does not dress as elaborately as his sixteenth century counterpart. Why do you think Western male twentieth century dress is more subdued?

2. Look at *plate #50*. What clothing clues indicate differences among the nobility and the servant class? Do the differences appear to be wide, or are there only slight gradations? What do the similarities and differences in dress tell you about the social and economic conditions in the late 1500s and early 1600s in England?

3. Look at *plate #51*. Note the differences in ecclesiastical vestments among the different church positions. Why did officials use clothing to delineate position in the church? Do some churches still follow this practice? What types of organizations should use clothing to differentiate rank or position? Defend whatever position you take with specific historical examples.

4. Look at *plate #53*. All of the people depicted are soldiers. From their uniforms, describe the type of war that their clothes are most suited or unsuited for.

5. Look at *plate #68*. How much has the military uniform changed between the first third of the seventeenth century and the first half of the eighteenth century? Note the changes in hand weapons.

6. Look at *plate #76* of France just before the Revolution. Compare the dress of the people in *plate #76* with *plate #77, Late Eighteenth Century— French Republic*. What differences do you see? What dress styles might

wealthy people be wearing in light of the recent revolution? Use these plates and other relevant ones to show how dress styles usually mirror political and economic conditions.

RELATED INTERNET SITE(S)

Costume History
http://members.aol.com/nebula5/tcpinfo2.html#history-17-18
Includes a set of links about fashion and dress during the Baroque and Restoration periods.

LETTER FROM LOPE DE AGUIRRE, REBEL, TO KING PHILIP OF SPAIN (1561)

URL ADDRESS: http://www.msstate.edu/Archives/History/ Latin_America/colonial.html

SITE SUMMARY: Lope de Aguirre was one of the most nefarious conquistadores in the discovery and exploration of South America. He was the subject of an outstanding film, *Aguirre, the Wrath of God*, by the famous director Werner Herzog. Power hungry and driven by a lust for gold and riches, Aguirre murdered the leaders of the Peruvian expedition in search of El Dorado and then went on to successfully navigate the Amazon, Huallaga, and Maranon rivers and to conquer a Spanish-settled island off the coast of Venezuela. He was finally killed by his own men. This letter to King Philip combines threats, demands for money, details of colonial Spanish corruption, and geographic details of previously unexplored lands and rivers.

DISCUSSION QUESTIONS AND ACTIVITIES

1. Aguirre refers to other rebels in his letter. Describe the conditions in colonial Peru that might have contributed to rebellion against King Philip of Spain.

2. In the first part of the letter, Aguirre makes reference to his and other explorers' assistance in ensuring that Francisco Hernandez would not become king of Peru. Why would this have become a problem for the king of Spain?

3. What do you think of Aguirre's attitude toward King Philip in this letter? Would Aguirre have been so bold toward the king if he had

not been thousands of miles away? From the tone of this letter, do you think that Aguirre ever intended to sail back to Spain?

4. Aguirre describes a very corrupt society ranging from local governors to Spanish officials and priests. Even if Aguirre's letter is somewhat exaggerated, why was there so much corruption?

5. There is also an air of genuine grievance in Aguirre's letter relating to, for example, a a lake teeming with fish. How do Spanish government officials seem to be exploiting the natural and human resources of the area?

6. Aguirre doesn't seem to hesitate to murder any adversary in his path. Could he have become such a renegade in his native Spain? Describe the conditions that, in your opinion, permitted Aguirre to become an outlaw.

RELATED INTERNET SITE(S)

The European Voyages of Exploration
http://www.acs.ucalgary.ca/HIST/tutor/eurvoya/columbus.html
   Presents an overview of the Spanish Empire during the 1500s.

SEVENTEENTH–EIGHTEENTH CENTURIES

THE GALILEO PROJECT (1564–1642)

URL ADDRESS: http://es.rice.edu/ES/humsoc/Galileo

SITE SUMMARY: Galileo was the first modern physical scientist, and his scientific knowledge far exceeded that of his contemporaries and the leaders of the Catholic Church. His method was to apply mathematics, experimentation, and inductive reasoning to existing phenomena. He made discoveries about the pendulum, invented a hydrostatic balance, and wrote a treatise on the center of gravity in solids. This site includes images and explanations of his inventions and the scientific instruments he used as well as maps of the surrounding Italian cities. A *receiving parlor* and *chapel* contain hyperlinked rooms that furnish information about Galileo's heresy trial and the church officials and astronomers who played a role in this part of his life.

DISCUSSION QUESTIONS AND ACTIVITIES

1. Select *Timeline of Galileo's Life & Era*. Discuss why Galileo was brought up so many times on charges by the Catholic Church concerning heresy about either his inventions or his theories.

2. Why did Galileo try to show that Copernican theory was consistent with both Catholic doctrine and biblical interpretation? Why was the church so close-minded about scientific discoveries? What did it have to lose by allowing free thinkers to develop, debate, and discuss their ideas?

3. Compare the trial of Galileo to the Scopes "monkey trial" and Darwin's theory of evolution. What aspects are similar?

4. Scroll to *Things* and select three inventions that Galileo either designed or improved upon. Discuss their significance and their contribution to the discipline of science.

5. Do you think that religion is naturally opposed to science? Does religion have any place in science? Conduct a debate with pro and con teams from your class. You may use examples from genetic engineering, euthanasia, cloning, or reproductive technologies to develop your argument.

6. Are literal belief in and interpretation of the Bible, the Koran, or the Torah necessary for either the Christian, Islamic, or Jewish faith, respectively? Defend and support the position that you take.

RELATED INTERNET SITE(S)

Catalog of the Scientific Community of the 16th and 17th Centuries
http://es.rice.edu/ES/humsoc/Galileo/Resources/galileo_links_tc.html
   Contains 631 detailed biographies of members of the scientific community during the sixteenth and seventeenth centuries.

UNITED STATES GAZETTES, NEWSPAPERS (1600–1900)

URL ADDRESS: http://www.msstate.edu/Archives/History/USA/gazette.html

SITE SUMMARY: Gazettes and newspapers from a specific historical period are some of the best primary sources for information about an event, person, or era. This site includes the full texts of hundreds of colonial gazettes and newspapers. Some of them feature only one article, such as *Major George Washington's Journals to the River Ohio in March 1754*. Another entire section is devoted to Ernest Hemingway's *Kansas City Star* stories along with related audio clips and articles about his life. Other sections contain America's first copyright law or articles about the running away of indentured servants or slaves. The site also contains articles that have cited various gazettes and journals. Students can learn how to use primary sources and develop thesis statements by reading selected articles.

DISCUSSION QUESTIONS AND ACTIVITIES

1. Click on the *Massachusetts Centinel Saturday, April 24, 1790*. You are an archaeologist who has just unwrapped this piece of newspaper from a glass jar at a dig site. What types of activities, events, crimes, etc., are described on this single page? What do you think of the sale of lottery tickets? What types of commerce do the people seem to be engaged in? What might you infer about how they live?

2. Select *The Maryland Gazette featuring George Washington's Journal* and click on *complete text*. George Washington was only twenty-one years old when he was asked to journey to the Ohio River to investigate the extent of French encroachment and deliver a letter to the French commander requesting that he cease and desist. What does Washing-

ton's account describe in detail that caused this publication to lead to the French and Indian War?

3. This account by George Washington reveals a great deal about his character and ability to persevere despite numerous physical hardships. You are a British lieutenant who has been asked to prepare a psychological profile of George Washington for General Cornwallis. How would you describe him based on this account? What do you think are his strengths and weaknesses?

4. Select *Clementina Rind's Virginia Gazette*. Mrs. Rind was the first woman in Virginia to publish a newspaper. How did she cover women's issues? Were her views ahead of her time? Why do you think she may have held these views?

5. Select *Benjamin Franklin's Pennsylvania Gazette January 2, 1750*. Read the articles that pertain to the importation of various goods. What items did the colonials have to import from England? Were there items that they could have manufactured themselves? Discuss the dangers of importing goods and materials from other countries. What are the advantages and disadvantages economically and militarily?

6. Select *The London Gazette November 9, 1694*. Read through the articles about the situation in different European countries. It is 1694 and you are a publisher of a new gazette. Describe how you are going to get stories from different parts of the world. How will you try to remain competitive with other gazettes? How will the information be delivered to you? Is it reliable? How current will it be?

RELATED INTERNET SITE(S)

Main London Gazette Page
http://www.history.rochester.edu/London_Gazette/
    Presents a short history of the *London Gazette*.

Good Reference Sources
http://www.msstate.edu/Archives/History/USA/gazette.html
    This site can be found at the end of the newspaper listings. It provides additional periodical-related primary source links.

ACCOUNT OF THE GREAT FIRE OF LONDON (1666)

URL ADDRESS: http://members.aa.net/~davidco/History/fire1.htm

SITE SUMMARY: In two years one of the great cities of the world, London, suffered two calamities that would change it more rapidly than at any other period in history. In 1665 the plague struck and killed over a hundred thousand victims, one of every three Londoners. In 1666 a fire destroyed eighty-nine churches in four days, leaving four-fifths of the city charred embers. This site provides the original description of the fire as published in the *London Gazette* from Monday, September 3, to Monday, September 10, 1666.

DISCUSSION QUESTIONS AND ACTIVITIES

1. Why was the fire able to spread so quickly? What did the fire feed upon? What were the methods used to fight fires in the seventeenth century?
2. Based on this account of the fire, draw a map of London showing all of the places mentioned.
3. Assess the role of King Charles during the fire. Was he encouraging?
4. You are a reporter for another London newspaper. Describe the fire in twentieth century terms, including the rumors about how it started.
5. Compare the London fire of 1666 to the ones in late 1940 when the Germans bombed London repeatedly.
6. You have been assigned to a fire-post. Describe your responsibilities.

RELATED INTERNET SITE(S)

The Great Fire of London Full Text: 1995 British Heritage Feature
http://www.thehistorynet.com/BritishHeritage/articles/1995_text.htm.
    Provides full-text journal entries of the diarists John Evelyn and Samuel Pepys concerning the great London fire.

Sir Christopher Wren—Great Buildings Online
http://www.greatbuildings.com/gbc/architects/Sir_Christopher_Wren.html
    Consists of a multimedia site that shows images of the churches and buildings rebuilt by Sir Christopher Wren.

ACCOUNTS OF LOUIS XIV (1671)

URL ADDRESS: http://history.hanover.edu/early/louisxiv.htm#simon

SITE SUMMARY: Capturing the decadence and hypocrisy of life in the court of Louis XIV is best done in these two translated accounts by Saint-Simon and Madame de Savigne, respectively. The first letter is a totally fulsome description of Louis XIV's virtues, beneficence, and character. The second letter describes the suicide of Vatel, the maître d' for a banquet held for Louis XIV at Chantilly in 1671. Vatel throws himself on his sword because the roast was not sufficient to feed several unexpected guests, the clouds dulled the fireworks display, and he lacked confidence that there would be enough fish for the morning meal.

DISCUSSION QUESTIONS AND ACTIVITIES

1. Saint-Simon was an influential court noble, but he had no official court position. How might his lack of position color his opinion of Louis XIV?

2. From Saint-Simon's letter, how would you describe the character of Louis XIV? Would you rely solely on this source or search elsewhere for personal accounts?

3. Did Louis XIV have mistresses? If he did, were his affairs with them conducted in private? You are Marie Thérèse, the wife of Louis XIV. Write a short diary describing your husband's affairs and your feelings about them. How does your view compare with Saint-Simon's?

4. Madame de Savigne's letter about the death of the maître d' Vatel provides a glimpse of the decadence of Louis XIV's reign. Write a society column in the manner of a style feature editor describing the party.

5. Do you think that a king like Louis XIV actually felt any remorse over the death of Vatel? Conduct a debate among your peers.

6. Why did the French people accept such lavish parties and entertainments? Could any American presidential parties, inaugural balls, or similar functions be compared to any of the French king's? Would Americans have tolerated such parties?

RELATED INTERNET SITE(S)

Louis XIV
http://www.geocities.com/TimesSquare/Labyrinth/1332.cultura.html
   Contains brief background material about Louis XIV and Cardinal Mazarin.

Louis XIV, King of France
http://www.knight.org/advent/cathen/09371a.htm
   Includes a short biographical sketch of Louis XIV.

ESSAY ON EAST-INDIA TRADE (1697)

URL ADDRESS: http://www.yale.edu/lawweb/avalon/econ/ eastindi.htm

SITE SUMMARY: The English East India Company was chartered by Elizabeth I in 1600 and remained a governmental commercial enterprise until 1873. Unlike contemporary American companies that are dedicated solely to business enterprises, the East India Company had governmental functions including the acquisition of territory, issuance of currency, negotiation of treaties, collection of taxes, waging of war, and administration of justice. This site contains the opinions of Charles D'Avenant, a trusted government official, on the pros and cons of the East India trade. His analysis is in the form of considered advice to Lord John Marquis of Normanby. It shows a level of economic sophistication and political foresight that has implications for England and its future colonies in the eighteenth and nineteenth centuries.

DISCUSSION QUESTIONS AND ACTIVITIES

1. What countries does the region known as the East Indies consist of? Draw a map showing the approximate location of these countries and their boundaries in the late 1600s.

2. You are the author of a bill "prohibiting the wearing of all East India and Persia wrought silks, bengals, and dyed, printed or stained callicoes." Formulate and deliver an oral argument defending your view to Parliament based on the danger of reliance on foreign imports and the need for consumers to purchase English-made goods.

3. As a member of Parliament, you are against the bill prohibiting the wearing of East India materials. Formulate and deliver an oral argument defending your view before Parliament based on the facts presented in D'Avenant's essay.

4. What are the drawbacks of protectionist and isolationist policies? Compare this proposed bill with the Smoot-Hawley Tariff Act passed by the U.S. Congress in 1930. What effect did this act have on the Great Depression?

5. In the late 1600s, England was at war with France. A rival East India company offered to lend the government a substantial sum of money to pay off its war debts in exchange for a charter for East India trade. Discuss the implications of government and business collaborations. What are the advantages and disadvantages?

6. Explain Charles D'Avenant's rhetorical question, "Is there anything in the world, that should be more thought a matter of state than trade, especially in an island"?

RELATED INTERNET SITE(S)

East India Company
http://www.hyperhistory.com/online_n2/History_n2/a.html
Use the right-hand scroll screen and click on the word *India*. Select *1500—1998* and when India comes up as a section, select *East India Company* for brief background material.

LIBERALISM (1700s–1800s)

URL ADDRESS: http://history.hanover.edu/modern/liberal.htm

SITE SUMMARY: Liberalism is characterized by the ideas of freedom, equality, and opportunity. These concepts also have economic and political implications. In the late 1700s and early 1800s, liberalism simply meant the establishment of governments based on the rule of law and by the consent of the governed. At first it meant enfranchising only the landowner class, but after a time came to include all adult citizens. This site contains primary texts by Thomas Malthus, John Stuart Mill, David Ricardo, Alexis de Tocqueville, Jeremy Bentham, and Klemens von Metternich.

DISCUSSION QUESTIONS AND ACTIVITIES

1. Select John Stuart Mill and click on *On Liberty*. Write an essay about the struggle between liberty and authority based on Mill's opinions. Do you agree or disagree with his views?

2. Click on Mill's writings concerning *Representative Government*. What does Mill consider to be a representative government? Does it correspond to our current ideas of representative government? Does Mill seem to be accepting of different forms of government? Based on Mill's writing, defend the communist government of China. Why might Mill be tolerant of this form of government?

3. Liberalism as a political philosophy also included the concept of personal freedom. Select Jeremy Bentham and click on *Offences Against Oneself (1785)*. In this writing, Bentham posed the first known argu-

ment for homosexual legal reform. What are his grounds for opposing punishment?

4. Select Alexis de Tocqueville and click on *Democracy in America*. Scroll down to Section 4 and click on *What sort of Despotism Democratic Nations have to Fear*. Do you agree or disagree with de Tocqueville's opinion that the United States is susceptible to this type of despotism?

5. Scroll down to Section 3 of *Democracy in America* and click on *Education of Young Women in the United States*. In light of today's society, would you describe de Tocqueville's views on women as conservative or liberal?

6. You are an opponent of Klemens von Metternich and have just received a leaked copy of *Political Confession of Faith, 1820*. What parts of his memoirs will you send to the newspaper as evidence of his antiliberal political views and beliefs?

RELATED INTERNET SITE(S)

Liberalism
http://tqd.advanced.org/3376/Genktk5.htm
Provides a hyperlinked essay about the concepts of liberalism and the philosophers, politicians, and writers associated with this form of political thought.

NATIVE AMERICAN HISTORY ARCHIVE (1700s–1980s)

URL ADDRESS: http://www.ilt.columbia.edu/k12/naha/natribes.html

SITE SUMMARY: This site is evolving. It contains a broad collection of information about many different Native American tribes and provides links related to their contemporary home pages. The best approach is to click on *Tribes* and follow the alphabetical index, accessing individual tribes when necessary. Under the Crow tribe, for example, are the tribal court decisions and the scope of rights furnished them by the Indian Civil Rights Act of 1968. The Eskimo (Inuit) site features images of a kayak, an igloo, and clothing plus speeches from an audio archive. The site requires diligent pre-searching, however, before using it as a primary sources teaching database.

DISCUSSION QUESTIONS AND ACTIVITIES

1. The persecution of Native Americans did not begin in the 1800s. It began with the first contacts that various tribes had with Europeans.

Select *Tribes* and click on *Cherokee*. Select *A Cherokee History Timeline*. Study the timeline and construct graphs that show the resultant loss of land, life, and property that the Cherokees experienced as a result of their encounters with European settlers. Discuss the demographic, social, and political patterns that emerge from your research.

2. Select the Creek tribe and click on *1815 Map of Cherokee and Creek Lands*. Compare this map to a current one showing present-day Native American reservations within the states shown on the 1815 map. Give a geographical history lesson of the Creek nation that provides evidence of the loss of their original lands to the United States government.

3. Select the Seminole tribe and click on *Seminole*. Examine the Seminole artifacts that are listed at this site. You are an archaeologist who has been asked to assess Seminole society based on these finds. Look at the types of materials used and their design, quality, and craftsmanship. Write a profile of the type of society you think existed at the time these artifacts were being used.

4. Select the Sioux tribe and click on *History & Culture of the Sisseton-Wahpeton Sioux Tribe*. Enlarge the images from the Minnesota Historical Society. What illustration details reveal the possible dates of the events depicted? What details in the illustrations provide an indication of how developed the Sioux tribe was? Look at transportation, housing, care of children, style of dress, weapons, material constructions, and other items for evidence to support your conclusions.

5. Even in the 1800s the stereotype of Native Americans as a savage and uncivilized people persisted. Select the Wyandot tribe and click on *Wyandot Migration to Kansas by Lucy B. Armstrong*. From this personal account, describe the level of development of Wyandot society based on housing construction, self-government, language, trade, religion, and literacy.

6. Click on *Wyandot Treaties*. Select treaties within a chronological order. You are a Wyandot historian who has been asked to analyze the treaties and report on their contents. How were your ancestors treated by the United States government over the period of time you chose to study? Were they paid for the lands that the government took from them? Did the government take advantage of them? If so, how? Was there any way that they could have protected themselves tribally against this encroachment?

RELATED INTERNET SITE(S)

Native Americans Documents Project
http://www.csusm.edu/projects/nadp/nadp.htm#report

Provides primary sources about the role of the Commission of Indian Affairs with regard to various Native American tribes, particularly in the late 1800s.

SLAVERY RESOURCES ON-LINE (1700s–1800s)

URL ADDRESS: http://vi.uh.edu/pages/mintz/gilder.htm

SITE SUMMARY: Originating from the Gilder Lehrman Institute of America within the Pierpont Morgan Library in New York, this site contains one of the richest online collections of excerpts from slave narratives. They are well organized under the headings enslavement, the middle passage, arrival, conditions of life, childhood, family, religion, punishment, resistance, flight, and emancipation. In addition there is a syllabus for an intensive course on the origins and nature of New World slavery and two slavery bibliographies. The site also contains links to the Library of Congress WPA Histories project that features additional slave narratives.

DISCUSSION QUESTIONS AND ACTIVITIES

1. Select *Excerpts from Slave Narratives* and click on *European slave trader, John Barbot . . .* Even though Barbot portrays slavery in the most inhumane terms, why does he describe it from a business point of view?

2. Select *Gods A-Gwinteter Trouble de Water: The Middle Passage* and click on the account of *Olaudah Equiano.* What conditions on the boat led Olaudah to fear that he would be eaten?

3. Select *Dere's No Hidin' Place Down Here: Arrival.* Compare and contrast the account of Olaudah Equiano's arrival as a slave in the West Indies to that of the English physician Alexander Falconbridge.

4. Select *We Raise de Wheat, Dey Gib Us de Corn: Conditions of Life.* Read several accounts in this section. Your younger brother has just been sold to another plantation. You have only twenty minutes to give him counsel that you hope will enable him to stay alive. Describe what advice you would give him in terms of work habits, attitude toward his masters, and avoiding punishment.

5. Select *Like a Motherless Child: Childhood.* Read the accounts in this section. Analyze the ways that slave owners undermined the authority of slave parents. Why do you think that slave owners engaged in this practice?

6. Select *Nobody Knows de Trouble I See: Family.* Read the accounts in this

section. Based on these accounts, what do you think slavery did as an institution to destroy the concept of family?

RELATED INTERNET SITE(S)

Lest We Forget
http://www.coax.net/people/lwf
This extensive site contains related links to information about the history and culture of African Americans from the time of slavery to the present day.

THIRD PERSON, FIRST PERSON: SLAVE VOICES FROM THE RARE BOOK, MANUSCRIPTS, AND SPECIAL COLLECTIONS LIBRARY (1700s–1800s)

URL ADDRESS: http://scriptorium.lib.duke.edu/slavery/

SITE SUMMARY: The real life accounts of American slaves from the eighteenth and nineteenth centuries poignantly unfold from this extensive site, which shows original bills of sale, the work of slaves, and the types of freedom (manumission or running away) that slaves could work and yearn for. It also contains broadsides promising rewards for runaways, descriptions of groups of slaves, and excerpts from papers, books, and letters that address the problem of emancipation during the Civil War. More importantly, it provides a written record of people whose hopes and aspirations were to be considered, for all intents and purposes, invisible to the rest of society.

DISCUSSION QUESTIONS AND ACTIVITIES

1. Select *Caesar* and read through all of the correspondence concerning this slave. You are a distant relative of Caesar who is constructing a family genealogy. From the evidence that you possess, formulate some hypotheses about what happened to him. Do you think that he gained his freedom?

2. Select *Plantation America, the Work of Slaves*. From the evidence presented in this section, what type of work did slaves do on plantations? What were their general living conditions?

3. Select *The Age of Revolutions Two Kinds of Freedom*. From the evidence presented in this section, which type of freedom do you think was more common, and why?

4. Select *Black Sotherners in the Old South—The Slave Community*. From the evidence presented in this section explain why the idea of a "slave community" was a misnomer. What is your definition of a community?

5. Select *The Problem of Freedom*. From the evidence presented in this section, describe the social and political climate that former slaves experienced during and immediately after the Civil War. Why do you think there would be rumors about African Americans arming themselves and attacking white people?

6. From reading the evidence about slavery at this site, what do you think are some of its legacies? Be prepared to talk about racism, white people's guilt, and how costly discrimination has been to our nation.

RELATED INTERNET SITE(S)

The Amistad Research Center
http://www.tulane.edu/~amistad/

Besides containing excellent information about the *Amistad* slave revolt, this collection includes manuscripts about African Americans in all occupations and careers. It also features works by Harlem Renaissance painter Aaron Douglas, oral history interviews, and historical exhibits.

THE AGE OF ENLIGHTENMENT IN THE PAINTINGS OF FRANCE'S NATIONAL MUSEUMS (1715–1799)

URL ADDRESS: http://www.culture.fr/files/imaginary_exhibition.html

SITE SUMMARY: Paintings can be viewed as primary sources that accurately depict an event, person, or time period. They can also be indicative of a period of economic poverty or prosperity. For France, the period between the death of Louis XIV and the reign of Napoleon was an era of relative domestic peace. Salons of philosophy, cafes, and clubs helped create a middle-class society that desired freedom from monarchical rule. This site provides excellent historical background about the Enlightenment, a genealogical chart of the Bourbons from Louis XIV onward, and a list of Enlightenment artists with hyperlinks to their respective paintings.

DISCUSSION QUESTIONS AND ACTIVITIES

1. A hierarchy of genres dominated the French Enlightenment period of painting. In order of importance were history painting, portraiture,

genre painting, still-life, and landscape. Why did French academicians impose these genre hierarchies on painters?

2. You are an aspiring and extremely ambitious French Enlightenment painter. What genre do you wish to excel in to have a prosperous career? Why is the genre you have chosen considered the noblest form of art?

3. Many French people were not prosperous during the Enlightenment. As a painter, how would you depict these people before the French Revolution in your paintings? What kind of clothes would they wear? What expressions might be on their faces? What would they be doing in your paintings? What would their houses and living conditions look like?

4. The French Enlightenment encompassed the rococo and neoclassic schools of painting. Select paintings at this site from each school and show how the styles changed with the coming of the French Revolution.

5. Discuss how eighty years of domestic peace and economic prosperity contributed to the French Enlightenment. What were the social and political effects on France when it did not have to be concerned with waging war? Discuss the proliferation of salons, cafes, and clubs. Who were some of the philosophers, writers, and well-known artists of this period?

6. Despite some reforms during the Enlightenment, class structure remained extremely rigid. You are an art historian who has been asked to present a lecture on how this structure was imposed on artists. What classes of people were not depicted in Enlightenment paintings? How were people, objects, themes and landscapes depicted during this time? Were paintings that depicted, for example, scenes of rural poverty exhibited at galleries?

RELATED INTERNET SITE(S)

Artists & Works by Chronology
http://humanitas.ucsb.edu/shuttle/art.html#artists
Select *Artists and Works by Chronology* at this site and click on the *18th Century*. Divided by country, it includes images of art by painters of this period. It is an excellent site for creating comparative art questions.

COLONIAL LIMA (1748)

URL ADDRESS: http://www.msstate.edu/Archives/History/lima.html

SITE SUMMARY: Excerpted from the 1748 book *A Voyage to South America* by Jorge Juan and Antonio de Ulloa, this passage describes the physical characteristics, family customs, class systems, commercial enterprises, dress, and lifestyle of the various ethnic groups in colonial Lima. While the descriptions provide helpful evidence of urban Peruvian life during the 1700s, they also reveal the authors' biases toward various ethnic groups and their ideal of beauty, fashion, and treatment of classes of people.

DISCUSSION QUESTIONS AND ACTIVITIES

1. Colonial Lima suffers from a caste system in this account. What is it based on? Which ethnic groups seem most favored?

2. Based on this account, write an imaginary character sketch of a powerful person in colonial Lima. Be sure to include his or her ethnic background, living quarters, dress, and other important aspects that would be historically accurate and pertinent to the individual's position.

3. Why is engaging in commerce not considered a disgrace in colonial Lima as it was in Spain?

4. You have been invited to a ball at the home of a wealthy colonial. Draw a design of your dress complete with jewelry, hair ornaments, and shoes. What is there about your dress that would appear indecent if you were a recent Spanish arrival?

5. Based on the class system that the authors describe, prepare an employment handbook for different classes showing their typical occupations and their earning potential.

6. The authors stress the existence of a class system that even includes slaves. It is 1748. You are a Catholic priest who is outraged by this system. Preach a sermon on its evils and predict the future for colonial Lima if the citizens continue to condone it.

RELATED INTERNET SITE(S)

Library of Congress Country Studies
http://lcweb2.loc.gov/frd/cs/cshome.html
   Includes a country studies handbook for Peru and many other Latin American countries. Each book contains a lengthy chapter about the early history of the country.

REVERIES ON THE ART OF WAR (1757)

URL ADDRESS: http://www.hillsdale.edu/dept/History/Documents/War/18e/1757-Saxe.htm

SITE SUMMARY: The art of war and leadership during war have been written about by famous military historians and statesmen such as Niccolo Machiavelli and Sun Tzu. This account by Field Marshall Hermann-Maurice de Saxe (1696–1750) is his reflection on the requirements of war. Written in 1732, it was published in 1757, after his death. Field Marshall de Saxe distinguished himself in the War of Austrian Succession (1740–1748) when Maria Theresa ascended to the throne after being supported by Great Britain. Comparisons and connections with other classic military texts can be combined into an interesting discussion lesson about the universality of military strategy laws.

DISCUSSION QUESTIONS AND ACTIVITIES

1. Field Marshall de Saxe makes a comment in his opening sentence to the effect that no rules of conduct can apply to the rules of war. Give your opinion on this statement and make reference to the Geneva Conventions of August 12, 1949.

2. What do you think of the field marshall's recommendation that a country have a tive-year draft? Research the history of mandatory military service at various periods in the United States. Choose one in which you think the government was justified in drafting soldiers and one in which it was not.

3. De Saxe recommends a classic style of battle, in Article 6, with lines of soldiers facing each other. When do you think this tactic would be dangerous and self-defeating? Provide examples from wars such as the French and Indian War and the American Revolutionary War to support your argument.

4. "War is an honorable profession," declares de Saxe. What is your opinion of this statement in today's society? Are U.S. soldiers respected and admired for their service?

5. Is there such a discipline as the "science of war"? Explain how war might or might not be made to follow specific principles and rules.

6. Compare these sections of de Saxe's reveries to parts of Sun Tzu's *The Art of War*. Why does de Saxe address the art of war so directly, whereas Sun Tzu seems to devote more words to avoiding it?

RELATED INTERNET SITE(S)

Hermann-Maurice, count de Saxe (1747), Marshall of France
http://babelfish.altavista.com/cgi-bin/translate
Provides a translated hyperlinked biographical sketch of the author.

THE INDUSTRIAL REVOLUTION (1760–1848)

URL ADDRESS: http://humanitas.ucsb.edu/shuttle/science. html#industrial-revolution

SITE SUMMARY: The term "Industrial Revolution" describes the rapid changes in methods of production and technology that began to appear in England about 1760. Essentially, domestic work or piecework was replaced with some form of mass production or factory system. New inventions such as James Watt's steam engine and Edmund Cartwright's power loom hastened cataclysmic changes in work, accumulation of wealth, and society. This excellent gateway site provides extensive background and overview material beginning with a timeline, a list of preconditions for industrialization, and a series of Power Point slides outlining the main points of this age. Primary sources consist of excerpted readings about the life of an industrial worker and lectures from the time period.

DISCUSSION QUESTIONS AND ACTIVITIES

1. Select *The Life of the Industrial Worker in 19th-Century England*. Click on *Evidence Given Before the Sadler Committee*. Based on the child labor conditions described in this testimony, draft a new law that provides children with better working hours and conditions.

2. You are a factory owner who is intent on defeating the new law drafted by your classmate. Write a speech for your appearance in Parliament that expresses your opinion about the pattern the Industrial Revolution must take if Great Britain is to remain a prosperous nation.

3. You are an expert on repetitive stress injuries and have been asked to testify before the United States Senate. A Senate committee member asks you to compare this new occupational hazard with some of the kinds of physical deterioration seen in textile and cotton workers during the Industrial Revolution. How would you compare them?

4. Modern-day workers fear that robots or other forms of automation will replace them in the workplace. Read *Opposition to the Chimney Sweepers' Regulation Bill*. When do machines offer a human being relief against intolerable working conditions? Write an essay about the benefits of the Industrial Revolution from a technology standpoint.

5. Read *Testimony Gathered by Ashley's Mines Commission*. Based on this testimony, draft an occupational health and safety law that would protect people from some of the dangers in this industry.

6. Refer to the Power Point slides by K. Austin Kerr entitled *The Industrial Revolution*. Compare and contrast the Industrial Revolution and the Computer Revolution in a similar presentation.

RELATED INTERNET SITE(S)

Industrial Revolution
http://www.letsfindout.com
Provides an elementary overview of the people and events associated with the Industrial Revolution.

Notes on the American Industrial Revolution: The Threads of Change
http://www.etsu-tn.edu/scitech/technol/entc3020/hemphill/amindrev/tsld001.htm
Includes a Power Point presentation with short, key sentences about the main events and inventions related to the American Industrial Revolution.

LORD JEFFREY AMHERST'S LETTERS DISCUSSING GERM WARFARE AGAINST AMERICAN INDIANS (1763)

URL ADDRESS: http://history1700s.miningco.com/index.htm

SITE SUMMARY: Lord Jeffrey Amherst was the general in charge of the British forces during the final campaigns of the French and Indian War (1754–1763). His victories against the French allowed the British to acquire Canada. His reputation was shaded by stories that he condoned gifts of smallpox-infected blankets as a form of germ warfare against the Ottawa Indian tribe led by Chief Pontiac. In 1763 Pontiac led a rebellion against the English in a futile attempt to reestablish the Ottawas' autonomy. This site contains the letter showing that Lord Amherst did countenance the "distribution of blankets to inoculate the Indians." Use the search function and type in *Lord Jeffrey Amherst* to retrieve this site.

DISCUSSION QUESTIONS AND ACTIVITIES

1. You have been asked to investigate whether Captain Simeon Ecuyer and Lord Jeffrey Amherst should be indicted by a British war crimes tribunal for deliberately distributing blankets infected with the small-pox virus to members of Chief Pontiac's tribe. Most of your evidence rests on the correspondence between Colonel Henry Bouquet and Lord Amherst. Write a report based on these letters and give your opinion whether grounds for indictment exist.

2. Select various members of the class to serve as judges, lawyers, eye-witnesses, smallpox survivors, Indian massacre survivors, and so on, and conduct a mock trial of Captain Ecuyer and Lord Amherst for war crimes.

3. You have a Ph.D. in ethics. Is there any time when you think that the use of germ warfare would be justified?

4. Find other periods in history when biological weapons have been used against either a military or a civilian population. Examples exist from World Wars I and II and Iraq's war against the Kurds.

5. Write a law banning the use of germ warfare under any circum-stances. Include penalties for any nation that engages in it.

6. Argue that the use of nuclear weapons constitutes a form of germ warfare because of the radioactive injuries, increased incidence of can-cer in future generations, contamination of the surrounding land, and so on.

RELATED INTERNET SITE(S)

Pontiac's Rebellion
http://history1700s.miningco.com/index.htm
    Gives accurate background information about the history and culture of the Ottawa tribe.

ARCTIC DAWN REPORT (1768)

URL ADDRESS: http://web.idirect.com/~hland/sh/title2.html

SITE SUMMARY: Arctic Dawn contains the exciting diary entries of the eighteenth century explorer Samuel Hearne as he traveled through the Arctic in 1768. It provides a fascinating glimpse into an explorer's mind that reflects the beliefs and attitudes of a society that considered itself more advanced than the indigenous peoples with which it came in contact. Hearne's diary includes many "sexist and racist" remarks about various Indian tribes. At the same time, it reveals the violence of life during his century and the tremendous surprise that the vast natural wonders of the New World presented.

DISCUSSION QUESTIONS AND ACTIVITIES

1. Based on Hearne's expeditionary accounts, draw a map showing his route and the rivers and indigenous peoples that he encountered on his way.

2. Why did the Hudson's Bay Company feel obliged to "extend the boundaries of the British Empire"? What countries were competing against them during this time?

3. Hearne lived during the time of the fur-trapping trade. What furs were most prized in Europe during this period? Based on Hearne's accounts, describe the trials and tribulations of fur trappers who needed to get their furs to Prince of Wales Fort in Hudson's Bay. How did the publication of Hearne's book help them?

4. What is Hearne's attitude toward the Native Americans with whom he interacts? Is he respectful? condescending? Why might he think that he is superior to the indigenous people? What customs do the various Native Americans practice that Hearne might think are evidence of an inferior culture?

5. Your name is Matonabbee. You have been accompanying Samuel Hearne on a great portion of this journey. Write several diary entries that include your opinion of the social customs that Hearne practices. What is your attitude toward Hearne? Do you think that he is stupid to go exploring? Does he seem greedy to you? What acts does he engage in that you think are evidence of an inferior culture?

6. What is Matonabbee's attitude toward women? Does Hearne share it? You are an Indian woman on one of Hearne's expeditions. Describe some of your travels and travails.

RELATED INTERNET SITE(S)

Arctic Exploration
http://www.library.yale.edu/beinecke/native2.htm
   Provides images by George Heriot and other painters of Native Americans from his book, *Travels Through the Canadas*.

1788 to 1868. Be sure to account for peaks in numbers, different settlement areas, and other important demographic information.

2. You are a former Australian convict. Tell the class about the length of prison terms and the types of crimes that people served time for, and give information about convict life. Were you ever permitted to return to Great Britain?

3. Read the passages from Charles Dickens's *Great Expectations* about the character Abel Magwitch's sentence to the Australian colonies. Imagine that you are Magwitch. Using a Dickensian style, write a letter to your friend in London describing your voyage.

4. Select *Convict Tales*. What is your opinion of these criminals? Do you think the types of crimes they have been deported for merited such punishment? Explain your reasoning.

5. You are a convict who has just been granted his freedom in Australia after serving a sentence of seven years for theft. Why do you see Australia as a place for a new, crime-free life? Why do you never want to see England again?

6. A new planet that supports life has just been discovered. A congressman has proposed that the United States empty its prisons and send all of our criminals to this planet with no opportunity for return. Argue the pros and cons of this plan. If you support it, would you make distinctions among certain types of crimes, or would you send everyone who has been convicted? Do you think that deportation to a new planet would serve as a deterrent to crime? If yes, why? If not, why not?

RELATED INTERNET SITE(S)

British Imperial Convicts Transported to Western Australia from 1850 to 1868
http://users.wantree.com.au/~reginald/convicts.htm
   Includes a list of convicts who were transported and are either not included or readily available in other Australian convict-related archives.

PORTRAITS OF THE PRESIDENTS AND FIRST LADIES (1789–1992)

URL ADDRESS: http://rs6.loc.gov/amhome.html

SITE SUMMARY: Culled from the Library of Congress "popular demand images" file, this site would be especially timely to use during a presidential election year. It contains 156 black and white portraits of thirty-five presidents and thirty-six First Ladies. Although the primary focus rests on the First Ladies' faces, one scene showcases the wedding of Frances Folsom and Grover Cleveland. The site can be used to study the "patriotic and commercial roles of presidential portraiture" as presented by a variety of styles, poses, and different photographers. The artists include Mathew Brady, employees of the company of N. Currier, and appointed White House photographers.

DISCUSSION QUESTIONS AND ACTIVITIES

1. Compare the portrait of Abigail Adams to that of Dolley Madison. Gilbert Stuart painted both. What personal qualities are transmitted to the viewer? Compare and contrast the interests and activities of each First Lady.

2. Look at the portrait of Mrs. Franklin Pierce. Read about her life and times in Washington, D.C. Was she happy in the capital? Compare what she is wearing in her portrait to what most women were wearing at this time. Does her clothing reflect the era, or does it provide clues to Mrs. Pierce's personal disposition?

3. Select *Grover Cleveland* and click on *The President's Wedding*. Grover Cleveland was forty-eight years old when he married Frances Folsom, who was twenty-one. Look at their wedding portrait. Do you see a stark difference in age between the two of them? If not, why? How does President Cleveland look to you? Describe how he seems to feel about himself. Why do the guests look so solemn?

4. Select portraits of various First Ladies from each of the three centuries. Notice how few are posed with a smile. Why do you think so many are posed unsmiling?

5. First Ladies assume many duties when they move into the White House. They have served as unpaid ambassadors for our country and continue to elicit aid and support for charitable causes and issues of national interest. Why are all of them posed without trappings that would identify them as having an official government position, such as the flag, the Presidential Seal, or a working desk?

6. Of all the First Lady portraits, do any look like those of "career women"? If so, write an editorial expressing your opinion that this portrait was meant to send a message to Americans of both genders concerning the different role of a First Lady.

RELATED INTERNET SITE(S)

Presidents and First Ladies Topics
http://mckinley.netcom.com/magellan/Reviews/Politics_and_Law/
Governments/United_States/Federal/Presidents_and_First_Ladies/
index.magellan.html
   This site features reviews of various U.S. Presidents and First Ladies.

POTUS Presidents of the United States
http://www.ipl.org/ref/POTUS
   An extensive site that includes background information, election results, cabinet members, important events, and other interesting facts
about each President of the United States.

THE FRENCH REVOLUTION (1789–1799)

URL ADDRESS: http://history.hanover.edu/modern/frenchrv.htm

SITE SUMMARY: The French Revolution, which lasted from 1789 to
1799, was a cataclysmic event and resulted in great changes in the governance and society of France. More important, it had significant consequences for the rest of Europe. Although it introduced the concepts of
democracy, it did not create one in France. It did, however, end supreme
rule by French kings and caused all European royalties and aristocracies
to heed the need for *liberté, egalité*, and *fraternité*. This site features
twenty-five primary documents directly relating to the Revolution, including the Tennis Court Oath of 1789, the Decree Abolishing Feudalism
of 1789, the Declaration of the Rights of Woman, and the reports and
grievances of various French social classes.

DISCUSSION QUESTIONS AND ACTIVITIES

1. Select one or two of the Cahiers of 1789. You are a French peasant
   who has just learned to read and write. What would you like written
   in your local village cahier?

2. What is the significance of *The Tennis Court Oath*? What in Louis XIV's
   background, royal birth, education, and upbringing caused him to
   pretend that the Tennis Court Oath had never occurred?

3. Read *The Decree Abolishing the Feudalism of 1789*. As a peasant, what
   are the immediate benefits to you? How will your life change? As a
   nobleman, do you see any benefits from this decree? How will your
   life change as a result of it?

4. Select *The Declaration of the Rights of Woman, 1791*. It was written in response to the Declaration of the Rights of Man. Why do you believe Olympe de Gouges was tried and executed for treason by writing this document?

5. Select *Maximilien Robespierre: Justification of the Use of Terror*. Argue the pros and cons of the quotation "virtue without which terror is fatal; terror without which virtue is powerless." What general conclusions about all revolutions can be drawn from the Terror?

6. The French Revolution did not bring about a democracy in France. Write an editorial expressing the opinion that the French did, however, receive benefits from Revolution, and so did the rest of the world.

RELATED INTERNET SITE(S)

Links on the French Revolution
http://www.hs.port.ac.uk/Users/david.andress/frlinks
   Provides substantial background and overview materials about the important dates, people, and events of the French Revolution.

UNITED STATES HISTORICAL CENSUS DATA BROWSER (1790–1970)

URL ADDRESS: http://fisher.lib.virginia.edu.census/

SITE SUMMARY: It is sometimes difficult for students to manipulate the variables in census data. At this site, however, students can select ten-year intervals from 1790 to 1970 for each state and county. Then they may choose up to fifteen variables and request that the material be displayed in various graphs. Within the year 1860, for example, users have a choice of categories, including free colored population, slave population, white population, education, literacy, marriage, and births and deaths. Within these categories are drop-down menus that support further delineation by age, gender, and so on.

DISCUSSION QUESTIONS AND ACTIVITIES

1. Select the *census years 1790–1850*. For each census year select the variable *total number of slaves*. Click on *graph states*. Note the demographic patterns that emerge as you graph each census year. What states are experiencing the largest gains in slave population? Which state has

the most slaves for the census year 1850? Research this factor and each state's position on slavery.

2. Select *census years 1790–1850*. For each census year, select the variable *no. of white slaveholding families*. Click on *graph states*. Note the demographic patterns that emerge as you graph each census year. What states are experiencing the largest gains among white slaveholding families? What are some of the reasons for this demographic pattern? From these data, what would you predict might happen during the Civil War in those states?

3. Compare these data with the variable *no. of white non-slaveholding families* for the *census years 1790–1850*. What patterns emerge among various states? What problems would you predict are going to occur from viewing these data?

4. Select the *1850 census year* and choose the variable *total no. of white adults who cannot read or write*. What states have the highest illiteracy rates? What states have the lowest rates? What conditions may have accounted for these rates? Be sure to look at patterns of immigration in those states for that particular period of time.

5. Select the *1870 census year* and choose the variable *no. persons born in Ireland*. What states have the largest numbers of people who were born in Ireland? How do you account for this demographic distribution?

6. Select the *1960 census year* and choose the variable *no. persons of foreign stock reporting ireland (eire) as country of origin*. What states have the largest numbers of people who were born in Ireland? Why might the demographic distribution be different from that of the 1870 census year? What conditions in Ireland changed that probably affected the rate of immigration?

RELATED INTERNET SITE(S)

U.S. Census Bureau
http://www.census.gov/

Contains the home page for all U.S. Census information. Several links are especially suited to secondary school students.

Ask a Census Expert
http://www.census.gov/ftp/pub/main/www/ask.html

Provides excellent assistance for general and specific questions relating to all aspects of the Census Bureau.

A VINDICATION OF THE RIGHTS OF WOMAN WITH STRICTURES ON POLITICAL AND MORAL SUBJECTS (1792)

URL ADDRESS: http://www.columbia.edu/acis/bartleby/ wollstonecraft/

SITE SUMMARY: Published in 1792, Mary Wollstonecraft's revolutionary book presented a powerful argument for the establishment of legal, political, and social equality between men and women. Wollstonecraft was one of the first women to articulate in print the institutionally and culturally sponsored oppression of women. Her work employs Thomas Jefferson's Declaration of Independence and the natural rights theory of John Locke to support her premise concerning the total equality between the sexes. In addition to the full text of her work, this site also includes an introduction, Wollstonecraft's dedication of her work to Monsieur Talleyrand, Bishop of Autun, and some study questions.

DISCUSSION QUESTIONS AND ACTIVITIES

1. Write a short biographical sketch of Mary Wollstonecraft. Discuss how her childhood and her experiences may have contributed to her writing this work.

2. Click on *Chap. XII On national education.* What is Wollstonecraft's opinion on coeducation? Would she approve of women attending the Virginia Military Institute or the Citadel?

3. Click on Chap. II, *The prevailing opinion of a sexual character discussed.* Do you agree or disagree with Wollstonecraft's statement that women are told from infancy how to gain the protection of a man by displaying weakness and softness of temper? Was this statement true only in previous centuries, or might it carry weight in today's society as well?

4. What is the overall tone of Wollstonecraft's book? Is she an angry person? Would you call her a feminist?

5. Imagine that you are Mary Wollstonecraft and that you have just been introduced to Betty Friedan and Gloria Steinem. What issues would you have in common? What issues would you think were totally unrealistic?

6. Wollstonecraft has definite ideas concerning gender roles. Compare

her ideas with the gender roles portrayed in Jane Austen's book *Sense and Sensibility*.

RELATED INTERNET SITE(S)

Mary Wollstonecraft and Frankenstein
http://www.dessert-fairy.com/maryshel.html
  Presents a well-linked biographical sketch of Mary Wollstonecraft and includes information about the most important people, events, times, and places in her life.

Study Questions for Wollstonecraft's *A Vindication of the Rights of Woman*
http://www.stark.kent.edu/~jmoneysmith/rights.htm
  Provides a chronology of Mary Wollstonecraft's life with an emphasis on her publications.

T. ROBERT MALTHUS HOME PAGE (1798)

URL ADDRESS: http://msumusik.mursuky.edu/~felwell/http/malthus/index.htm
SITE SUMMARY: Thomas Robert Malthus, an English curate, economist, and scholar, wrote several books on political economy. His most famous work was *An Essay on the Principle of Population*. His thesis was that population, when unchecked, tends to increase geometrically, while the means to feed the population tends to increase arithmetically. To offset this eventually deadly cycle of overcrowding, poverty, disease, and war, Malthus proposed that measures be taken to prevent overpopulation. This site contains the full text of the essay plus twelve population-related pamphlets. It also provides an excellent introduction to the social theory that Malthus espoused.

DISCUSSION QUESTIONS AND ACTIVITIES

1. Research the socioeconomic conditions in Great Britain at the time Malthus wrote his essay on population. Was population in Great Britain increasing geometrically while food production increased at an arithmetic rate?

2. What is the current rate at which the world' population doubles? Is the Malthusian theorem still a realistic one?

3. Malthus is still remembered for this essay even though he later changed his mind and rewrote it. Find the parts that he changed and

write a retraction for him that will be printed in the local newspaper. Why do you think that people always refer to his first essay?

4. Karl Marx called Malthus's essay "a libel on the human race." Explain what he meant by this charge.

5. What technological, biological, and agricultural discoveries and practices may have prevented Malthus's theory from becoming a reality in many parts of the world? Some considerations should include birth control, improved agricultural methods, the invention of specific machines, and improved transportation.

6. In 1968 Paul Ehrlich published a book entitled *The Population Bomb* in which he stated that "the battle to feed humanity is over." Why have we not yet experienced this prophesied population Armageddon?

RELATED INTERNET SITE(S)

Thomas Malthus on Population and Consequences
http://www.tdd.lt/sdib/html/malthus.htm

This is an outstanding overview site about the Malthusian theory of population. It reviews England's economic situation at the beginning of the nineteenth century, the Malthusian theory, and the pros and cons of the theory, and discusses it within the context of other economic concepts and characteristics of the period.

NATIONALISM (1800s)

URL ADDRESS: http://history.hanover.edu/modern/national.htm

SITE SUMMARY: Nationalism reflects a people's sense of belonging together as a nation. The feelings of loyalty to one's country and pride in its culture and history are sometimes evoked to inspire a people to seek national independence. Nationalism is an important factor in international relations and has changed the maps of continents several times. As a movement it also has its negative side, sometimes producing rivalry and tensions among nations. This site includes primary texts from German, Jewish, Irish, and Italian patriots. They were all written in the 1800s, a time when nationalistic movements were widespread.

DISCUSSION QUESTIONS AND ACTIVITIES

1. Abbé Sieyes excluded the nobility and clergy from his definition of the Third Estate (see French Revolution, http://history.hanover.edu/ modern/frenchrv.htm). How does Mazzini's view in *On Nationality, 1852* differ from that of Sieyes?

2. Select Johann Gottlieb Fichte's address, *To the German Nation, 1806.* What words, phrases, and thoughts in this address make it more nation-centered than Mazzini's view of nationality?

3. Select Theodor Herzl's *On the Jewish State, 1896.* Herzl seems to base his justification for a Jewish state on the continued persecution and anti-Semitism directed at Jewish people over the centuries. Do you think that persecution should be a main requirement for nationhood? Can you think of other countries that were founded principally because its people were discriminated against or persecuted by others?

4. Select Daniel O'Connell's address *Justice for Ireland, Feb. 4, 1836.* Compare this address to Theodor Herzl's pamphlet *On the Jewish State, 1896.* Both of these writings indicate a significant degree of persecution and discrimination by people in the majority. Yet O'Connell pleads for simple justice under British law, whereas Herzl is seeking the creation of a new country. Why do you think O'Connell still seems to want to work within the system, while Herzl has given up hope for that?

5. Of all the writings at this site, which one do you think is the most idealistic in its interpretation of the political concept of nationalism? Why?

6. Of all the writings at this site, which one do you think is the most pragmatic in its interpretation of the political concept of nationalism? Why?

RELATED INTERNET SITE(S)

19thC Liberal Europe Nationalism
http://chomsky.arts.adelaide.edu.au/person/Dhart/ClassicalLiberalism/LiberalEurope/Bibliography/Index.html

Contains a short description of European nationalism along with some stimulating study questions and a bibliography of related books.

AFRICAN AMERICAN PERSPECTIVES (1818–1907)

URL ADDRESS: http://rs6.loc.gov/amhome.html

SITE SUMMARY: Pamphlets, because of their ephemeral nature, are a treasured commodity within the genre of primary sources. The Daniel A. P. Murray Pamphlet Collection is part of the Library of Congress's American Memory Project. The collection comprises 351 pamphlets published from 1818 to 1907. Broadly, the topics encompass African Americans, the arts, ethnicity, religion, politics and government, and war. Most of the collection spans the period 1875–1900. Among the published African American authors are Booker T. Washington, Ida B. Wells-Barnett, Benjamin W. Arnett, Frederick Douglass, and Emanuel Love. A multitude of African American associations and organizations, viewpoints, proceedings, and position statements are also included. A search engine makes it possible to search by keyword, subject, and author.

DISCUSSION QUESTIONS AND ACTIVITIES

1. Type in the word *lynching* as a keyword and click on *The blood red record: a review of the horrible* . . . . Why did so many lynchings take place in the South? What motives inspired most lynchings?

2. Read several of the pamphlets about lynching. You are the mayor of a southern city. You know that there is a federal statute punishing lynching under the Fourteenth Amendment, but wish to have other city plans in effect to prevent such murders. What would you do in

the way of education, media coverage of crimes, local laws, and so on to prevent such a horrible event from occurring in your community?

3. Under the subject *United States—History—Civil War, 1861–1865—Afro-American Troops*, select *The Negro as a Soldier*. Read through the history of African American participation in America's wars from the Revolutionary War to the Civil War. Why do you think the role played by African Americans in these past wars has not received much coverage in books or periodicals? As a freelance writer, use excerpts from this account to express your indignation that their valorous history has been neglected by previous historians.

4. Type *John Brown* as a keyword search and click on *John Brown: an address by Frederick Douglass.* . . . At one time Douglass was mobbed in Boston for praising John Brown. In this speech Douglass describes him as a true hero. Why was even the mention of John Brown's name such a threat to the people of Boston at that time?

5. In the search box, type *Draft riot, 1863*. Write a newspaper article describing the draft riots in New York City in 1863. Make sure that you emphasize the plight of the victims, how much damage was done, and how many people were killed. Write a conclusion that recommends that a committee of merchants take up a collection to help African Americans who were hurt most either physically or monetarily.

6. In the search box, type *underground railroad*, and in the *A History of Oberlin* . . . section, read Delazon Smith's opinion of Oberlin College's position on abolition and its participation in the Underground Railroad. What is his attitude toward the college in these two areas?

RELATED INTERNET SITE(S)

Attend a Meeting of the National Afro-American Council
http://memory.loc.gov/ammem/aap/aapexhp.html

This site contains a simulated discussion of the ideas and concerns that were voiced at the National Afro-American Council meeting in 1898. The writings mirror the opinions expressed in the African American Perspectives Pamphlets.

CONFESSIONS OF AN ENGLISH OPIUM EATER (1822)

URL ADDRESS: www.lycaeum.org/~sputnik/Ludlow/?Texts/Opium/index.html

SITE SUMMARY: The search for relief of pain has led to the use and, unfortunately, the abuse of many types of drugs. Opium was widely prescribed for various ailments in the 1800s until its addictive qualities became known. Thomas De Quincey (1785–1859) was a famous essayist and reporter. He became addicted when he experimented with the drug to relieve a stomach ailment. By 1813 his daily allowance had reached a total of 8,000 drops. His book on the pleasures and miserable pains of opium is enlightening reading to say the least. It is also a first-person account by a British freelance writer in an age when imaginative prose was the order of the day.

DISCUSSION QUESTIONS AND ACTIVITIES

1. De Quincey traces his use of opium to a stomach ailment that began during childhood. You are a psychoanalyst and you are in great disagreement with De Quincey. Provide an expert opinion that it was the nature of his childhood rather than a stomach ailment that may have made him prone to taking opium.

2. Where might De Quincey have purchased his tincture of opium or laudanum? Was it legal at that time? What trade was it a part of?

3. It is 1822 and you are a member of a book club that is discussing De Quincey's book. As a book club member, what do you think of his book? Would you censor it so that children would not be allowed to read it? Write a book review that expresses your opinion.

4. You are a local magistrate who has just finished reading the part of the book concerning "the pains of opium." You are making up your mind whether to propose a bill banning sale of the drug and making it a criminal offense to dispense it without a doctor's prescription. What aspects of using opium trouble you most?

5. It is 1822 and you are De Quincey's closest friend. He confides in you that he is an opium addict and that he wishes your help in quitting this horrible habit. How would you go about helping him?

6. You are a nineteenth century bookseller who has just received De Quincey's manuscript. Write an essay about the pros and cons of publishing it.

RELATED INTERNET SITE(S)

Opium Wars
http://www.wsu.edu:8000/~dee/CHING/OPIUM.HTM
    Gives an overview of the Opium Wars between Great Britain and China. It also emphasizes the despicable role that England played as a major drug trafficker in the 1830s.

THE CONFESSIONS OF NAT TURNER (1831)

URL ADDRESS: http://odur.let.rug.nl/~usa/D/1826-1850/slavery/ confes02.htm

SITE SUMMARY: As the abolitionist movement grew, William Lloyd Garrison, one of the most strident of orators, called for the immediate freedom of all slaves. Rumors flew that others would incite slaves to murder their masters. In 1831 Nat Turner, a literate slave from Southampton, Virginia, led such a revolt with six confederates. Turner's group killed his owner and the rest of the family and then went on to murder other whites on neighboring farms. This site contains his story as told by Thomas Gray, an attorney seeking to discover the reasons for the insurrection.

DISCUSSION QUESTIONS AND ACTIVITIES

1. Nat Turner was referred to in the newspapers of 1831 as "General Nat." In his confessions, what qualities and characteristics does he display that make this an apt title?

2. Write an editorial expressing the view that Nat Turner's rebellion was a moral success and that he should be considered one of the greatest social reformers of the day.

3. Compare and contrast the rebellions of Nat Turner and the Roman slave Spartacus. Were both men justified in their actions?

4. Why does Nat Turner express no remorse for the murders he committed?

5. Describe what might have happened in 1831 in Virginia if Nat Turner's revolt had never taken place. Was there a movement in Virginia for gradual emancipation? Were Virginians expressing abolitionist sentiments in the local newspapers or other public means of communication?

6. Imagine that you are Nat Turner. Why have you decided to give an interview to Thomas Gray, an attorney who is not even representing you?

RELATED INTERNET SITE(S)

Slave Narratives
http://vi.uh.edu/pages/mintz/primary.htm

Provides life narratives of former slaves that relate to their living and working conditions.

THE VICTORIAN WEB (1837–1901)

URL ADDRESS: http://www.stg.brown.edu/projects/hypertext/landow/victorian/victov.html

SITE SUMMARY: Victorianism encompassed a period of sixty-three years when Queen Victoria of England reigned and Britain reached the height of its power, becoming a great colonial power and enjoying a tremendous industrial expansion at home. Brown University has a comprehensive site filled with primary and secondary sources concerning architecture, design, the idea of race in thought and science, information about social classes, religion, literature, and the Queen herself. Users can select from broad subject categories such as economics, philosophy, politics, or gender matters to help narrow their searches.

DISCUSSION QUESTIONS AND ACTIVITIES

1. Select *Social Context* and click on *A Timeline of British History*. Scroll down to 1837, the year Queen Victoria assumed the throne. Design an annotated timeline of the important events, people, legislative acts, inventions, wars, revolutions, mutinies, and triumphs up until 1901, the end of the Victorian Age.

2. Select *Social Context* and click on *Corn Laws*. You are an economist who has been asked to testify before Parliament about the negative aspects of the Corn Laws. You must present your information by using graphs and charts since the members are not well versed in economic theory. Be sure to include information about the effects of the Corn Laws on employment, wages, the price of food, and the economic burden on the lower classes and the poor.

3. The Victorian Age saw a great economic disparity between classes of people. Many were very rich, and many more were very poor. Why did England not experience a revolution similar to the French Revolution?

4. Select *Philosophy*. You are an editor of a new encyclopedia and have been asked to choose four people whom you believe most influenced the Victorian Age for the good. Write a biographical sketch of each that will be included in the encyclopedia.

5. Select *Literature*. Conduct interviews with three fiction authors who,

in your opinion, wrote about the problems, events, and people of their age. What do you believe was their influence on society? Did any of them help get legislation passed as a result of their fiction books? Select three classmates to act in the persona of these authors.

6. Write a dramatic monologue in the persona of a Victorian gentleman. Describe how you usually spend your day. Give your opinion of other classes of people, and how you conduct your life in general.

RELATED INTERNET SITE(S)

Related Victorian Web Resources
http://www.stg.brown.edu/projects/hypertext/landow/victorian/misc/related.html
   Provides a set of links to information about Victorian literature, arts, and culture.

THE MARX/ENGELS ARCHIVE (1843–1888)

URL ADDRESS: http://csf.colorado.EDU/psn/marx/

SITE SUMMARY: On November 24, 1842, Karl Marx and Friedrich Engels met for the first time. From 1842 until Marx's death in 1883 these German revolutionists and co-founders of scientific socialism collaborated on several works that were to dramatically change governments around the world and influence world history in profound ways. Comprehensive in scope and still under construction, this site provides a chronology of Marx and Engels's working and writing relationship, biographies of both men, and the full text of all important works including correspondence, articles, position papers, and essays. An excellent search engine supports keyword querying of 40,000 pages of their collected works.

DISCUSSION QUESTIONS AND ACTIVITIES

1. Using the Marx/Engels Thumbnail Chronology and onsite interviews, write psychological profiles of Karl Marx and Friedrich Engels. Describe the social and economic conditions that they would have observed growing up that may have influenced them to write *A Manifesto of the Communist Party.*

2. If Karl Marx and Friedrich Engels were alive today, would they be surprised at the collapse of communism in the Soviet Union? Why or why not?

3. Karl Marx spent his life trying to figure out why the French Revolution had failed to bring about social changes. Refer to *A Manifesto of the Communist Party* and describe his plan for political and social success.

4. Select *Library* and click on *Capital, volume 1.* This book was also known as *Das Kapital.* It is considered a book that changed the world because it challenged every type of government to eliminate poverty. Write an editorial for a conservative journal expressing the view that this book was really an idealistic set of ideas that never had any chance of coming to fruition because of the acquisitive nature of the human race.

5. Select *Library* and click on *1871 Interview with Marx* and *1879 Interview with Marx,* respectively. Why do the reporters go to great lengths to describe Marx's appearance and the comforts of his home? What other questions do they ask that might lead you to believe that they may be trying to point out the hypocritical nature of his writings in light of his way of life?

6. Select *Library* and click on the *1892 and 1893 interviews with Friedrich Engels.* He seems sure of himself and has ready explanations for riots in Paris, famine in Russia, and many other disturbing events. Imagine that he has come back to life and has agreed to an interview with you. What questions would you like to ask him about twentieth century history? What replies would you predict you would receive based on his writings?

RELATED INTERNET SITE(S)

The Marx-Engels Correspondence
http://www.marxists.org/Lenin/Archive/1913-mec.htm
   Contains the correspondence of Marx and Engels together with helpful commentary. This is the highlighted version of the Marx/Engels Archive.

Marx/Engels Photo Gallery
http://marx.org/Bio/Photo/36km1.htm
   Features photographs of Marx and Engels and the houses where they were born, worked, or lived.

VIEWS OF THE FAMINE (1845–1851)

URL ADDRESS: http://vassun.vassar.edu/~sttaylor/FAMINE/

SITE SUMMARY: Views of the Famine lends itself nicely to classroom and group activities because of the sheer number of primary sources.

The site contains seventeen selected articles from *The Illustrated London News* related to the Irish potato famine from 1845 to 1851. The articles also include links to seventy-two corresponding engravings, which are indexed in the site. A second selection features all the articles from the *Cork Examiner* from January 1847 to December 1947. Section 3 contains links to engravings about the famine in the *Pictorial Times* from January 24, 1846, to October 30, 1847. Section 4 furnishes full-page cartoons with some selected articles from the magazine *Punch* related to the famine. A master picture list and a list of related Internet sites conclude this large database of primary sources.

DISCUSSION QUESTIONS AND ACTIVITIES

1. Select *The Illustrated London News* and click on *Index to Illustrations.* Scroll down to *Famine Period* and choose several engravings that show the Irish famine victims starving, begging, attending funerals, or receiving charity. Using the criteria of medium, composition, color, light and shadow, and style, respond to the following questions: What emotions do these engravings evoke? Are there scenes that appear almost biblical in context? If so, why? What response might the artists be hoping to elicit from those who look at the pictures? What medium would you use to depict such a disaster? Why?

2. What was the potato disease? Why was it so disastrous to Ireland? Can you think of any other countries where a disease affecting one staple crop could bring about a deadly famine? As a United Nations committee chairperson, what advice would you give to these present-day countries?

3. Select *The Cork Examiner* and read through the articles relating to the conditions of the famine. Write a press report for the *New York Times* that describes everything you witnessed.

4. You are a poor Irish farmer who has a brother living in New York City. He has asked you to emigrate. Why have you decided to leave Ireland?

5. Select *Punch*, the satirical British periodical. Why did it choose to depict the Irish in an unsympathetic light? Use examples to support your answer.

6. What do you think are the legacies from the Irish famine? Discuss the great emigration to the United States, Canada, and Australia; enmity toward the British for not providing sufficient aid, and the everlasting potential for secession by Northern Ireland from the United Kingdom.

RELATED INTERNET SITE(S)

Histories of the Famine
http://www.toad.net/~sticker/nosurrender/History.html

Gives an overview of the Great Famine and a list of hyperlinks to primary accounts.

The National Archives of Ireland, the Great Famine 1845–1850
http://www.kst.dit.ie/nat-arch/famine.html

Primary sources also abound at this site. Most of them concern government papers and records dealing with emigration, the transportation of Irish convicts to Australia, and the Relief Commission.

Related Materials
http://vassun.vassar.edu/~sttaylor/FAMINE/Related.html

This excellent compilation of related Irish famine links is broken down by categories ranging from extensive articles to nonprint media productions, poetry, memorials, and bibliographies about the famine.

SCIENTIFIC AMERICAN OF THE 19TH CENTURY
(1845–1859)

URL ADDRESS: http://www.history.rochester.edu/
Scientific_American/

SITE SUMMARY: The periodical *Scientific American* of the nineteenth century bears little resemblance to the technical and scholarly publication of the current century. Instead, users will find poetry, religious news, miscellanea from around the country, and technical news and instruction. This site contains fourteen volumes from August 1845 through December 1859. A keyword-type search engine supports querying of Volumes 3 through 14. A cursory search of several volumes yielded articles on the Mexican War, the magnetic telegraph, the price of flour, and gold being exported from Russia to London at the rate of $500,000 per month.

DISCUSSION QUESTIONS AND ACTIVITIES

1. Select *Volume 1* and click on *No. 1 August 28, 1845*. Read some of the articles on this page. You are a marketing executive who has been asked to define the type of readership that *Scientific American* would appeal to based on the articles it publishes. Who might be its main

readers? Where might they live in 1845? What types of things might interest them?

2. Select several articles from Volume 1. If you had been alive in 1845, would you have believed everything you read in *Scientific American*? What articles would you have been skeptical about, and why?

3. What articles in this magazine make its title, *Scientific American*, a misnomer?

4. There are a great many inventions described in various articles as well as a listing of patents awarded for the year 1844. What types of things are being invented? How are most of them driven?

5. Based on the invention-related articles, how would you characterize the age people are living in? Are they in a totally agrarian period or an industrial one? Does it seem to be a transitory period between the two? Support your thesis with articles cited from the periodical.

6. As the owner of a large conglomerate of periodicals and newspapers, explain why the nineteenth century version of *Scientific American* in its present form must change in order to be profitable. You may base your arguments on the look, content, and audience of present-day magazines.

RELATED INTERNET SITE(S)

The Penny Magazine
http://www-engl.cla.umn.edu/LKD/pm/PMI.1.btml
Contains selected 1832 articles from the *Penny Magazine*, a British publication. The breadth of subject matter and treatment of issues are similar to the nineteenth century *Scientific American*.

United States Gazettes, Newspapers (1600–1900)
http://www.msstate.edu/Archives/history/USA/gazette.html
Includes articles from a host of nineteenth century gazettes and newspapers, many of which can be used for comparison questions.

VOTES FOR WOMEN: SELECTIONS FROM THE NATIONAL AMERICAN WOMAN SUFFRAGE ASSOCIATION COLLECTION (1848–1921)

URL ADDRESS: http://rs6.loc.gov/amhome.html

SITE SUMMARY: The women's movement has been characterized by periods of great national programs that achieved such things as the right to vote and by periods of almost complete dormancy, as during the

1950s. This collection contains 167 books, pamphlets, and other ephemera that document the National American Woman Suffrage Association's campaign to obtain the right to vote for women. The writings of famous suffragists such as Elizabeth Cady Stanton and Susan B. Anthony are included. A timeline of one hundred wars toward suffrage helps place the movement in perspective. A subject and author index and search engine are also included. This site can easily be used in conjunction with another Library of Congress site, Votes for Women Suffrage Pictures, 1850–1920.

DISCUSSION QUESTIONS AND ACTIVITIES

1. Select *Time Line: One Hundred Years Towards Suffrage*. The timeline ends at this site in 1923 with a proposal for an Equal Rights Amendment (ERA). Why was the ERA never ratified in 1923, and why was it not ratified again in 1970?

2. Using the *Time Line*, construct one with similar annotations for the years 1924–1998 that reflects the events, people, lawsuits, legislation, and other important matters related to the women's movement.

3. Select *Subjects* and click on *Education of Women*. This lengthy series of essays is entitled *Women and the Alphabet*. It was written by a man in 1859. What is his attitude toward educating women? In the nineteenth century he would have been considered enlightened. Why? What parts of his essay do you find sexist in light of the time you are living in?

4. Select *Subjects* and click on *Free Love*. This speech, entitled "And the Truth Shall Make You Free," was delivered to a packed house in Steinway Hall, New York City, in 1871 by Victoria Woodhull. It was considered so shocking that it contributed to her eventual ostracism by several women's rights associations. What principles of social freedom did Woodhull recommend that people adopt that were so avant-garde? Why were her sentiments so disturbing to women? How would Woodhull's speech be viewed in the 1990s?

5. Select *Search the collection* and type in *blue book*. This document is a history of women's suffrage by Frances Maule. Scroll to page 17 of the document. Maule titles this passage "Preference for the Negro." In it she states that women were unwilling to work for the suffrage movement if it would "embarrass them in regard to their work for Negroes." Why do you think women passed up the opportunity to have their suffrage rights included in the Fourteenth and Fifteenth Amendments? What were the dynamics of the movement that hindered this achievement?

6. Select *Subjects* and click on *Feminism—United States*. The article "Enfranchisement of Women . . ." contains a list of women's rights. How many of these rights do you think have been achieved? Which ones have been only partially achieved? What rights would you add to this document?

RELATED INTERNET SITE(S)

History of Women's Suffrage
http://www.rochester.edu/SBA/historysba.htm
Provides a list of historic women's suffrage sites, a history of the women's suffrage movement with specific links to the Seneca Falls Convention, a history of women's emancipation in Great Britain, and the text of the 1992 New York State of Appeals case involving the "Topfree Seven."

Votes for Women Suffrage Pictures, 1850–1920
ammem/vfwhtml/vfwhome.html
Presents thirty-eight pictorial portraits of women suffragists and scenes relating to this powerful movement to obtain for women the right to vote.

CALIFORNIA AS I SAW IT: FIRST-PERSON NARRATIVES OF CALIFORNIA'S EARLY YEARS (1849–1900)

URL ADDRESS: http://rs6.loc.gov/amhome.html

SITE SUMMARY: Rich in textual materials and illustrations, this site contains 190 eyewitness accounts and works that document California's history through the exciting Gold Rush period to its emergence as a state and the epitome of the American Dream. For those students who may be unfamiliar with California's history, the site contains a section overview that places the first-person narratives in historical perspective. Overview sections also include Spanish California, the Forty Niners, the Miners, California government and law, and summaries about the development of towns and cities. The search engine supports keyword, author, subject, and title queries.

DISCUSSION QUESTIONS AND ACTIVITIES

1. Select *Subject* and click on *California—Gold discoveries*. Read the introduction and the letter from the Placerville gold miner. What do you

think Mr. Shufelt misses most, and why? Does Shufelt still think that it was worth leaving everything he had behind to seek his fortune in the gold mines? Read through some of the other descriptions of gold mining. Write a letter to someone you love describing your experiences as a gold miner in a typical California gold mine.

2. Select *Subject* and click on *Donner Party*. Why did Eliza P. Donner Houghton write this book? What was the controversy surrounding the tragic story of the Donner party? Why were the soccer players who survived the October 13, 1972 Andes plane crash treated more humanely for their survival skills than members of the Donner party?

3. Select *Subject* and click on *Yosemite Valley*. This book by Lafayette Houghton Bunnell, a member of the Mariposa Battalion sent to hunt Native Americans involved in recent raids was published in 1892. It contains parts concerning the discovery of Yosemite. Select *Chapter V* and scroll down to page 54. Imagine you are Captain Bunnell. Based on what you have seen in this beautiful valley, how would you go about obtaining the support of government officials, the current president, and others to purchase Yosemite as a national park?

4. Select *Subject* and click on *San Gabriel Mission*. Read parts 3–5 of Hugo Reid's letter about the Indians of Los Angeles County that contain sections relating to the Native Americans' way of life. Why do you think the Native Americans' way of life was bound to clash with that of Spanish, Mexican, and American settlers? Is this always an inevitable outcome when cultures are at different stages of development?

5. Select *Subject* and click on *San Francisco—Crime and Criminals*. Choose *Chapter 5, The Reminiscences of Henry Hiram Ellis*. What were the types of crimes that Ellis, as a policeman, was dealing with? Does San Francisco strike you as being particularly lawless during this period? Why do you think it was?

6. Select *Subject*, click on *Agriculture*, and choose *Life Sketches of a Jayhawker of '49 by L. Dow Stephens*. What is a jayhawker? Would you have liked to lead the life that L. Dow Stephens led? Why or why not?

RELATED INTERNET SITE(S)

Diary from the Gold Rush

http://uts.cc.utexas.edu/~scring/index.html

Contains the memoirs of a California gold miner and his experiences in Panama and Mexico.

VALLEY OF THE SHADOW (1850–1865)

URL ADDRESS: http://jefferson.village.virginia.edu/vshadow2/

SITE SUMMARY: The heart-rending story of the American Civil War is seen through the public sources left by people who lived in either Franklin County, Pennsylvania, or Augusta County, Virginia, from 1850 to 1865. The counties were separated by only a few hundred miles, but they lay on either side of the Mason-Dixon Line. Of all the excellent Internet sites about the Civil War, this is the most outstanding. It's a virtual cornucopia of primary sources such as public records, letters and diaries, newspapers, church records, maps, and images. The site also contains an "Interpretations" section that features Civil War histories, essays, and papers by college and high school students.

DISCUSSION QUESTIONS AND ACTIVITIES

1. Enter the *Valley of the Shadow Archive* and select *The Eve of War*. Click on *Newspapers* and select *Newspaper Transcriptions for Augusta and Franklin Counties*. Click on *Newspaper Transcriptions Index by TOPIC* and click on *African-Americans/Race Relations (Augusta or Franklin counties)*. Choose several articles about the same African American–related subject from both counties. Compare the vocabulary, description of the story, and the writer's opinions of these stories. Are there any differences between how African Americans are depicted in these two counties?

2. Remain in the *Newspapers* section of this database and click on *Augusta*. Click on *The Spectator, August 2, 1859*. Read the article that describes the lynching of a black man. Describe the attitude of the reporter to this horrible event.

3. Remain in the *Newspapers* section of the database and click on *Franklin*. Click on *Valley Spirit, April 20, 1859*. Why does the reporter seem so gleeful in showing that this escaped "hero" slave has "feet of clay"?

4. Enter the *Valley of the Shadow Archive* and select *Letters & Diaries*. Select *Franklin County* and click on *Letters Written to Henry Bitner, 1861–1863*. The first six letters are from Alex Cressler. What are his opinions of the Civil War?

5. Remain in the *Letters & Diaries* section and select *Augusta County*. Click on *Michael Reid Hanger, 1861*. What are his opinions of the war? How does he seem to feel at the beginning of his enlistment? Compare his description in the beginning to the ones after he has participated in

more battles. What do you think would be Michael Reid Hanger's advice to his son if he had to go to war?

6. Enter the *Valley of the Shadow Archive* and select *Maps & Images*. Using the maps at this site, produce a chronological history of the damage done to both counties by the Civil War. Damage may include the burning of farms and the destruction of crops as well as damage caused by battles.

RELATED INTERNET SITE(S)

Civil War Photographs at the Library of Congress
http://rs6.loc.gov/cwphome.html

Features a searchable keyword index of Mathew Brady's collection of Civil War photographs.

Civil War (including battlefields) Sites in the Shenandoah Valley
http://www.cr.nps.gov/catsig.htm#civilwar

Sponsored by the U.S. National Parks service, this site contains accurate maps and descriptions of numerous Civil War battle sites in Maryland, Pennsylvania, and Virginia.

United States Civil War Center
http://www.cwc.lsu.edu/

This is an excellent gateway site about all aspects of the Civil War.

SECTIONAL CONFLICT (1850–1877)

URL ADDRESS: http://scriptorium.lib.duke.edu/collections/civil-war-women.html

SITE SUMMARY: This Civil War archive collection features scanned pages and excerpted texts of the writings of several women during the American Civil War. The current contents include the papers of "Wild Rosie" O'Neal Greenhow, a well-known Confederate spy; Sarah E. Thompson, a Union spy and organizer of Union sympathizers in a rebel area around Greenville, Tennessee; and the diary of sixteen-year-old Alice Williamson, a witness to the occupation of Gallatin, Tennessee, by Union forces. The site also provides many additional links to other Civil War sites of educational and historical value.

DISCUSSION QUESTIONS AND ACTIVITIES

1. Select *Rose O'Neal Greenhow Papers*. Why do you think Wild Rosie was a Confederate sympathizer? Look at the United States Historical Cen-

sus Data Browser site (http://icg.fas.harvard.edu/~census//) and determine the slave population in Maryland, where she was born.

2. Why do you think Wild Rosie was exiled to the Confederacy after serving a second term in prison? Why wasn't she executed for treason? Compare her treatment to that of Ethel Rosenberg, who was executed for treason in 1953 for passing secrets about the atomic bomb to the Soviet Union.

3. Read the letters concerning Wild Rosie's spy activities. You are a Union judge who has been asked to conduct a hearing on whether there is sufficient evidence to convict Wild Rosie O'Neal Greenhow for spying. Write a brief outlining the charges based on your reading of the evidence.

4. Select *Sarah E. Thompson Papers*. What motivated Sarah Thompson to become a spy? How do you compare her motive to Wild Rosie's motive?

5. You are a Confederate soldier who has just arrested Sarah E. Thompson for spying. What evidence do you think is the most incriminating?

6. Select *Alice Williamson Diary*. Using quotations and other anecdotes from the diary as evidence, how does Alice Williamson feel about the occupation of her hometown? What things seem to bother her the most, and why?

RELATED INTERNET SITE(S)

Women and the Civil War
http://scriptorium.lib.duke.edu/women/civilwar.html
This site contains a helpful annotated bibliography of books about women and their involvement in the Civil War. It also contains links to Duke University's manuscript collections on the same topic.

SECTIONAL CONFLICT, AFRICAN-AMERICAN WOMEN (1850–1877)

URL ADDRESS: http://scriptorium.lib.duke.edu/collections/african-american-women.html

SITE SUMMARY: This easy-to-use site includes the eighty-five-page, handwritten memoirs of Elizabeth Johnson Harris. She started writing them at the age of fifty-five in 1923. It describes her early childhood, her view of race relations, and her feelings about her place as an African American in a racist society. It also furnishes several of her published poems and anecdotes. A second link presents a letter written in 1857 by Vilet Lester, a slave owned by a family in Randolph County, North Carolina. It offers a unique opportunity to visualize slave life through her eyes. The third link contains the letters of Hannah Valentine and Lethe Jackson, house slaves at a home in Abingdon, Virginia. Both were left behind to take care of the home when their owners moved to the Governor's Mansion in Richmond, Virginia. Their letters, written between 1847 and 1850, convey valuable information about the relationships between slaves and owners.

DISCUSSION QUESTIONS AND ACTIVITIES

1. Select *Elizabeth Johnson Harris: Life Story*. How would you describe Elizabeth Johnson Harris to a friend? Is she ambitious for herself or just for her children? What do you think are her aspirations? If she had lived in a time of less discrimination, what do you think she would have become based on the qualities and characteristics she possesses?

2. What role does the church play in the life of Elizabeth Johnson Harris besides a religious one?

3. What do you think is the status of race relations in this area based on her memoir?

4. Select the *Vilet Lester Letter*. Why are slave letters considered rare documents? What have we, as a country, lost because we have so few records of these people?

5. In this letter, Vilet writes of being sold a number of times. What effect do you think these moves and the separation from loved ones, including a daughter, had on her life? Imagine that she was your friend. Do you think that she would be trustful? How do you think she would tend to behave in new situations and with people whom she has just met?

6. Click on *Hannah Valentine and Lethe Jackson: Slave Letters*. Hannah Valentine is a slave in the Campbell home. She is in charge of the other slaves and of maintaining the home while her owners are in the Governor's Mansion in Richmond, Virginia. From her letters written to the Campbells, how would you describe their relationship?

RELATED INTERNET SITE(S)

African American Women's History
http://ublib.buffalo.edu/libraries/units/ugl/center/blkwomen.html

Includes an extensive series of annotated links to other Internet sites that contain information about African American women from different periods in history.

EVOLUTION OF THE CONSERVATION MOVEMENT
(1850–1920)

URL ADDRESS: http://rs6.loc.gov/amhome.html

SITE SUMMARY: As the status of our environment becomes front-page news on a daily basis, students are becoming more interested in the history of the powerful conservation and environmental movement, especially in the United States. This site, sponsored by the Library of Congress, features photographs, full-text government documents, and manuscripts that discuss the conservation movement in the United States. It also contains a special album of images and scientific reports from the 1899 Harriman expedition to Alaska. A convenient hyperlinked chronology helps students to narrow their topics, and an extensive annotated bibliography provides additional primary and secondary sources by such authors as John Burroughs, George Perkins Marsh, John Muir, and Henry David Thoreau.

DISCUSSION QUESTIONS AND ACTIVITIES

1. Select *Chronology of Selected Events in the Development of the American Conservation Movement, c. 1850–1920*. Complete a similar timeline for the years 1921–1999.

2. Select *Subject* and click on *Big Game Hunting*. This document discusses the role President Theodore Roosevelt played in preserving natural resources for big game as well as his affinity for hunting. Why would today's conservationists look askance at the hunting and collecting practices of President Roosevelt?

3. Select *Subject* and click on *Game-laws—United States. American Big Game in its Haunts* was written in 1904 by George Bird Grinnell. It was an "alarm call" to warn Americans about the pollution of their natural resources and the eradication of species. How does it compare to Rachel Carson's *Silent Spring*?

4. Select *Subject* and click on *Hetch Hetchy Valley, Cal.* These documents, published in the early 1900s, are about a decision to build a dam and reservoir in Hetch-Hetchy Valley in Yosemite National Park to provide water for San Francisco. What is the current situation with regard

to Hetch-Hetchy? What do you think of the decision to build the dam in light of the current problems?

5. Select *Subject* and click on *Indians of North America—Land Tenure*. Native Americans have been the true stewards of the land in America. This section contains a series of statutes that changed the boundaries of various Indian reservations or national forests for governmental purposes. Discuss the positive and negative aspects of selected statutes. Did Native Americans gain or lose by most of them?

6. Select *Authors* and click on *Muir, John 1838–1914*. You are a leading Brazilian conservationist. How can you use John Muir's "Our National Parks" to instill in people the desire to establish similar parks in Brazil? What parts of the sketches may appeal to them?

RELATED INTERNET SITE(S)

Learning Page of the Library of Congress
http://memory.loc.gov/ammem/ndlpedu/index.html
This site is an outstanding one for additional lesson plans and questions about the evolution of the conservation movement.

ORIGIN OF SPECIES BY CHARLES DARWIN (1859)

URL ADDRESS: http://www.mpiz-koeln.mpg.de/books/books.html

SITE SUMMARY: The creation of the human race as described in the Bible was accepted by Christians as literal truth until Charles Darwin published his seminal work about evolutionary biology. Although preceded by works by several other naturalists who had observed similar patterns in evolving species, Darwin's book also set forth the idea that apes and humans were descended from a common ancestor. The firestorm of controversy that followed this assertion continues to this day. At this site, students can read the full text of Darwin's work. They will need to use the additional related Internet sites for background, biographical, and pro and con information.

DISCUSSION QUESTIONS AND ACTIVITIES

1. What is meant by the term Social Darwinism? How does Chapter 5 of Darwin's book, "Natural Selection," apply to it?

2. After his trip to the Galapagos archipelago, Darwin never accepted the teaching of Genesis that every species had been created whole and

had come down through the centuries unchanged. If he had appeared as a witness in the Scopes "Monkey Trial," what would he have said in favor of Scopes's teaching?

3. Why do you think *Origin of Species* generates so much controversy even today?

4. Based on the principles Darwin sets forth in *Origin of Species*, would he be in favor of cloning human beings? Why or why not?

5. You are a school board member in a "Bible Belt" area of the United States. A parent has asked you to officially ban *Origin of Species* from all school library media centers. What will be your decision based on the laws in the United States, the local community's feelings, and your personal opinions on censorship?

6. Establish a forum to discuss the misuses of Darwin's book to justify oppression as nature's way. Provide examples of how it has been used to justify genocide, fascism, and ruthless business practices involving monopolies.

RELATED INTERNET SITE(S)

Human Prehistory: An Exhibition
http://users.hol.gr/~dilos/prehis.htm
   Provides excellent images showing the stages of the evolution of the human species.

Popular Phenomenon of Charles Darwin
http://www.csuchico.edu/anth/CASP/Pearce_A.html
   Presents a lengthy paper relating to the continued interest in Charles Darwin's seminal work.

Quotes on Creation & Evolution
http://net1.netcentral.co.uk/steveb/create/quotes.htm
   Includes quotes by famous paleontologists, naturalists, and evolutionists that explain terminology concerning natural selection, survival of the fittest, and much more.

LONDON LOW-LIFE: BEGGARS AND CHEATS (1860)

URL ADDRESS: http://library.byu.edu/~rdh/eurodocs/uk/lowlife.html

SITE SUMMARY: The Industrial Revolution that started around 1748 emphasized the use of scientific method. Henry Mayhew, a journalist, applied scientific method to defining and characterizing various classes of society. Mayhew's in-depth interviews focused on the lower classes. His four-volume account, *The London Labour and the London Poor*, is a priceless picture of daily life for the lower classes in Victorian times. The site contains a lengthy excerpt from Volume 4, *Those that Will Not Work*. It also includes interviews with beggars of all types and with cheats such as the broken-down tradesman.

DISCUSSION QUESTIONS AND ACTIVITIES

1. Based on Mayhew's sketch of the "Decayed Gentleman," write a skit that involves him crashing a country weekend party at the home of an English lord.
2. Choose a partner and write a scam that the "Broken-Down Tradesman" could use to his advantage. What types of people might be easy victims for this type of criminal?
3. Of all the types of beggars described in the passages under *London's Underworld*, which type do you think might earn the most money, and why?
4. What do Mayhew's descriptions tell you about the Victorians' attitude toward poverty, petty crime, or those who might genuinely be down on their luck?
5. Do Americans distinguish between the deserving and undeserving poor? How have our social programs changed in this regard?
6. Mayhew goes to great lengths to describe the criminal class's clothing, state of health, personal habits, and even mannerisms. We would accuse him of negatively stereotyping people. What are the dangers in that practice?

RELATED INTERNET SITE(S)

The Victorian Web
http://www.stg.brown.edu/projects/hypertext/landow/victorian/victov.html
  This is a comprehensive site about the literary, social, cultural, political, and economic aspects of the Victorian Age.

LETTERS FROM AN IOWA SOLDIER IN THE CIVIL WAR (1862–1865)

URL ADDRESS: http://bob.ucsc.edu/civil-war-letters/home.html

SITE SUMMARY: The series of letters that Newton Robert Scott, a private in the 36th Infantry Iowa Volunteers, wrote to Hannah Cone, a neighborhood friend, are rich in detail and bring the years 1862–1865 to life again. From his obvious homesickness to his sarcasm when his sweetheart jilts him to marry another, the universal sufferings of war are movingly depicted. Scott's letters also provide evidence of the contagious diseases in Federal camps in Mississippi, Missouri, Iowa, and Arkansas that may have taken more lives than the fighting itself. Easily accessible, this site features a hyperlinked table of contents plus Scott's service record, and obituaries of himself and his friend.

DISCUSSION QUESTIONS AND ACTIVITIES

1. In his first two letters, Scott mentions the death of soldiers from disease. What types of diseases were killing them?

2. Scott's letter written from Helena, Arkansas, tells of the burning of rebel property and the eating of "good chicken." What was the Union's policy on damaging enemy property? Did it change officially or unofficially as the war dragged on?

3. On February 14, 1864, Scott mentions that approximately 100 Confederate men who were classified as deserters joined the Union Army. Why are these men deserting, and why are they signing up to fight against the South?

4. On November 3, 1864, Scott writes of his hopes that the reelection of President Abraham Lincoln would shorten the war. What was the military situation at that time between the Union and the Confederacy? Were his hopes unrealistic at that time?

5. Scott's letters are redolent with memories of home and all of the daily aspects of home life that he misses. Why do you think so many men enlist in wars rather than waiting to be drafted? What might draw them to fight in a war before they absolutely have to?

6. Imagine that you are Hannah Cone. Write a letter to Newton Robert Scott telling him about your life and describing what it is like now that so many men are away at war.

RELATED INTERNET SITE(S)

American Civil War Homepage
http://sunsite.utk.edu/civil-war/warweb.html
Provides a host of primary sources in the form of diaries, letters, eyewitness accounts, and regimental histories.

Civil War USENET
USENET Alt.war.civil.usa

Contains an FAQ archive about the Civil War, a search engine for keywords, and a reading list.

NATIVE AMERICAN DOCUMENTS PROJECT (1870s)

URL ADDRESS: http://www.csusm.edu/projects/nadp/nadp.htm

SITE SUMMARY: This Internet project continues to expand as it makes available more documents about the history of federal policy on indigenous peoples. The site contains three sets of data. Indexed are published reports of the Commission of Indian Affairs and the Board reports of various Indian Commissioners for 1871. The reports treat most aspects of Indian policy at that time. The second set of data comprises ten quantitative tables, with explanations, termed allotment data. Allotment is the name of the process that allowed most of the land left to Native Americans in the latter part of the nineteenth century to pass into other hands. The third set of data includes indexed documents pertaining to the Rogue River War and Seletz Reservation collection. All documents contain explanatory materials and relevant maps. The site also features topical and tribal indexes.

DISCUSSION QUESTIONS AND ACTIVITIES

1. Click on *Report of the Commissioner of Indian Affairs*. In it the commissioner names the Apaches in the territories of Arizona and New Mexico as being one of the more difficult tribes to manage. Your name is Cochise. You are shocked at how you have been described in this report and demand to attach a letter that presents your views of the situation. Your written response should include as many facts as you can find concerning the United States government's negative policies, as well as treaties and laws relating to the Apaches.

2. On page three of the report, the acting commissioner, R. Clum, states that the Kiowa and Comanche tribes have also proved most troublesome. He recommends that the criminal laws of the United States be enforced for all Indians caught committing crimes. You are a Kiowan who has been asked to talk to the commissioner to tell him why your tribe will not obey any American laws. State your reasons in a short written brief.

3. Refer to page five of the report. You are the secretary of the interior and have just finished reading this section of the report. Give your opinion of the situation involving the Sioux. Do you anticipate any future troubles based on your analysis of this report?

4. In 1887 Congress passed the Dawes Act. It dramatically altered the relationship between the U.S. government and Native Americans. It also changed the relationship between individual Native Americans and their respective tribes. Analyze the impact that this act had in these two areas.

5. Within the same section, click on *Comparing Allotment and Homesteading, 1900–1915*. Use the data from these tables to make a graph that shows how Native Americans were at a distinct disadvantage to their homesteading counterparts.

6. Select *A Brief Interpretative History of the Rogue War and Siletz Reservation to 1894*. This is an extensive site with many primary sources behind each initial link. You are a historian who has been asked to study the history of attacks on the Rogue River Valley Indian people. Prepare an outline listing all of these attacks and show how they were meant to instigate an Indian war.

RELATED INTERNET SITE(S)

Index of Native American Indian Resources
http://indy4.fdl.cc.mn.us/~isk/mainmenu.html
   Contains more than 300 pages worth of links to information about Native American tribes, arts, literature, education, history, and science.

United States Laws Relating to Indian Nations and Tribes
http://law.house.gov/31.htm
   Provides collections of treaties, laws, resolutions, and papers relating to United States government dealings with various Native American tribes.

TEMPERANCE AND PROHIBITION (1873–1928)

URL ADDRESS: http://www.cohums.ohio-state.edu/history/projects/prohibition/

SITE SUMMARY: Temperance and Prohibition is a multimedia site filled with statistical data about the growth of the brewing industry and saloons. It has information about the people who were either involved with or opposed to the temperance movement and includes photographs of saloons and first-person accounts of family life with loved ones addicted to alcohol. The site also contains excellent background materials on why the United States had a prohibition movement. Within the background materials are hyperlinks to the primary sources that support the rationales and assertions in the text.

DISCUSSION QUESTIONS AND ACTIVITIES

1. Draw a flow chart showing the correlation between technological changes such as the telegraph, railroads, and mechanical refrigeration and the growth and development of the brewing industry.

2. You are about to start an Anti-Temperance Union in your city because of the constant abuse of alcohol by so many people in your community. At your first meeting, attended mainly by women, you are asked to describe what saloons are like because most of the women have never been in one. Paint a picture of how bad they really are.

3. You are a social worker who has been asked to testify before a congressional committee about the impact of alcohol abuse on the family. Use sources at this site to write the testimony you would present orally to the committee.

4. You are a German immigrant who has finally realized his American dream—to open up a saloon in America. The only problem is that you have too much competition. What enticements will you provide to ensure a steady flow of customers?

5. Based solely on statistical evidence that you can display in various charts and graphs, formulate an argument in favor of prohibition and for passage of the Eighteenth Amendment.

6. You are a noted historian who is well aware of the problem of making laws in the "climate of the times" that may be unenforceable. Argue against the passage of the Eighteenth Amendment based on the difficulty of regulating social behavior. What other events or movements do you think are going on that may have undue influence on the passage of this amendment?

RELATED INTERNET SITE(S)

The Ram's Horn
http://www.history.ohio-state.edu/projects/Ram's_Horn/
This social gospel magazine was published in the 1890s. It contains groups of images of various social classes from the period, including "the wealthy," "immigrants," "smokers," and "political bosses." It was considered a very conservative periodical even in its day.

JACK LONDON (1876–1916)

URL ADDRESS: http://sunsite.berkeley.EDU/London/

SITE SUMMARY: Jack London was not just a writer who lived vicariously through the characters he created. Indeed, most of his works are filled with people, events, and places of which he had personal knowledge. London actually traveled to the South Seas and won a prize from a newspaper for his captivating description of a typhoon off the coast of Japan. He also mined for gold during the Klondike gold rush. An extensive collection of letters, telegrams, manuscripts, and papers relating to his life and work are maintained at this comprehensive site. It also provides a biographical sketch, photographs, an audio and video of London's century, and a chronology about his life.

DISCUSSION QUESTIONS AND ACTIVITIES

1. Jack London's life was considered reflective of the Progressive Era. Summarize how some of his writings, both fiction and nonfiction, were characteristic of the general beliefs of this period.

2. Select *Writings* and click on *War of the Classes (1905)*. Select *The Scab*, a speech London gave before the Oakland, California, Socialist Party local in 1903. What is his attitude toward strikebreakers, labor unions, and the big trusts such as the Standard Oil Company?

3. Select *Writings* and click on *War of the Classes (1905)*. Select *The Class Struggle*, a speech that London gave in the Hotel Metropole. What are his beliefs about the class system? What is going on in society with regard to labor unions and the big trusts to cause London to hold these beliefs?

4. Select *Writings* and click on *War of the Classes (1905)*. Select *The Tramp*, a speech that London gave at the Academy of Sciences Hall in San Francisco in 1902. If London were alive today, what would be his position on the homeless? What would he think that the government should do for them?

5. Select *Writings* and click on *War of the Classes (1905)*. Select *How I Became a Socialist*. London describes his background to which he attributes his conversion to socialism. Did he conduct his life the way one would expect of a socialist? Argue the pros and cons that London was either a practicing socialist or "cocktail socialist."

6. Jack London ran unsuccessfully for mayor of Oakland, California. Would you have voted for him or against him? Why?

RELATED INTERNET SITE(S)

Jack London Campfire Chat
http://killdevilhill.com/jacklondonchat/wwwboard.html
   Provides an Internet-based discussion of Jack London and his writings.

Jack London State Historical Park
http://www.parks.sonoma.net/JLPark.html
   Furnishes an extensive description of Beauty Ranch and a fairly lengthy biography of London.

THE NORTHERN GREAT PLAINS (1880–1920)

URL ADDRESS: http://rs6.loc.gov/amhome.html

SITE SUMMARY: Usually students do not think of photographs as potential primary sources. This outstanding collection of 900 photographs, however, depicting rural and village life at the turn of the century on the northern Great Plains, is a valuable resource. It provides students with the opportunity to analyze the effects of geography and climate on early settlements. The site also contains information about Dakota Territory and eventual statehood, ranching, North Dakota politics, and contemporary North Dakota. The exceptionally clear black and white photographs are taken from the Fred Hulstrand History in Pictures and the F. A. Pazandak Photograph Collection. A special presentation section includes a helpful North Dakota history overview and information about Native American Dakota tribes such as the Sioux and the Cree.

DISCUSSION QUESTIONS AND ACTIVITIES

1. Select *Fred Hulstrand History in Pictures Collection* and click on *Browse the Subject Index*. Click on *Agricultural Laborers—North Dakota* from different periods of time. You should also look at the pictures from the F. A. Pazandak Picture Collection. You have been asked to give a visual presentation to the class showing how changes in farming methods were influencing agricultural communities as early as the 1890s. Select images that show how machinery that was horse-driven, for example, is now motor-driven. Be sure to point out that motor-driven machines required fewer laborers.

2. Click on *Architecture, Ukrainian—North Dakota—1960–1969*. From what period does the log and plaster U.S. post office look like it is from? What does the picture tell you about how developed the area is? What

do you think the main occupations of the local residents might be? Look for some census information and find out how populated the area is presently. Was it ever heavily populated?

3. Click on *Baby Carriages—1890–1899*. These are not just pictures of individual baby carriages. Instead, the entire family is shown along with many of their belongings. Why would families have their pictures taken this way? What were they trying to show other people and relatives?

4. Click on *Bison—North Dakota—Casselton—1900–1909*. This picture of the last buffalo killed in North Dakota is symbolic of the idea that man has finally conquered his environment. Why did the settlers feel the need to slay so many of the indigenous creatures? Why could they not live in harmony with them as did Native Americans?

5. Click on *Blizzards—North Dakota—Milton*. What type of weather did these settlers, in their sod houses, have to contend with? What did the government do by way of the Homestead Act to get them to settle such a harsh place?

6. Browse through *Subjects* and note the names of various cities and towns. Look at the conditions during that time and find out the present population. There is a movement to return this sparsely settled land back to prairie grass and bison. Based on the evidence you have amassed, give your opinion.

RELATED INTERNET SITE(S)

North Dakota State History
http://www.lib.ndsu.nodak.edu/ndirs/travel.html

Presents the history of North Dakota, complete with a list of governors, maps of Civil War battles, and evidence of the Lewis and Clark expedition.

Northern Great Plains Public Hearings
http://www.rrtrade.org/ngp/Hearings.htm

Provides the testimony from the Northern Great Plains Initiative for Rural Development Commission by various city and town representatives. It sheds light on the current problems facing rural areas of the northern Great Plains.

JACK THE RIPPER (1888)

URL ADDRESS: http://ripper.wildnet.co.uk/casebook.html

SITE SUMMARY: Students fascinated by criminal history and determined to complete an assignment about this topic may wish to access this comprehensive but rather macabre site. Between August 31 and November 9, 1888, five female prostitutes were brutally stabbed to death in the Whitechapel district of London's East End. The identity of the killer, known as Jack the Ripper, was never established. From a primary source perspective, this site includes letters by Jack the Ripper, the full-text documents of the case, witness descriptions, and a list of suspects. It's a crime solver's dream.

DISCUSSION QUESTIONS AND ACTIVITIES

1. Select *An Introduction to the Case*. What do you think was the role of the press in this case? How did they go about making sure that the murders stayed uppermost in the news? You are the editor of an 1888 London tabloid. How would you tell your reporters to cover the story so that it stayed on the front page?

2. You are in charge of the investigation to capture Jack the Ripper. Remember that fingerprinting and forensic science are not yet in use. How would you go about assembling and deciphering your evidence based on all of the clues? Make diagrams of the crime scene, draw a map showing the areas where the killer has struck, and analyze the letters for similarities in handwriting and content.

3. Based on the letters, evidence left at the murder scene, and victim autopsies, write a psychological profile of Jack the Ripper. What do you think his childhood was like? How was he raised? What type of occupation may he be practicing? What might his views be on prostitutes? What situations might anger him?

4. At one of the murder scenes, graffiti attributed the murder to Jews. Sir Charles Warren made the decision not to leave it up to the police to photograph it for fear of riots against Jewish people living and working in that area of London. Click on *Official Documents of the Case*. Read *Warren's Report to the Home Secretary 11/6/88*. Were his reasons for tampering with the evidence justified or unjustified?

5. Select *Witness Descriptions*. For years, police have known that eyewitness testimony can be quite unreliable. Look at all the witness descriptions. Why do you think that eyewitness descriptions are unreliable? What types of descriptions would you tend to believe? Why?

6. Select *Contemporary Accounts of the Crimes*. Choose newspaper articles from the same day from a variety of newspapers and periodicals that were covering the story. Analyze the coverage in terms of sensationalism, instilling fear, or how they reported the facts of the case.

RELATED INTERNET SITE(S)

Casebook Timeline
http://ripper.wildnet.co.uk/timeline.html
   Although this is available at the home site, it provides an excellent timeline of the events and can help students who need to assemble evidence and put other aspects of the case in perspective.

HOW THE OTHER HALF LIVES (1890)

URL ADDRESS: http://www.cis.yale.edu/amstud/inforev/riis/title.html

SITE SUMMARY: Known as "The Great Emancipator of the Slums," Jacob Riis was a tireless campaigner for freedom from poverty. His main focus was the tenements of New York City, which teemed with disease, filth, and despair. He sought to eradicate them by publishing books and articles as a reporter for the *New York Tribune* and the *Evening Sun* that pulled at one's heartstrings. They depicted the life of the poor, especially their children, in living quarters that not even a family pet would tolerate. This site contains a hypertext version of one of Riis's great books. The links also feature photographs of the slums he wrote about and additional historical information.

DISCUSSION QUESTIONS AND ACTIVITIES

1. Select the Introduction to *How the Other Half Lives*. What are the main issues that Riis seeks to address in his book?

2. Select "Genesis of the Tenements." You are an urban planner who has been asked to analyze rapid changes in demographic patterns that are occurring as the wealthy flee from certain areas of the city, where tenements are then established. Draw or find maps to show the changes and shifts in population. What do you think are the main causes for this shift?

3. New York City has been called a "melting pot." Read several chapters about various ethnic groups living in the city. Would you agree or disagree with this statement? Why?

4. You are a slum landlord and have just finished reading Jacob Riis's book. What is your opinion about the amount of profit you feel entitled to make? What problems do you have when people don't pay the rent? What do you think of his book from an owner's standpoint?

5. This question is for two students. Choose a partner to act as a reporter

for the *New York Tribune*. Use the site's descriptions of immigrants to make your selection. Interview a recent immigrant from an ethnic group of your choosing. Have this person describe the living and working conditions in a tenement in Hell's Kitchen.

6. You have been asked by the mayor of New York City to chair a committee to outline reforms for the city's slums. What things would you do immediately to improve conditions? What things would you try to do within the next five years? Be sure to address issues of landlord profit margins, rent control, eradication of rats and other pests, and so on.

RELATED INTERNET SITE(S)

Muckrakers
http://www.digisys.net/users/benwood/progressivism/webdoc3.htm
Although this is a personal site, it contains many useful Internet-related sites about this period of American history.

POTUS
http://www.ipl.org/ref/POTUS
POTUS is an acronym for Presidents of the United States. When students select *President Theodore Roosevelt*, they can obtain additional information about his role in urban reforms.

THE GEORGETOWN AUDIO-VISUAL ELECTRONIC LIBRARY PROJECT FOR THE STUDY OF EMILE ZOLA AND THE DREYFUS CASE (1894–1899)

URL ADDRESS: http://www.georgetown.edu/guieu/libproj.htm

SITE SUMMARY: In 1894 Captain Alfred Dreyfus, a member of the French General Staff, was accused of writing a letter to the German military attaché in Paris disclosing French military secrets. Dreyfus, who was Jewish, was convicted with totally inadequate evidence and condemned to life imprisonment at the infamous French penal colony of Devil's Island. Upon his conviction, a wave of anti-Jewish demonstrations broke out all over France. This site explores the climate of the times that permitted Dreyfus to be falsely accused. It includes scholarly papers written about various aspects of the affair, Emile Zola's famous essay, *J'Accuse!* (in French), and a statement by President Jacques Chirac admitting the French government's dreadful complicity in the tragedy.

DISCUSSION QUESTIONS AND ACTIVITIES

1. Click on *Basic Chronology*. Prepare a similar one describing the climate of the times in France, touching on their fear of war with Germany, their feelings toward Jewish people, and previous scandals. Be sure to include the Boulanger affair, the Wilson case, and bribery of government officials involved with the building of the Suez Canal. Analyze these factors for possible causative relationships to the Dreyfus affair.

2. Read *J'Accuse!* by Emile Zola. In it, he accuses high government officials, military staffers, and handwriting experts of obfuscating the truth about Captain Dreyfus. Why was he sued for libel? What was the outcome of the case, and what happened to Zola not long afterwards?

3. Select *Learn more about Emile Zola, Capt. Dreyfus and "The Affair" (Links)* and click on *"The Affair" (English)*. Read the article that appeared in *Time* magazine on September 25, 1995. Why do you think that this case attracts attention today? Why do you think President Jacques Chirac felt the need to issue an apology?

4. Dreyfus was a member of an unpopular minority group, as were Sacco and Vanzetti in America. Compare their trial to the Dreyfus court-martial.

5. You are a French historian. Write a short report on the role of the media during the Dreyfus affair. How did they fan the flames of anti-Semitism? Were they neutral regarding Captain Dreyfus until he was proven guilty, or did they help convict him with their articles?

6. Draw a political cartoon for a French newspaper illustrating a particularly perfidious aspect of the trial.

RELATED INTERNET SITE(S)

The Dreyfus Affair: A Chronology
http://www.wls.lib.ny.us/libs/white-plains/gallery/dreyfus_chronology.htm

Supplies a detailed chronology of all the people, issues, and events involving the Dreyfus affair.

French Army Concedes that Alfred Dreyfus Was Innocent
http://wol.pace.edu/csis/dyson/pdbh1.html

This is another site where students will find the *Time* magazine article of September 25, 1995, describing Defense Minister Charles Millon's apology to the French Jewish community concerning the Dreyfus affair.

GOLD IN THE KLONDIKE (1896)

URL ADDRESS: http://www.halcyon.com/rdpayne/kgrnhp.html

SITE SUMMARY: On July 17, 1877 the *Seattle Post-Intelligencer* reported that a steamship bound for Seattle "has passed up Puget Sound with more than a ton of gold on board and 68 passengers." The Klondike gold rush had begun in earnest. A lengthy overview at this site furnishes students with information about the nature of the gold rush and emphasizes the impact it had on Seattle, Washington, the key embarkation city. All articles feature excerpts from local newspapers about outfitting the miners and the economic benefits that the event bestowed on Seattle. A related Web site contains full-text articles from the *Seattle Times* about the size of gold nuggets, sense of adventure, miners' luck and misfortune, and other interesting facts.

DISCUSSION QUESTIONS AND ACTIVITIES

1. Based on the description supplied by Gold in the Klondike, draw a map showing the important areas where the gold lay, the best route to get there, and the best place to stock up on provisions. Refer to http://www.nps.gov/klse/klse_vvc.htm for additional information and maps.

2. At the bottom of this site, click on *Return to Klondike Gold Rush NHP*. Click on *Klondike Gold Rush National Historical Park (Seattle Unit)*. Why did the Canadians require that each miner have sufficient provisions for one year before they could enter the country?

3. At this same site, read the statistics on one's odds of finding gold and actually keeping it. Use other sites to find out what the climate is like in this area of Canada and what the physical hardships were like. Write a letter to your brother describing them and begging him not to go on a gold rush.

4. From the *Klondike Gold Rush NHP* site, click on *Centennial Series* (http://www.seattletimes.com/klondike/). Read the articles from the *Seattle Times*. What do you think was the role of the press in ensuring that there was a gold rush in the Klondike? What type of stories did they publish? Do you think that this was responsible journalism?

5. Using the site above, read the account of James S. Cooper and others who journeyed to the Klondike. Despite your advice to the contrary, your best friend has decided to make the trip. What provisions, med-

ical supplies, weapons, and so on, would you tell your friend to take with him? Be sure to include everything he will need to survive.

6. Seattle was recovering economically from the Panic of 1893. What did it stand to gain from the Klondike gold rush? Did it have an undue interest in making sure that it continued as long as possible?

RELATED INTERNET SITE(S)

Centennial Series (*The Seattle Times*)
http://www.seattletimes.com/klondike/
Provides excellent newspaper articles about various miners' adventures and misadventures in the Canadian gold fields.

Klondike Gold Rush National Park (Seattle Unit)
http://www.nps.gov/klse/klse_vvc.htm
Presents pictures and text about early Seattle and the Klondike gold rush.

EMMA GOLDMAN (1869–1940)

URL ADDRESS: http://sunsite.Berkeley.EDU/Goldman/

SITE SUMMARY: Emma Goldman was a radicalized version of the "Renaissance Woman." She was active at the turn of the century criss-crossing the United States while she lectured about birth control, women's equality, union organization, and the need for an eight-hour workday. Labeled and vilified as an anarchist, Goldman, a Russian émigré, was eventually arrested for sedition during World War I and deported. She is the only woman to be buried in the Kremlin Wall alongside other noted communist leaders. This site provides an overview of Goldman's life and sample documents from the book edition of *The Emma Goldman Papers*. It also contains a curriculum guide for secondary school students to help explore freedom of speech, women's rights, and antimilitarism issues.

DISCUSSION QUESTIONS AND ACTIVITIES

1. Why was Emma Goldman so feared as an anarchist? Why was anarchy seen as a foreign movement? Discuss the following people and events and their relationship to Goldman: Johann Most; the bombing of Haymarket Square; the assassination of President William McKin-

ley by Leon Czolgosz; and the attempted assassination of Henry Clay Frick by Alexander Berman.

2. Click on *Selections from Emma Goldman's Writings* and click on *Anarchism and Other Essays*. What is Goldman's definition of anarchy? How does it compare to one in a dictionary or an encyclopedia of political thought?

3. Click on *Selections from Emma Goldman's Writings* and click on *Prisons: A Social Crime and Failure*. What is Goldman's opinion of prisons? Imagine that she is alive today and has been asked to deliver a speech before the A.C.L.U. (American Civil Liberties Union) on stricter prison sentences and the "three strikes and you're out" law. What would she say?

4. Click on *Selections from Emma Goldman's Writings* and click on *Patriotism: A Menace to Liberty*. Why does Goldman believe that patriotism is dangerous to democracy? Does she equate this term with nationalism?

5. Read some of Emma Goldman's other writings or speeches. You are the judge in the Palmer Raids and must decide whether to deport Goldman on what was known as the "Soviet Ark." Would you deport her? Write a brief defending your decision.

6. Outline Emma Goldman's position on women's suffrage and other rights. Argue that she may have been deported because she was so threatening to the position and power that men had established over women in various professions and other areas of life.

RELATED INTERNET SITE(S)

Emma Goldman Photos
http://www.pitzer.edu/~dward/Anarchist_Archives/goldman/goldmangraphicstable.html
   Contains a virtual photo tour of Emma Goldman at different stages of life along with her friends and family.

The Failure of Christianity
http://au.spunk.org/library/writers/goldman/sp001501.html
   Provides the full text of Emma Goldman's opinions about religion as published in the April 1913 issue of *Mother Earth*, a journal she founded.

ANTI-IMPERIALISM IN THE UNITED STATES (1898–1935)

URL ADDRESS: http://home.ican.net/~fjzwick/ail98-35.html

SITE SUMMARY: The isolationist movement has deep roots in American political traditions and foreign policies. The pros and cons of this policy were hotly debated in journals, newspapers, and public discourse as America began to gain status as a world power. It also had its origins as direct opposition to the Philippine-American War of 1899–1902, and it resulted in the formation of the Anti-Imperialist League. The league focused primarily on issues involving economic imperialism during its last ten years, and by the 1920s another generation of anti-imperialist organizations was founded in response to U.S. involvement in World War I. The documents in this site contain a collection of pro- and anti-imperialist literature from 1898 to 1935. They take the form of organized platforms, speeches, pamphlets, photographs, and political cartoons. The site also includes a search engine, bibliography, related literary essays, and excellent background material.

DISCUSSION QUESTIONS AND ACTIVITIES

1. Select *Platforms* and click on *Platform of the American Anti-Imperialist League*. Based on this platform, what subsequent wars or undeclared wars would the United States never have become involved in? Give your reasons for each one that you list.

2. Select *Unified Contents* and click on *Anti-Imperialism Cost Lives . . . .* Compare the rhetoric in this address to speeches given by pro–Vietnam War supporters. What are the similarities and dissimilarities?

3. Select *History* and click on *Filipinos in the Debate About Imperialism.* Choose several essays, letters, or speeches that support the important role that Filipinos played in the anti-imperialist movement.

4. How did the Anti-Imperialist League prevent the United States from becoming a classic colonial power in the image of Great Britain and other European countries?

5. On July 4, 1821, John Quincy Adams stated that "America goes not abroad in search of monsters to destroy. . . . She might become the dictatress of the world but she would no longer be the ruler of her own spirit." How does this quote apply to the philosophy of the Anti-Imperialist League?

6. Based on the policies and platforms of the Anti-Imperialist League, what should be our foreign policy toward Iraq and the countries that used to comprise Yugoslavia?

RELATED INTERNET SITE(S)

Connections + (History: Anti-Imperialism in the United States)
http://www.mcrel.org/resources/plus/anti.html

Provides links to lesson plans, activities, and teachers' guides about anti-imperialism in the United States.

"THE WHITE MAN'S BURDEN" AND ITS CRITICS (1899)

URL ADDRESS: http://www.boondocksnet.com/kipling/kipling.html

SITE SUMMARY: Rudyard Kipling's 1899 poem "The White Man's Burden" rationalized colonial imperialism, and in turn generated a deluge of responses both pro and con. Imperialists in the United States used the poem to justify the acquisition of Puerto Rico, Guam, and the Philippines. Anti-imperialists parodied the poem, noting the hypocrisy in it and the inherent greed of military power and commercial markets. This site provides the full text of the poem, and subsequent essays, cartoons, and interviews.

DISCUSSION QUESTIONS AND ACTIVITIES

1. Read Kipling's poem and click on the cartoon about it from the *Detroit Journal*, February 1899. What message do you think the artist is trying to convey?
2. Draw four cartoons that interpret both the imperialist and the anti-imperialist view of Kipling's poem.
3. Look at the advertisement of Admiral George Dewey washing his hands with Pears' soap. What illustrations, symbols, and words are used to convey the imperialist message of "The White Man's Burden"? Write an editorial to the editors of *McClure's* magazine protesting the publication of this advertisement based on your analysis of it.
4. Read some of the responses that were written in 1899. Write your own response as an anti-imperialist to the poem.
5. Mark Twain was a well-known anti-imperialist. What did he mean when he said, "The White Man's Burden has been sung. Who will sing the Brown Man's?"
6. Write your own parody of Rudyard Kipling's "The White Man's Burden."

RELATED INTERNET SITE(S)

Anti-Imperialism in the United States, 1898–1935
http://www.rochester.ican.net/~fjzwick/ail98-35.html
Contains an extensive collection of anti-imperialist history and literature from 1898 to 1935 in the form of organized platforms, speeches, pamphlets, photographs, and cartoons.

LIFE AUTOMOBILE PAGE (1901–1995)

URL ADDRESS: http://www.pathfinder.com/Life/cars/classic/classichome.html

SITE SUMMARY: The development of the automobile has had an enormous impact on people's way of life throughout the world. Acquiring one and having an appropriate infrastructure of roads, bridges, and the availability of fuel gave people the opportunity to change their lives in a variety of ways. They could accept a new job, travel to distant parts of the country, or move away from an undesirable location. This archive contains a photo history of the evolution of the American car as pictured in *Life* magazine from 1901 to 1995. The pictures, some of them by famous photographers such as Dorothea Lange and Margaret Bourke-White, also provide a slice of Americana during these years.

DISCUSSION QUESTIONS AND ACTIVITIES

1. Select *1901*. What does the photograph of the disassembled Curved Dash Olds tell you about the mechanical simplicity of one of the first automobiles in the United States? What are the implications for mechanical simplicity in terms of mass production, ease of repair, self-service, and the like?

2. Select *1936*. How did the production of cheap automobiles alter the demographic pattern of the Great Plains states during the Dust Bowl years?

3. Select *1941* and other relevant years. How did the automobile improve recreational opportunities for Americans? Discuss the role of the automobile in developing the suburbs and in the exodus from large cities.

4. Select *1947*. What were the advantages and disadvantages of an interstate highway for drivers, towns and cities, businesses, and the oil industry?

5. As the automobile evolved from Henry Ford's basic black to ones with different designs and colors, it became more of a status symbol. What do you think are the pros and cons of this change?

6. Look at several automobile photographs. Where was the woman's place in American car culture? How were women used to advertise and display cars? How often do you see them photographed in the driver's seat? Why?

RELATED INTERNET SITE(S)

Life of Henry Ford
http://www.hfmgv.org/histories/hf/henry.html
   Provides a biography of Henry Ford and covers the events relating to his production of the Model T.

World Transportation Photographs
http://memory.loc.gov/ammem/wtc/wtchome.html
   This site features 900 images of all types of transportation by American photographer William Henry Jackson.

SAN FRANCISCO GREAT EARTHQUAKE AND THE FIRE OF 1906 (1906)

URL ADDRESS: http://www.sfmuseum.org/1906/06.html

SITE SUMMARY: At 5:12 A.M., April 18, 1906, San Francisco was struck by the most disastrous earthquake in the history of North America. While the earthquake caused comparatively little damage, the broken water mains left the city virtually defenseless against the fires that followed. This site contains a treasure trove of primary sources. It includes a map of the quake epicenter, the seismograph readings of the 1906 and 1989 earthquakes, and a chronology of events. Additional materials provide a list of the dead; San Francisco police and fire department reports; eyewitness accounts; the military's role during the quake and subsequent fire; engineering and scientific reports; newspaper clippings about the earthquake; and photographs.

DISCUSSION QUESTIONS AND ACTIVITIES

1. Where was the epicenter of the 1906 San Francisco earthquake? Design maps showing which areas of the city were damaged the most and what eventually happened to some of the larger buildings as a result of the fires.

2. What was the approximate seismographic reading of the 1906 earthquake? On a world scale, should it be termed a "great earthquake"?

Look in an almanac or at an earthquake-related Internet site and design a chart showing the relationship of its magnitude and loss of life to other recorded earthquakes.

3. Read some of the eyewitness accounts of the earthquake. What are the similarities in these accounts? Which ones seem the most reliable to you, and why?

4. A decision was made to dynamite selected buildings to stop the spread of the fire. Unfortunately, some of the dynamite was in powder form rather than stick form and very unstable. Many of the soldiers had never used it before and were untrained in its application. Discuss how these two factors may have contributed to more loss of property. (Refer to the accounts given by First Lieutenant Raymond W. Briggs within the link *Progress of the Fires* by Lawrence J. Kennedy.

5. Select *Relief and Recovery Efforts*. How do you think the city handled citizen relief? What do you think would happen today if San Francisco experienced an earthquake on this scale?

6. Chinatown was completely destroyed in the fires that followed the earthquake. How did people and individual surrounding communities treat the inhabitants of Chinatown? You are a literate Chinese immigrant. Write an editorial expressing your opinion of the treatment of the Chinese after the earthquake.

RELATED INTERNET SITE(S)

1906 San Francisco Earthquake Photo Page
http://www.eas.slu.edu/Earthquake_Center/1906EQ/1906thumb.html
    Features photographs from 1906 of the damage caused by the earthquake not only to San Francisco but also to surrounding communities.

Scenes in San Francisco—Early Motion Pictures
http://rs6.loc.gov/ammem/ndlpedu/sffilm/sffile.htm
    Presents a brief, downloadable film from the Library of Congress American Memory Collection about people evacuating San Francisco and camping outside.

THE MIDDLE EAST: DOCUMENTS (1907–Present)

URL ADDRESS: http://www.mtholyoke.edu/acad/intrel/meres.htm

SITE SUMMARY: This site is a compilation of primary documents relating to the creation of the state of Israel and the subsequent problems associated with the status of Palestine. Beginning with the Anglo-Russian Entente and Agreement on Persia of 1907, there follow documents such as the Balfour Declaration of 1917, various British White Papers concerning Palestine, the Israeli Declaration of Independence, the Palestine Mandate, and the National Charter. Contemporary documents such as the Israeli–Palestine Liberation Organization Agreement and the United Nations Security Council Resolutions relating to the Middle East are also included.

DISCUSSION QUESTIONS AND ACTIVITIES

1. Select *The Balfour Declaration, November 2, 1917*. What was going on in the Middle East when this declaration was issued by the British government? What do you think the British were hoping to gain from it? If you were a Jewish person, how would you have interpreted this document? If you were an Arab, how would you have interpreted it?

2. Select *King-Crane Commission Report, August 28, 1919*. Until 1946 this was the only official American study of the Palestine problem. What were the findings of the commission concerning the creation of a Jewish state? What factors would change America's position regarding the establishment of a Jewish state?

3. Select *San Remo Conference, 1922*. The Arabs accepted the Balfour Declaration and the results of the assigned mandate of Palestine to the British. Why did they believe that their rights were going to be safeguarded? How many Jews were returning to this ancestral home during this period?

4. Select *Anglo-American Committee of Inquiry—Chapter I*. In the *Recommendations and Comments* section, the committee members recommended that entrance certificates be given to 100,000 Jews who had been the victims of Nazi persecution. The Zionists agreed with this recommendation, but rejected the other nine. Why do you think the other nine recommendations were rejected?

5. Select Report of the *Anglo-American Committee—Chapter III*. Based on this report, how would you describe the political situation in Palestine in 1946? If you were Great Britain, what would you have done to bring about peace in the region in 1946?

6. Pretend you have the power, with the exception of the Holocaust, to revise history up until 1946. What should various governments have done differently to have prevented the problems that the Middle East is experiencing today?

RELATED INTERNET SITE(S)

Middle East Studies Association of North America
http://www.mesa.arizona.edu/links.htm
   Provides information on the Middle East Studies Association of North America, various Middle East conferences, and, most important, related links to this world problem area.

MEXICAN REVOLUTION (1910)

URL ADDRESS: http://www.msstate.edu/Archives/History/ Latin_America/Mexico/revolution.html

SITE SUMMARY: Mexico has had several revolutions. This site covers the one in 1910 when Francisco I. Madero, a liberal landowner, decided to run against Porfirio Diaz and was jailed. He fled to the United States and issued a call for revolution. Insurgencies developed throughout Mexico, culminating in temporary power for Madero, followed by his murder under the dictatorship of General Victoriano Huerta. This comprehensive site includes pictures of and biographical information on Huerta, Pancho Villa, and Francisco Madero. It also features photographs of the Mexican Revolution, the Plan de Ayala (the insurgents' plan for liberty and democratic reform), the full text of the Zimmermann telegram, and a translation of the Constitution of 1917.

DISCUSSION QUESTIONS AND ACTIVITIES

1. What were the economic and social conditions that led to the Mexican Revolution of 1910?

2. Select *Plan de Ayala*. As a historian, how do you account for the failure of Don Francisco I. Madero's leadership? Why was he unable to unify the country?

3. Imagine that you are Gustavo A. Madero, the brother of Francisco I. Madero. Your brother has been spectacularly unsuccessful in stopping the fighting that has broken out in various Mexican states. There is great economic and social instability. He has decided to appoint Victoriano Huerta chief of the armed forces. Argue against this decision and explain to your brother why it may cost him his life.

4. What was the role of the United States ambassador, Henry Lane Wilson, in the Mexican Revolution of 1910? Do you think that he acted under the auspices of the United States government when he con-

spired with Porfirio Diaz and General Huerta to bring down Madero's government, or did he overstep his authority as an ambassador?

5. Discuss the role of the United States and German governments in the Mexican revolutions of 1910–1917. What do you think is the legacy of the political and sometimes military interference, especially by the United States? Should the United States have involved itself in the internal politics of Mexico?

6. If Mexico were to experience another similar revolution, what do you think the role of the United States should be?

RELATED INTERNET SITE(S)

Mexico
http://www.msstate.edu/Archives/History/Latin_America/Mexico/mexico.html
Provides several links to additional primary source materials about Mexico from the pre-Columbian period to the nineteenth century.

EYEWITNESS: A NORTH KOREAN REMEMBERS (1911–1955)

URL ADDRESS: http://www.kimsoft.com/korea/eyewit.htm

SITE SUMMARY: This site contains much more than a first-person account by Kim Young Sik of the turmoil, disruption, and pain of war. It provides voluminous materials about the last days of the Yi dynasty, the history of anti-Japanese movements in Korea from 1911 to 1935, the Japanese occupation of 1940–1945, liberation, and the Soviet and United States occupation of 1945–1946. It also includes materials covering Korea under communism, the Korean War, Kim's life as a refugee, and his work with the Central Intelligence Agency. It concludes with information about North Korean spy operations and a detailed bibliography for further research.

DISCUSSION QUESTIONS AND ACTIVITIES

1. Select *Anti-Japan Movement: 1911–1920*. Why was the suppression of the nationalist movement in Korea by the Japanese so severe? Do you think it was justified?

2. Select *Anti-Japan Movement: 1911–1920*. In 1919 the first Korean Com-

munist Party was formed in Irkutsk, Siberia. Why did the Koreans ally themselves with the communists?

3. Select *US Military Government—1945*. On November 12, 1945, General Hodge tells General Douglas MacArthur that "the U.S. occupation of Korea under present conditions and policies is surely drifting to the edge of a political-economic abyss." What policies is the United States pursuing at this point that are leading to the Korean War?

4. Select *Korean War Starts*. Why did President Truman commit United States forces to assist South Korea without seeking congressional approval? Using a debate format, argue that President Truman either engaged the country in an illegal war or was protecting our country from the spread of communism.

5. Some historians have said that our involvement in Korea and Vietnam came about because the United States has never been able to delineate clearly the currents of nationalism, communism, and imperialism that flow into one another. Based on these two wars, what do you think should be our foreign affairs policy with regard to foreign civil strife?

6. What do you think is the attitude of Kim Young Sik toward the Korean War? Why has he gone to all this trouble to place his autobiography on the Internet?

RELATED INTERNET SITE(S)

History of Korea
http://violet.berkeley.edu/~korea/history.html
    Provides an unannotated series of links on the dynastic history of Korea.

The History of Korea
http://www.kbs.co.kr/pr/history/history.htm
    Sponsored by Radio Korea International, this site features images of Korean history from prehistoric times to the present day.

History of Korea World History Archives
http://www.hartford-hwp.com/archives/55a/index.html
    Includes links to retrospective histories of pre- and post-1953 Korea. It also contains a site about the abuse of Korean women as Japanese prisoners of war during World War II.

ENCYCLOPEDIA TITANIC (1912)

URL ADDRESS: http://www.rmplc.co.uk/eduweb/sites/phind/

SITE SUMMARY: Students reluctant to use primary sources may be enticed by this well-organized, accessible site about the ill-fated maiden voyage of the great cruise ship *Titanic*. The largest sections of the site contain passenger and crew lists broken down by classes and occupations, respectively. Lists of survivors are also included along with links to their biographies. Other resources provide the full text of Walter Lord's *A Night to Remember*, newspaper articles, and accounts by survivors and survivors' descendants. Another section features interactive deck plans, links to photographs, and computer images of various parts of the ship. A site index makes navigation a breeze.

DISCUSSION QUESTIONS AND ACTIVITIES

1. Select *Misc.* and click on *Titanic Chronology*. Design a timeline that shows the departure and route of the *Titanic* up until the time it sank.

2. You have been named chief of a board of inquiry to investigate the reasons for the sinking of the *Titanic* and the great loss of life. Write a detailed outline for your fellow board members concerning the eyewitness testimony you are going to permit and the engineering evidence you will allow to be heard about the ship's construction. Be sure to include information about the safety procedures which were or were not followed, the weather conditions at the time of the accident, and other important factors.

3. As a member of a board of inquiry, you must decide which factors were most important in contributing not only to the sinking of the *Titanic* but also to the great loss of life. In your opinion, what were the most critical mistakes? What recommendations would you make for future cruise ships so disasters of this kind can be avoided?

4. The *Titanic* could be described as a metaphor for the class system. Use the first, second, and third class passenger lists to determine which class experienced more deaths. Explain your findings by making appropriate charts and graphs that indicate percentages and totals by passenger class.

5. Use the deck plans and the position and capacity of the lifeboats to produce your own evacuation plan. Could you have saved more lives with your plan? Remember, you have only two hours and approximately forty minutes to effect your plan.

6. You are the first reporter to meet *Titanic* survivors as they disembark from the *Carpathia*. Write a story for the front page of a New York newspaper describing the disaster.

RELATED INTERNET SITE(S)

Titanic
http://www.nara.gov/exhall/originals/titanic.html

Features a U.S. Navy memorandum referring to the collision of the *Titanic* with an iceberg on April 15, 1912, and some brief background material.

Titanic Home Page
http://seawifs.gsfc.nasa.gov/OCEAN_PLANET/HTML/titanic.html
   Contains an excellent set of *Titanic*-related Internet links.

The Titanic Information Site
http://www.netins.net/showcase/js/titaniclinks.shtml
   This is another outstanding comprehensive site about the sinking of the *Titanic*. It also contains survivor lists, eyewitness accounts, and the unfinished biography of Molly Brown, an American passenger whose life was the basis for a famous musical.

TRENCHES ON THE WEB (1914–1918)

URL ADDRESS: http://www.worldwar1.com/

SITE SUMMARY: Trenches on the Web is a well-maintained and well-organized multimedia site for historical information about World War I. A documents section contains prewar documents followed by French and German mobilization orders, copies of German newspaper articles about the war with France, the Austrian declaration of war on Serbia, and the Zimmermann telegram. Besides documents, the site features primary sources in the form of original charts, maps, images, and posters. It also provides a search engine, a discussion forum site, book reviews, and a virtual reality link that includes World War I weapons, zeppelins, airplanes, and boats.

DISCUSSION QUESTIONS AND ACTIVITIES

1. Select *Pre-War Documents*. Analyze the American political cartoon about Bismarck. What do you think is the message of the cartoon? Look at how Bismarck is depicted on a teeter-totter. Describe your emotions upon viewing him in this position. Would you be optimistic or pessimistic about Bismarck avoiding war in Europe?

2. Select *Pre-War Documents*. Analyze the French political cartoon about Franz Josef grabbing Bosnia-Herzegovina. Draw one in a similar fashion that would show the dismay of contemporary countries as they witness present-day Bosnia-Herzegovina being torn away from Yugoslavia.

3. Select *Timeline* and click on *1839–1914: The Long Fuse*. What do you

see as the role of any of the United States presidents during this time in helping to avoid war in Europe? Were there events that they could have influenced and did not? Were there times when they should have spoken out and did not? Could any of them have had that much influence with these war-prone European political leaders?

4. Select *Timeline* and click on *July–1914: The July Crisis*. Who do you think the principal players were in moving Europe toward World War I, and why?

5. Select *Timeline* and click on *8-June-1915—The Boston American*. World War I has been going on since 1914. How does this American newspaper describe the war? Are Americans involved yet? How are the combatants depicted? Does the coverage seem fair to you? What is the general feeling of the article? If you were a young man of draft age, would you be concerned about future military service in this war?

6. Select *Timeline* and click on *British Trench Warfare 1917–1918*. What was the purpose of trench warfare? Why was it such a hardship on the infantry? Why was this type of warfare responsible for such high casualties rates in World War I?

RELATED INTERNET SITE(S)

The Great War 1914–1918
http://www.[itt.edu/~pitt.edu/~pugachev/greatwar/ww1.html
Provides poems, literary accounts, and historical sketches of World War I plus a series of related Internet sites.

Military History: World War I (1914–1918)
http://www.cfcsc.dnd.ca/links/milhist/wwi.html
Includes an overview of the major battles and other military events of World War I.

World War I Document Archive
http://www.lib.byu.edu/~rdh/wwi/
Includes many European documents related to World War I, a citation guide, and links to a mailing list.

BOLSHEVIK "COUP D'ETAT" (1917)

URL ADDRESS: http://www.yale.edu/lawweb/avalon/diplomacy/ forrel/1918rv1/18rv1men.htm

SITE SUMMARY: The Russian Revolution had a profound impact on other nations because it established communism as a form of government. Russia not only imposed communism on itself but also imposed it on neighboring countries that it acquired as the result of helping to win World War II. This site contains correspondence dating from November 7 through November 22, 1917, from various U.S. ambassadors to Russia, Sweden, and the Netherlands to the secretary of state. The letters tell how the Bolsheviks, under the leadership of Vladimir Lenin, seized power from Alexander Kerensky's democratically elected government. As soon as the Bolsheviks seized power, Russia and Germany signed the Treaty of Brest-Litovsk, which ended Russian participation in World War I and established their right to govern the Baltic states, Armenia, and Georgia.

DISCUSSION QUESTIONS AND ACTIVITIES

1. Select the telegram dated November 7, 1917, 5 P.M. Why does the aide de camp to Alexander Kerensky "accidentally" meet the United States ambassador and tell him that Kerensky's government will be deposed if they do not get reliable troops?

2. In this same telegram the United States ambassador mentions the Russian aide de camp's request that the United States not recognize the Soviet government if it is established in Petrograd. What do you think are the implications of the request? Would you recognize the Soviet government at this point if you were the president of the United States?

3. Select the telegram dated November 7, 1917, 6 P.M. In this telegram the ambassador reports that "Lenin made a peace talk that violently attacked the bourgeoisie and advocated the division of property." What were the social and economic conditions at this time for the majority of the Russian people? What is so appealing to most of them about Lenin's advocacy of dividing property?

4. Select the next telegram, dated November 8, 1917, 4 P.M. In this message, the ambassador reports that the coup d'etat was successful. Lenin has identified three problems facing Russian democracy. Which one(s) do you think may cause him the most problems? Why?

5. Select the next telegram, dated November 8, 1917, 4 P.M. (from Summers). Consul General Summers reports that the Bolsheviks have taken over the administration's post and telegraph and have closed the offices of all conservative newspapers. If you had received this message, what type of government would you think is taking power? Why?

6. Read some of the remaining telegrams. If you were the ambassador to Russia, what advice would you give to your government at this

time? What should the role of the United States be in this revolution based on this correspondence?

RELATED INTERNET SITE(S)

Chapter VIII The Conclusion with the Central Powers of the Peace of Brest Litovsk, March 3, 1918
http://www.yale.edu/lawweb/avalon/diplomacy/forrel/1918rv1/blmenu.htm
   Provides additional ambassadorial correspondence on the political situation leading to the signing of the Treaty of Brest-Litovsk, in March 1918.

Russia Under the Bolsheviks
http://maddenenterprises.com/Russian_Revolution/Books/Dioneo/Dioneo_03.html
   Contains the full text of a pamphlet by I. V. Shklovsky, a Russian exile in London, in which he outlines, rather onesidedly, the destructive aspects of Bolshevism.

LIBRARY OF CONGRESS SOVIET ARCHIVES EXHIBIT (1917–1991)

URL ADDRESS: http://www.ncsa.uiuc.edu/SDG/Experimental/soviet.exhibit/soviet.archive.html

SITE SUMMARY: When the Soviet Union collapsed in 1991, the control over its archives was transferred to a democratic state. This joint exhibit is meant to provide users with primary source documents that will enable them to understand some of the history of the Soviet Union. The site features documents spanning the October Revolution of 1917 to the failed coup of August 1991. Materials are provided from the Archives of the Communist Central Committee, the Presidential Archive, and the KGB (the former Soviet Union's secret police). Internal politics, foreign policy, and security operations are revealed along with the tyrannical practices of intimidation and terror that were also part of the Soviet Union.

DISCUSSION QUESTIONS AND ACTIVITIES

1. Select *Letter from Rykov*. Why do you think Stalin chose to execute so many members of the Communist Party rather than execute non-Party

members? What did he gain from unleashing a reign of terror? What other revolutions have had similar reigns of terror?

2. Read the section titled *Secret Police* and click on *United Press*. What does this correspondence tell you about the degree of censorship that existed in the USSR? What do you think the United States should have done about the deportation of "citizen Gullinger"? Should it have asked for a hearing and proof of these charges? As the United States ambassador to Russia, write a letter protesting the deportation of Gullinger.

3. Read the section titled *The Gulag* and click on *Collectivization of Livestock: Letter to Bolshevik*. What conditions in Russia probably drove the authors of this letter to commit the crimes that they served time for? What risk are they running by writing a letter about their experiences? What would be the best way to disseminate this information about the terrors of the Gulag to the rest of the world? Refer to the writings of Nobel Prize winner Alexander Solzhenitsyn for assistance in answering this question.

4. Read the section titled *Collectivization and Industrialization* and click on *Letter of April 9, 1932*. What was Stalin trying to accomplish by collectivizing farms? Why were his methods so unsuccessful, and why did collectivization result in a terrible famine? Trace the history of Russian agriculture pre- and post-communism. What years was Russia able to feed itself? What conclusions can you draw from this evidence?

5. Read the section about *Anti-Religious Campaigns* and click on *Letter from Gorky to Stalin*. Why was it necessary to eradicate religion under the communist government? Why were organized religions a threat to the communists?

6. Describe how you would try to survive under Stalin's regime as one of the following: a member of the Communist Party; a Kulak peasant; a member of the Politburo; or a non–Communist Party member.

RELATED INTERNET SITE(S)

A Chronology of Russian History
http://www.departments.bucknell.edu/russian/chrono.html
Provides major dates and events in Russian history and links to related Internet materials.

Russian History Home Page
http://www.msstate.edu/Archives/History/russia.html
Includes a history of Russia beginning with settlements by Slavs and Varangians through Gorbachev's resignation plus an exhibit of nineteenth-century Muslim life in the Russian Empire.

TREATY OF VERSAILLES (1919)

URL ADDRESS: http://www.lib.byu.edu/~rdh/wwi/versailles.html

SITE SUMMARY: While the Treaty of Versailles officially ended military hostilities against Germany in World War I, the provisions of the document in the way of monetary and military reparations and loss of land and colonies set the stage for Germany's future economic and political collapse. When inflation ran rampant and many Germans were bankrupted, the resentment against the Allies felt by many Germans sowed the seeds for a strong German Nationalist movement and the rise to power of Adolf Hitler. This site enables users to search captioned articles of the treaty relating to such issues as prisoners of war, reparations, and German rights and interests outside of Germany.

DISCUSSION QUESTIONS AND ACTIVITIES

1. Prepare a detailed outline showing all the monetary and military reparations that Germany had to pay and the location and amount of land and colonies that it lost.

2. The Treaty of Versailles was termed a "Carthaginian Peace." Write a diatribe on the treaty from a German perspective that denounces it as a heinous retribution for crimes that Germany did not commit.

3. You are a former German soldier who has just finished reading the Treaty of Versailles. What parts of it can you live with, and what parts are simply abhorrent to you?

4. Historians argue that this treaty sowed the seeds for a future world war because it caused deadly inflation that bankrupted Germany. Explain from an economic standpoint how this occurred.

5. You are a French soldier who lost his leg at the Battle of the Somme. You have just read the Treaty of Versailles. Write an editorial to a French newspaper praising the penalties served on Germany. Why do you think that this is a fair treaty? What do you hope will happen to Germany as a result of the treaty?

6. Write an outline of a peace treaty that you believe would have resulted in a more lasting peace and possibly have prevented World War II.

RELATED INTERNET SITE(S)

Conditions of an Armistice with Germany
http://www.lib.byu.edu/~rdh/wwi/1918/armistice.html

Presents the exact conditions under which the Allies would establish a cease-fire with Germany during World War I.

THE WOLF LEWKOWICZ COLLECTION (1922–1939)

URL ADDRESS: http://web.mit.edu/maz/wolf/

SITE SUMMARY: This online collection includes 178 letters from Wolf Lewkowicz of Poland to Sol J. Zissman, his deceased sister's son. Zissman immigrated to the United States as an eleven-year-old boy prior to World War I. The letters span the years 1922–1939 and began when Wolf was thirty-six years old and Sol was twenty and living in Chicago. Insightful and well-written, Wolf's letters reflect the economic and political crisis facing Jews living in Poland during a time of terrible persecution. Wolf's last letter was written in 1939. On September 1942, Wolf and his wife were forcibly transported to their deaths in the Treblinka concentration camp.

DISCUSSION QUESTIONS AND ACTIVITIES

1. Select *Letter 3 Lodz, 5 August 1922*. From this letter, how would you describe the conditions in Poland and Germany after World War I for Jews in particular? Are there any signs in this letter of the persecution that Jews in these countries will soon be facing?

2. Select *Letter 2 Lodz, 18 November 1922*. In it Wolf's nephew expresses his desire to send his uncle a ticket so that he can come to America. Why is it so hard for would-be emigrants to leave?

3. Select *Letter 151 Lodz, 6 January 1936*. How has the mood of Poland and Germany changed regarding Jewish people? Does Wolf suspect that the government is behind the anti-Semitism or powerless in the face of an epidemic of virulent prejudice against a minority group?

4. Select *Letter 164 Lodz, 12 September 1937*. What is the situation in Poland now regarding Jewish people? Why is Wolf's nephew trying to persuade him not to delay with the registration of his son, Joseph? Why is Wolf's nephew so fearful? Are his fears well grounded?

5. How do some of these letters compare to the diary entries of Anne Frank? How would you describe the mood of both writers? Discuss the similarities and dissimilarities in their writings.

6. Select *Letter 175 Opoczno, 7 April 1939*. In it Wolf describes the mood of the Polish people just after Hitler has invaded Czechoslovakia. How are Polish Jews reacting to this news, and why?

RELATED INTERNET SITE(S)

Simon Wiesenthal Center
http://www.Wiesenthal.com

Provides a virtual tour of the Museum of Tolerance. It is dedicated to educating people around the world about the need for tolerance. The site also includes biographies of children caught in the Holocaust, a glossary of Holocaust terms, and a bibliography.

To Save a Life: Stories of Jewish Rescue
http://www.humboldt.edu/~rescuers/

This site supplies narratives of people rescued from the Holocaust.

Warsaw Uprising
http://www.cs.princeton.edu/~mkporwit/uprising/august.html

Relates the story of the uprising in the Warsaw Ghetto of Poland by Jews. It lasted two months and resulted in the loss of 200,000 lives. The site contains maps, photographs, and background material.

HOWARD CARTER PERSONAL DIARIES (1923)

URL ADDRESS: http://www.ashmol.ox.ac.uk/gri/4sea1not.html

SITE SUMMARY: For seven years the archaeologist Howard Carter had searched for a royal tomb which he was convinced lay undiscovered in Egypt's Valley of the Kings. This site contains his diary entries from October 1922 to May 1923, when he was successful in uncovering the top of a flight of stairs leading down into the earth, where he discovered the tomb of the Pharaoh Tutankhamun. The tomb had lain undisturbed for over 3,000 years. The diary ends with Carter supervising the transport of Tutankhamun's remains and other artifacts to the Cairo Museum.

DISCUSSION QUESTIONS AND ACTIVITIES

1. From Howard Carter's archaeological site descriptions, draw an archaeological map of the Valley of the Kings showing where Tutankhamun's tomb was found.

2. Do you think that Howard Carter and Lord Carnarvon were right to open King Tutankhamun's tomb? Do you think that governments should allocate time and money for archaeological explorations of this kind?

3. How was Carter able to identify the tomb as belonging to King Tutankhamun? What knowledge did he have to have as an archaeologist?

4. Imagine that you are King Tutankhamun brought back from the dead for a trip down the present-day Nile. What things would be different on the river from when you were alive more than 3,000 years ago?

5. You are an archaeologist. Based on the discovery of Carter's diary, how would you go about scientifically dismantling the tomb so as to preserve everything for the story that it might tell?

6. As head of antiquities for an imaginary country brimming with ancient tombs and monuments, it is your job to review applications by archaeologists wishing to excavate the ruins of your country's previous civilizations. What requirements would you make in terms of their qualifications, salary (if any), preservation of future discoveries, and work methods? What are your demands concerning hiring workers, publicity, keeping any artifacts, conserving the site, and other items? Write a brief handbook containing your rules and regulations.

RELATED INTERNET SITE(S)

Egyptian Kings
http://touregypt.net/kings.htm
This site groups Egyptian kings within dynastic periods and includes a hyperlinked paragraph about each one.

Famous Pharaohs
http://www.skittler.demon.co.uk/pharaohs.htm
Includes long paragraphs about and images of famous Egyptian pharaohs.

In the Tomb of Tutankhamun
http://web1.getty.edu/0gci/conservation/7_3/
news_in_conservation.tut.html
Although this is a commercial site, it does contain excellent images and explanations of the contents of Tutankhamun's tomb.

CALIFORNIA GOLD NORTHERN CALIFORNIA FOLK MUSIC FROM THE THIRTIES (1930s)

URL ADDRESS: http://rs6.loc.gov/amhome.html

SITE SUMMARY: This is one of the sites within the Library of Congress American Memory Project. It is a compilation of sound recordings, still-life photographs, drawings, correspondence, and research materials. They were collected from a group of European ethnic communities in Northern California which were studied as part of the New Deal Work

Projects Administration (WPA) during the Great Depression. The collection contains thirty-five hours of folk music recorded in twelve languages, and it features 185 musicians. The search engine supports searches by keyword, subject index, ethnic group, performers, musical instruments, and audio title.

DISCUSSION QUESTIONS AND ACTIVITIES

1. Select *Subject* and click on *Bankers—California—Songs and Music—Texts*. What is the song at this site about? Why have there been bank failures, and why do the people believe that the banks have been the robbers?

2. Select *Subject* and click on *California—Gold Discoveries—Songs and Music—Musical Transcriptions*. How did the California Emigrant song, which swept the country, spread the contagion of gold fever? Find some other songs that contain legends about California that would have attracted prospective gold miners.

3. Select *Subject* and click on *Broadsides—Great Britain*. Listen to the song "The Drunkard's Dream." How did this song reflect the conditions connected with the temperance movement? What emotional strings does it attempt to pull by making references to the drunkard's wife and children? How would you describe its tone?

4. Select *Subject* and click on *Cowboys—Songs and Music—Texts*. City slickers thought the life of the cowboy to be a glamorous one, filled with rides through open country and cookouts and companionship over an open campfire. Describe the conditions of the cowboy's life based on your reading and on listening to the songs "Sam Bass" and "Cowboy's Lament."

5. Select *Musical Instruments*. Choose a stringed instrument that is used by several different ethnic groups. Select music by each group and show how the instrument was used to create different types of dances and songs that reflect each group's ethnic heritage.

6. Select music from a variety of ethnic groups. In tone, tempo, and emotion, how did their music help break the language barrier among American immigrants?

RELATED INTERNET SITE(S)

The Archive of Folk Culture
http://lcweb.loc.gov/folklife/archive.html
    This site provides links to other folk life–related Library of Congress

collections and also contains full-text publications from the American Folk-Life Center.

THE 1930s IN PRINT (1930s)

URL ADDRESS: http://xroads.virginia.edu/g/1930s/PRINT/printfront.html

SITE SUMMARY: This site is part of the American Studies Group at the University of Virginia. Its purpose is to promote better understanding of events, people, places, and attitudes that helped shape American history in the 1930s. The home page is designed in the form of a 1930s newspaper with four periodic flashing images that show President Franklin Roosevelt, a battleship, the explosion of the *Hindenberg*, productive factories, and an aerial view of Washington, D.C. A click on any of these pictures produces a useful 1930s timeline. Several articles are linked to additional sources pertaining to 1930s literature and the Great Depression. A linked bibliography is also part of this small but useful site.

DISCUSSION QUESTIONS AND ACTIVITIES

1. Select the *Timeline*. Choose six people from this timeline that you feel had significant influence, either positively or negatively, in the 1930s.

2. Click on the article *American People Struggle with Hardship and Depression*. What irony do you see in this picture that captures the Depression? How do you think many people felt about the "American Dream" during the 1930s?

3. Click on the article *Reviewed: GWTW and ABSALOM*. What lessons did the heroes and heroines of *Absalom, Absalom!* and *Gone with the Wind* have for people who were living in the 1930s? What psychological traits, such as optimism versus pessimism and the ability to remain flexible, probably helped people survive the Great Depression?

4. Click on the article *Reviewed: GWTW and ABSALOM*. The United States is in the midst of a computer revolution that is forcing many people to perform work differently, to learn new things, and to think of having multiple careers in a lifetime. What lessons do the main characters of *Absalom, Absalom!* and *Gone with the Wind* provide for people of the twenty-first century?

5. Click on the article *Resources for Research: Articles, Books and Links*. Click on the link *John Steinbeck: The California Novels* and choose *The Grapes*

of Wrath. From this chapter summary, what events have happened that typified the 1930s for many people?

6. Click on the article *Resources for Research: Articles, Books and Links*. Click on *The New Deal Network* and choose *Dear Mrs. Roosevelt*. You are a child in the Great Depression whose father has just lost his job. What would your immediate priorities be in terms of food, clothing, and shelter? What things would you sacrifice first so that you might survive? What items would you sell last?

RELATED INTERNET SITE(S)

The New Deal Network
http://newdeal.feri.org
   Provides an excellent database of photographs, political cartoons, texts (in the form of speeches and letters), and other historic documents about the New Deal.

Voices from the Dust Bowl
http://rs6.loc.gov/amhome.html
   Contains songs, photographs, and first-person accounts of migrant workers who left the Dust Bowl to work in California during the Great Depression.

THE FDR CARTOON ARCHIVE (1932–1943)

URL ADDRESS: http://www.wizvax.net/nisk_hs/fdr.index.html

SITE SUMMARY: Students do not usually think of political cartoons as potential primary sources. When grouped by subject matter or date, however, they can provide an interesting database to help students discern historical patterns or perspectives. This increasing collection includes newspaper clippings of hundreds of political cartoons featuring Franklin Delano Roosevelt and issues involving his administrations from 1932 to 1943. The cartoons are exhibited in nine categories ranging from "Waiting for the New Deal," "Foreign Relations," and "Farm Issues" to "The War Years." All have complete citations that include the cartoonist's name, newspaper affiliation, the caption, and a brief content note.

DISCUSSION QUESTIONS AND ACTIVITIES

1. Select *The Cartoons* and click on *Waiting for the New Deal*. From selected cartoons, what do you think people are hoping will happen when Roosevelt takes office? What issues do they want him to address?

2. In this same section, click on the cartoon *Seeking Advice on Bronco-Busting*. Interpret this cartoon in light of the symbols and words used in the picture. Which words or phrases are the most significant? Why do you think so? Describe the emotions that are portrayed in this cartoon.

3. Select *The Cartoons* and click on *The First 100 Days*. Choose the cartoon *Shade of T. R.* Which former president is the cartoonist referring to in this picture, and to what famous quotations by this former president is he comparing FDR's decisions? Would you describe this as a conservative or liberal cartoon? Why?

4. In this same section, look at several cartoons depicting FDR's First 100 Days. In general, how is FDR portrayed? Was he drawn as a confident president? How might these cartoons have reinforced the image that FDR wanted to project to the country during a time of national crisis?

5. Select *The Farm Problem* and click on the cartoon *The New Trend in Easter Fashions*. Draw your own cartoon using contemporary characters and words that will convey a message similar to the one in this cartoon.

6. Select *Foreign Issues* and click on the cartoon *Breaking Down Economic Isolation*. What was Roosevelt's policy on foreign trade? How does this cartoon reflect it or poke fun at it? What do you think is its purpose? Explain and clarify the issues dealt with in the cartoon.

RELATED INTERNET SITE(S)

Franklin D. Roosevelt Library and Museum
http://www.academic.marist.edu/fdr
Includes personal information about Eleanor and Franklin Roosevelt and indexes to various collections of the president's papers.

POTUS (Presidents of the United States)
http://www.ipl.org/ref/POTUS
Contains information about election results, cabinet members, presidential highlights, and other historical documents relating to FDR's presidency.

APPEAL TO THE LEAGUE OF NATIONS BY HAILE SELASSIE (1936)

URL ADDRESS: http://www.mtholyoke.edu/acad/intrel/selassie.htm

SITE SUMMARY: Ethiopia's heritage is a noble one in which their first emperor, Menelik I, was the son of the biblical Queen of Sheba and King

Solomon of Israel. The country was relatively free of domination by foreign powers until 1935, when Italy invaded it in an attempt to expand its colonies in Africa. The Ethiopians' weaponry was no match for that of their mechanized military counterparts. In courage, however, the Ethiopians were superior, even to throwing spears at invading Italian tanks. In June 1936, Emperor Haile Selassie fled Ethiopia and appeared before the League of Nations to ask for its support. This site contains the full text of his plea.

DISCUSSION QUESTIONS AND ACTIVITIES

1. Why did the Italians wish to acquire Ethiopia as another colony? Research the natural resources and geographic position of Ethiopia. What advantages did it have as a strategic base for future Italian conquests in Africa?

2. Was Italy justified in its use of mustard gas to help defeat the Ethiopians? What present-day countries have used biological weapons to fight wars?

3. Did Emperor Haile Selassie trust too much in the ability of the League of Nations to prevent war being waged on his country? If so, why?

4. Emperor Haile Selassie has come to you as head of the United States to beg for weapons to fight against the Italians. What are the pros and cons of any decision that you might make?

5. What message did the League of Nations send to other potential world aggressors when it failed to come to the aid of Ethiopia? Cite future world events involving Germany and the Axis powers.

6. Imagine that the League of Nations voted to aid Ethiopia against Italy. What form should the aid take? Consider money to purchase weapons, the installation of a peacekeeping force, international mediation, a sanctioned boycott of Italian exports, strategic bombing of Italian military sites, and other remedies.

RELATED INTERNET SITE(S)

Haile Selassie
http://ac.acusd.edu/History/text/selassie.html
    Provides an extensive biographical sketch of Emperor Haile Selassie that emphasizes his role upon the invasion of his country by Italy in 1935.

AMERICAN LIFE HISTORIES (1936–1940)

URL ADDRESS: http://rs6.loc.gov/amhome/html

SITE SUMMARY: Searchable by keyword and state, this massive site contains 2,900 first-person accounts and narratives of various Americans from an occupational or Great Depression perspective. The accounts are in the form of full-text documents and audio excerpts read by modern-day actors. The life stories of Americans from almost every walk of life are represented—for example, a maid in Massachusetts, a granite worker in Vermont, a textile factory worker in North Carolina, and a department store clerk at Macy's in New York. Ranging in length from 2,000 to 5,000 words, they take the form of dialogues, narratives, and case histories. Although they are personal in tone, the subject's family background, education, income, type of work, political opinions, religious views, medical condition, and outlook on life are neutrally detailed.

DISCUSSION QUESTIONS AND ACTIVITIES

1. Select the state of *Georgia* and click on *A Day in a Store*. Besides selling items that people need, how does this store serve the community? You live in a small town and are faced with the building of a Wal-Mart store right outside the downtown area. Argue how this store will have a negative impact on the community.

2. Select the state of *Utah* and click on *View Document George William Vogel*. Vogel comments that there seem to be millions of buffalo and that they could never become extinct. What type of hunting practices does he describe that would soon eradicate the buffalo completely from America? How does Vogel's environmental ignorance strike you in light of today's animal populations?

3. Select the state of *Rhode Island* and click on *Yankee Fisherman*. How are these people surviving the Depression? Why does their occupation offer more economic security in the Depression than other types of work? What are they dependent upon compared to other types of jobs?

4. Select the state of *Missouri* and click on *I Have Talked with Grandma Handy*. Why does Grandma Handy seem to show no remorse over her family's previous ownership of slaves? If you had to be a slave, would you have wanted to live on the Handy place? Provide reasons for your decision.

5. Select the state of *New Hampshire* and click on *Here We Can Be Glad #3*. What is the tone of this oral history? How do the reactions of the

millworker Katherine strike you when she is teased for being Polish? Why do you think immigrants from one ethnic group look down on another? Does this problem still exist in the United States?

6. Read several life histories from different states. Choose a colorful member of either your immediate or extended family and prepare questions to ask about his or her life.

RELATED INTERNET SITE(S)

Learning About Immigration Through Oral History
http://learning.loc.gov/learn/lesson97/oh1/ammem.html
Provides an excellent lesson plan for using *American Life Histories 1936– 1940*, to teach the oral history method.

THE NANJING MASSACRE (1937)

URL ADDRESS: http://japaneseculture.miningco.com/index.htm

SITE SUMMARY: No country in the world has a monopoly on either virtue or vice, and that is certainly true in the case of Japan during World War II. The Nanjing Massacre was one of the hidden holocausts of the war. When the Japanese army invaded the ancient Chinese city of Nanking (Nanjing), they systematically set about torturing and murdering 300,000 Chinese civilians. This site features photographs as primary sources. They may be too disturbing for adolescents to access without a teacher assigning some background and explanatory materials prior to an assignment. The site itself contains extensive overview material plus a map of the city as it existed at the time of the massacre.

DISCUSSION QUESTIONS AND ACTIVITIES

1. Why was this Asian holocaust referred to as "The Rape of Nanking"?

2. You have been appointed head of the Nanking War Crimes Investigatory Board and have been ordered to examine the degree to which there was a massacre in Nanking. What evidence in the photographs will you use to indict for war crimes the military officers who were in charge of the Japanese army that occupied Nanking?

3. Why do you think the Japanese soldiers were preconditioned to commit such atrocious crimes? How were they taught to view "the enemy"?

4. Select *The Nanjing Massacre Archive* and click on *Basic Facts on the Nan-*

jing Massacre and the Tokyo War Crimes Trial. Choose *The Tokyo War Crimes Trials.* What is your opinion of the justice that the war criminals received? Write an editorial for a Chinese newspaper giving your opinion of the trial and the verdicts. Were the sentences fair or too lenient? Should Japan have been forced to pay reparations to the victims' families?

5. You are the head of Amnesty International. Give a speech to members of the War College in Carlisle, Pennsylvania, warning them of the dangers of negative stereotyping of enemy forces. Do you think that the "fostering of the enemy as subhuman syndrome" should be made an international crime?

6. Find information about a similar massacre from any period of American, European, or Asian history. Compare the circumstances under which it occurred with those under which the Nanking massacre took place, noting the similarities and dissimilarities. Are there conditions that need to exist beforehand for massacres to take place? If so, identify them.

RELATED INTERNET SITE(S)

Basic Facts on the Nanjing Massacre and the Tokyo War Crimes Trials
http://japaneseculture.miningco.com/index.htm
   Provides Nanking massacre records, a chronology of events and summaries of the verdicts, and the sentences of the convicted Japanese war criminals.

Nanking
http://japaneseculture.miningco.com/index.htm
   Contains useful information and links by Princeton University students, who organized a conference about this horror-filled event.

U-BOAT WAR (1939–1945)

URL ADDRESS: http://uboat.net/

SITE SUMMARY: During World War II German submarines, hunting in groups called wolfpacks, sank thousands of merchant and Allied ships. This is one of the most comprehensive sites on the Web dealing with World War II convoy battles, submarine hunting areas, and wolfpack successes. It includes 100 photographs as well as lists of U-boat losses, captures, and other losses. Maps show where U-boats operated, and a section titled "Technologies" provides ship diagrams and torpedo

and other weapons diagrams. Another part contains twenty or more related Internet sites. A search engine supports queries by U-boat, commander, wolfpack, and more.

DISCUSSION QUESTIONS AND ACTIVITIES

1. Select *History*. Write a short military history paper showing how the
   Germans had the initial edge at the beginning of World War II because of their use of U-boats in World War I.

2. Select *Maps* and click on *US East Coast*. Identify the areas with the
   largest concentrations of U-boats. Why were the Germans placing
   their submarines in these areas?

3. Select *Maps*. Trace the sea routes that U.S. ships had to travel as part
   of the Lend-Lease Act to deliver defense materials to Great Britain
   and the Soviet Union. If you were the captain of a U.S. supply boat,
   which areas of the sea would you have feared the most? Why?

4. Select *The Laconia Incident*. In this incident there is guilt on the part of
   both the Axis and Allied powers. Because Germany lost the war, however, Admiral Donitz was found guilty of war crimes and served more
   than ten years in prison for them. Argue that the American bomber
   pilot was also guilty because he bombed boats that at the time were
   flying the Red Cross flag.

5. Select *U-boat Fates*. Prepare a statistics-based chart showing all of the
   U-boat losses and the areas in which they occurred. Based on your
   research, assess the chances of a German submariner surviving the
   war.

6. Select *The Peleus Affair*. In Chapter 2, the author cites examples of
   Allied submarine commanders gunning down defenseless Japanese
   sailors in lifeboats. Discuss the concept of scapegoating. Why do you
   think it is necessary that the victors in war publicly punish those they
   have vanquished? What purpose does it serve? What types of war
   crimes would you leave unpunished?

RELATED INTERNET SITE(S)

The U-Boat War in World War One
http://uboat.net/history/wwi/index.html
   This site provides an excellent overview of the World War I U-boat
battles. It documents the first use of the U-boat as an offensive weapon.

PRIMARY SOURCE DOCUMENTS ON THE HOLOCAUST
(1939–1945)

URL ADDRESS: http://www.lib.byu.edu/~rdh/eurodocs/germany.html

SITE SUMMARY: This site contains one of the most complete and organized sets of primary documents relating to the Holocaust. Any or all of them could be used for class discussion or assignments. Currently there are thirty-eight links that address issues such as Nazi statements on the Jewish Question, propaganda from *Mein Kampf*, the Wannsee Protocol, discriminatory decrees against the Jews, and Kristallnacht. It also includes information and documentation relating to euthanasia, the sterilization of Jewish workers, individual concentration camps, the Jager Report, crematorium construction, and a copy of the Eizenstat Report.

DISCUSSION QUESTIONS AND ACTIVITIES

1. Select *Primary Source Documents on the Holocaust* and click on *Nazi Statement on the Jewish Question*. Read several of the excerpted speeches by Hitler, Himmler, and others about their desire and plan to wipe out European Jewry. You are a young German Jewish doctor who has attended several rallies to hear Adolf Hitler speak. Tell your wife the type of things that you have heard. What is your opinion of Hitler?

2. Select *Hitler on Propaganda*. Based on his propaganda principles, choose an article about a recent crime from a local newspaper and rewrite it to Hitler's specifications. Distribute the article to your classmates and see if they can identify the parts that are propaganda.

3. Select *Wannsee Protocol*. Everyone denied that the Nazi regime had a systematic plan for Jewish genocide. You are a war crimes investigator who has just uncovered a copy of this protocol. What is the political significance of this document? What are the criminal implications for all the participants?

4. Select *Wannsee Protocol*. Why do you think that no one objected to the "solutions" proposed in this document? Do you know of any United States government official who objected to the internment of the Japanese in World War II? Although the Wannsee Protocol is clearly speaking of a plan for genocide, can you find any similarities between the German and American decisions?

5. Select *Discriminatory Decrees Against Jews*. Place these decrees in chron-

ological order and demonstrate with a chart or graph how the options for even life itself were systematically being denied Jews.

6. Select *Kristallnacht*. Was there anything "spontaneous" about this evening? Why were "healthy male Jews, not too old," to be arrested and transferred to concentration camps? What did the Nazis fear from them?

RELATED INTERNET SITE(S)

Cybrary of the Holocaust
http://remember.org/
This site contains full-text materials, images, eyewitness accounts, and bibliographies about the Holocaust.

Simon Wiesenthal Center
http://www.wiesenthal.com/
Dedicated to the concept of tolerance, this site chronicles the history of human rights and the Holocaust. It features exhibits, articles, glossaries, and links to other Holocaust sites.

CYBRARY OF THE HOLOCAUST (1939–1945)

URL ADDRESS: http://remember.org/

SITE SUMMARY: This extensive site is dedicated to the memory of the 6 million Jews and 5 million others who lost their lives in the Holocaust. The site is constantly being expanded by adding more Holocaust-related sites. An excellent search engine provides users with the ability to search for known items and keywords. The left column lists links to hundreds of primary sources. Beginning with photographs of the concentration camps Birkenau, Mauthausen, and Auschwitz, it moves to coverage of the trial of Adolf Eichmann. The trial site includes the list of charges, excerpted testimony of survivors, and the closing statement by Eichmann. Another part of the site contains additional eyewitness testimony by survivors, liberators, and other victims. A section called Historical Perspectives presents notes about the Wannsee Protocol, documentation pertaining to the liquidation of Lithuanian Jewry, and interviews with Holocaust historians.

DISCUSSION QUESTIONS AND ACTIVITIES

1. You have been asked to be on a television program to debate a Neo-Nazi who claims that he has proof that the Holocaust never happened.

What evidence will you use to refute this claim? Organize it into a detailed outline.

2. Use the outline developed in question 1 to prepare a television script showing the chronology of the Holocaust. Use the primary sources, including images, which are available at this site for your references.

3. Select *Witnesses* and click on *Survivors*. Based on the testimony that you have read, how would you describe the Nazi regime in terms of its technological approach to genocide? Why is the term "Holocaust" used to describe it?

4. Select *The Camps*. How close were Mauthausen, Birkenau, and Auschwitz to cities and towns? Based on their geographic location and the smoke emitted from the crematoriums, do you think the local population knew about the heinous crimes the Nazis were committing? If so, why do you think that they did nothing to stop them?

5. Select *The Trial of Adolf Eichmann*. What do you think of Eichmann's claim that he was powerless to resist orders from his military superiors? What evidence in the trial shows that he was one of Hitler's "willing executioners"?

6. Many people think that the Holocaust could never happen again. Juxtapose this statement against the evidence in Bosnia and other former Yugoslavian countries or the evidence in Burundi and Rwanda. What do you think should be the role of the United Nations in cases of genocide?

RELATED INTERNET SITE(S)

Holocaust: An Historical Summary
http://www.ushmm.org/education/history.html
    Provides an extensive full-text summary of people, places, and events relating to the Holocaust.

EDMC Holocaust Sites
http://coe.ohio-state.edu/edmc/websites/holocst.htm
    Includes a set of unannotated links to other online Holocaust sites.

POWERS OF PERSUASION POSTERS FROM WORLD WAR II (1939–1945)

URL ADDRESS: http://www.nara.gov/exhall/exhibits.html

SITE SUMMARY: On exhibit at the National Archives home page, this online site presents thirty-three American propaganda posters of World War II. A sound file with the song "Any Bonds Today?" is also accessible. The posters are divided into two subject categories. Posters in Part One were designed to imbue the viewer with patriotic feelings through the use of the colors in the American flag and pictures that conveyed physical strength. Part Two's posters show the horrors and carnage of war and were designed to elicit feelings of aggression toward the enemy.

DISCUSSION QUESTIONS AND ACTIVITIES

1. Look at the posters in *Part One* and *Part Two*. Which type of poster do you think might motivate the viewer to enlist as a soldier? Why?
2. Select *It's a Woman's War Too*. How did these posters glamorize secretarial and even factory jobs?
3. Select *It's a Woman's War Too*. Look at the poster of Rosie the Riveter. What happened after World War II to women who had wartime factory jobs? Look at some pictures of women in advertisements during the early fifties. How do they differ from the portrayal of Rosie the Riveter? Why do you think common stereotypes of women changed when the war ended?
4. Select *Warning! Our homes are in Danger*. The images of women and children in danger were based on results of a government study that found they were effective emotional devices. You are an ethicist. Write an article analyzing the emotional messages that are conveyed in this poster section and argue their immorality.
5. In Chapter 6 of Adolf Hitler's *Mein Kampf* he states that "all propaganda must be popular and its intellectual level must be adjusted to the most limited intelligence among those it is addressed to." What was the U.S. government's purpose in disseminating these posters?
6. Why do you think propaganda is considered a subtle kind of warfare?

RELATED INTERNET SITE(S)

Earth Station's Propaganda Poster Page
http:earthstation1.simplenet.com/warpostr.html
Contains additional images of American propaganda posters from World Wars I and II.

JAPANESE INTERNMENT (1942)

**URL ADDRESS: http://www.davison.k12.mi.us/academic/
hewitt11.htm**

SITE SUMMARY: After the signing of Executive Order 9066 by President Roosevelt on February 19, 1942, the U.S. Army began an immediate involuntary evacuation of approximately 120,000 Japanese Americans from their West Coast homes. They were transported to primitive relocation centers in some of the most desolate parts of the country. Since they were allowed to take only what they could carry, many lost all of their personal and real property. More than 70,000 of these internees were American citizens who were totally denied their rights under the Fourth Amendment to the U.S. Constitution. This site includes a timeline, an exclusion poster, a copy of Executive Order 9066, pictures and descriptions of life in several camps, and much more.

DISCUSSION QUESTIONS AND ACTIVITIES

1. Select *Executive Order 9066*. Does any part of the order indicate that it applies only to those of Japanese ancestry? Why did the United States concentrate on evacuating the Japanese and not those of German or Italian ancestry?

2. Select *Timeline*. Show that there was an increasing pattern of discrimination against the Japanese that goes back as far as 1912. Be sure to include information about the California Alien Land Law.

3. Select *An Exclusion Poster*. You are an American citizen of Japanese descent living in San Francisco who has just read Exclusion Order No. 27. You will be taken to an internment camp in Arkansas within the next twenty-four hours. Make a list of the things you will try to do to save the store and the house you own, your household goods, and other business investments of prime importance to you. Who in the way of neighbors, business colleagues, friends, clergy, or lawyers might be willing to help you?

4. You are a Japanese American who has two elementary school age children when you receive the order of internment. Describe the journey to one of the concentration camps shown at this site. Describe the living conditions once you arrived. Were your children able to go to school? What did you do during the time you were interned? How did you feel toward the United States when you were freed?

5. Select *The 442nd Go for Broke*. This was the most decorated unit of World War II. In reality, they fought on two fronts, one in Europe and one at home. Present the pros and cons of enlisting as a Japanese American in World War II. In the end, what would have been your personal decision?

6. Was the government justified in violating the Fourth Amendment in the case of the internment of those of Japanese ancestry? If your answer to this question is no, then do you think that the government

should have to pay reparations to all those who were interned and pay for lost property and profits during that time? Can you think of any time in the future when an order such as Executive Order 9066 might need to be enacted?

RELATED INTERNET SITE(S)

Japanese Internment
http://www.northcoast.com/~bbn.ako.html
Contains an emotional and powerful account of a Japanese American's internment during World War II and the effect that it has had on his parents' life and his own.

Museum of the City of San Francisco
http://shell3.ba.best.com/~sfmuseum/hist1/subjects.html
Provides an extensive collection of primary sources, including hundreds of newspaper articles grouped by year and week, relating to the internment of the Japanese during World War II.

WORLD WAR II (1939–1945)

URL ADDRESS: http://www.yale.edu/lawweb/avalon/wwii/wwii.htm

SITE SUMMARY: Although there are thousands of documents concerning World War II, students are usually introduced to ones that are considered by historians to be significant to the conduct and cessation of the war. This site features many of these documents. Within alphabetized links are thirty-seven documents. Included are the Atlantic Charter as well as documents from the Cairo Conference, the Casablanca Conference, and the Potsdam Conference. The site also includes the declarations of war with Japan, Germany, and Italy; documents concerning Germany's invasion of Poland; the Master Lend-Lease Agreement; Pearl Harbor documents; and documents related to the Yalta Conference.

DISCUSSION QUESTIONS AND ACTIVITIES

1. Select *The Atlantic Charter*. The war was far from over when President Roosevelt and Prime Minister Winston Churchill signed this document. Although it was meant to rally support for the war effort, it has a postwar perspective. What parts of it seem to be postwar plans?

2. Select *British War Blue Book* and click on *No. 9: Speech by the Prime Minister at Birmingham on March 17, 1939*. What is Prime Minister Neville Chamberlain's view on Hitler's taking over Czechoslovakia? Why does he keep referring to the agreement at Munich?

3. Select *Agreement between the United Kingdom and the Union of Soviet Socialist Republics: July 12, 1941*. Why did Stalin sign a nonaggression pact with Hitler in 1939 and this one with Great Britain in 1942? Did Stalin buy any time by siding with Hitler initially?

4. Select *France's Response to Germany's Invasion of Poland* and read the correspondence. Although France was pledged to help Poland if the latter was attacked by Germany, France did not come to the aid of Poland. Instead, two days after the attack, France declared war on Germany. Imagine that France had helped Poland defend itself militarily. Would the progress of the war have been any different?

5. For a time, President Roosevelt tried to fight the war by making the United States "an arsenal of democracy." Select various documents and correspondence that support that statement.

6. Select *Yalta Conference*. Compare this agreement to the Atlantic Charter. Where were there loopholes for Stalin to control most of Eastern Europe? How would you have rewritten the Yalta Conference agreement? What territories, if any, would you have given to the Soviets and the British?

RELATED INTERNET SITE(S)

World War II Archive
http://www.msstate.edu/Archives/History/USA/WWII/ww2.html
Contains documents, pictures, and Quicktime and MPEG movies of World War II.

World War II Page
http://gi.grolier.com/wwii/wwii_mainpage.html
Includes articles, photographs, air combat film clips, bibliographies, and a World War II quiz.

Yahoo! World War II
http://www.yahoo.com/Arts/Humanities/History/20th_Century/World_War_II/
This is an excellent gateway site to World War II archives, battles and campaigns, Japanese war crimes, personal accounts, prisoners of war sites, and much more.

WHAT DID YOU DO IN THE WAR GRANDMA? WOMEN AND WORLD WAR II (1939–1945)

URL ADDRESS: http://www.stg.brown.edu/projects/WWII_Women/ tocCS.html

SITE SUMMARY: While American men fought in various overseas battles and came home as decorated heroes, American women took their jobs in the many civilian and defense positions that were created as the United States shifted from a peacetime to a wartime economy. American war production exceeded that of the three Axis nations combined thanks to the efforts of millions of American women. The most valuable parts of this site are the interviews conducted with women who worked in the factories and at other jobs during this stressful period. The site also contains an excellent introduction about the contribution American women made to the war effort, a brief timeline of World War II events, a glossary of terms, a bibliography, and links to other World War II Internet sites.

DISCUSSION QUESTIONS AND ACTIVITIES

1. How did the war broaden women's horizons? What opportunities did it give them that they had never had before? What types of jobs had they previously been confined to, and at what level of pay? Write a letter to your granddaughter telling her how working in a factory during the war changed your life.

2. What motivated millions of women to go to work? Was it patriotism and war propaganda, or was it the pay, the feeling of independence, companionship, and the chance to learn new skills?

3. Select *Table of Contents* and click on *Coming to Terms with the Holocaust . . . and Prejudice at Home*. What were the lessons that Judith Weiss Cohen learned in World War II? How did moving to Georgia for basic training change her?

4. Select *Table of Contents* and click on *Washington Was As Far As She Got*. This interview describes women so dedicated that they keep secrets that even impact their personal lives. Do you think that Americans would be that patriotic and obedient if a similar war were fought today? Why or why not?

5. Prepare a chart showing how the war helped lift America out of the Great Depression. Include factors such as the lifting of price controls; the need for increased production of all kinds of war materials and foodstuffs; higher wages; and the shortage of labor.

6. How do you think women felt after the war when most left their jobs and became homemakers again? Discuss the loss of wages, independence, personal freedom, and other ideas you have about what may have affected them. What problems may they have experienced in their marriages?

RELATED INTERNET SITE(S)

Women at War (at Redstone Arsenal)
http://www.redstone.army.mil/history/women/welcome.html
This site contains extensive text and several photographs discussing and showing the work that women did in a $40 million war plant in Huntsville, Alabama.

VOICES FROM THE DUST BOWL (1940–1941)

URL ADDRESS: http://rs6.loc.gov/amhome.html

SITE SUMMARY: The Great Depression was partially caused by a disastrous combination of climactic and economic factors that led to a demographic shift in population from states affected by drought and soil erosion to western states. This collection features the songs, dances, meetings, conversations, and first-person accounts of migrant workers in the central California camps established by the government in 1940 and 1941. The site is browsable by keyword, song text, photographs, performers and interviewees, and audio titles. The song collection is particularly rich in evoking feelings of sadness and the mournful tone of people forced to leave their homes and start their lives over again with almost nothing.

DISCUSSION QUESTIONS AND ACTIVITIES

1. Select *Migrant Experience*. Describe the "Dust Bowl" syndrome. What economic, geographic, and agricultural factors led to it?

2. Remain in *Migrant Experience*. Why did so many Dust Bowlers head for California? Include the titles and words to folk songs that they may have heard which described the nice life in California. Why has this state seemed to be the destination of so many people in search of the American Dream?

3. Why were the Anglo migrants referred to as "Okies" even though only 20 percent of them came from Oklahoma? What background and

economic and social conditions did the Anglo migrants have in common that caused people to negatively stereotype them?

4. California also had a non-Anglo migrant population. They were primarily from Mexico and the Philippines. From the interviews and photographs in *Migrant Experience*, how did the Mexicans feel about discrimination and life in the camps? Since they were not newcomers, how might they have felt toward the Anglo migrants?

5. What purpose did the Farm Security Administration camps serve in helping migrants adjust to their new surroundings, jobs, and poor living conditions? Find songs that support your description of the migrant experience and cite some of the lyrics, or play them as part of an oral presentation.

6. You are a migrant worker from a farm in Arkansas. Write a song that expresses the homesickness or depicts the discrimination you feel in California.

RELATED INTERNET SITE(S)

The American Experience
http://www.pbs.org/wgbh/pages/amex/dustbowl/interviews.html
   Contains interviews of Americans who survived the Dust Bowl.

California Gold: Northern California Folk Music from the Thirties
http://rs6.loc.gov/amhome.html
   This site is part of the Library of Congress American Memory Project. While the majority of folk music is of different ethnic groups, there is a section of music from the Anglo tradition that captures life in the thirties.

Dust Bowl Disaster
http://www.letsfindout.com/subjects/
   Provides an overview and background material about the conditions that produced the Dust Bowl.

VENONA PROJECT (1943–1980)

URL ADDRESS: http://www.nsa.gov.8080/docs/venona/venona.html

SITE SUMMARY: Secret codes, espionage, and treason are the ingredients for one of the most exciting collections of primary source documents about the U.S. Signals Intelligence Service's involvement with Soviet KGB code messages from the 1940s. The purpose of the project was to read and exploit, when necessary, Soviet diplomatic communications. The results were astounding. In 1947 message traffic showed that someone on the U.S. War Department General Staff was a spy and that Julius and Ethel Rosenberg were involved in serious espionage. The site contains monographic materials by several people who worked on the project along with pictures of the messages, images of the code traffic, telegrams, and declassified government documents. A helpful index by year, month, and day is also included.

DISCUSSION QUESTIONS AND ACTIVITIES

1. Select *Images of the Venona Documents* and click on the year *1944*. Choose *July 26*. "Antenna" was the trade or code name for Julius Rosenberg. How would you use this correspondence as evidence against Julius Rosenberg if you were the prosecutor trying him for espionage? How would you explain its contents if you were Emanuel Bloch, the lawyer who defended Rosenberg?

2. Select *Images of the Venona Documents* and click on the year *1944*. Choose *May 5*. What background and predisposition to possible re-cruitment as a Russian agent did Alfred Sarant exhibit to Julius Ro-senberg? Describe the educational background and personal qualities that you would look for when recruiting spies on behalf of the United States government for espionage in Iraq.

3. Select *Images of the Venona Documents* and click on the year *1944*. Choose *June 14*. Imagine that you have successfully identified Antenna as the code name for Julius Rosenberg. How would you interpret the message dated June 14, 1944?

4. Select *Images of the Venona Documents* and click on the year *1944*. Choose *June 15*. The Russian code name for the Manhattan Project was ENORMOZ. What was happening in Russia at this time? Why, if they were considered our allies, were the Russians being left out of the loop with regard to the latest developments in the Manhattan Project?

5. Select *Images of the Venona Documents* and click on the year *1944*. Choose *June 28*. Who was Donald Maclean? What do you think his reasons were for treason? What role did he play in the spy case in-volving Kim Philby, one of the most remarkable double agents of the twentieth century?

6. Imagine that you are the head of a Venona-like project that has been ordered to monitor electronic, print, and other forms of correspon-dence between Iraq and the United States. What kinds of information would interest you the most? How would you go about recruiting people for an Iraqi-based spy network? Which Iraqis, and in what

positions, would you monitor for suspicion of espionage against the United States?

RELATED INTERNET SITE(S)

Images of the Trial of Julius and Ethel Rosenberg
http://www.law.umkc.edu/faculty/projects/ftrials/rosenb/
ROS_CT.HTM
Contains the full text of the court decisions affirming the convictions of the Rosenbergs.

Trial of Julius and Ethel Rosenberg—Biographies of Participants
http://www.law.umkc.edu/faculty/projects/ftrials/rosenb/
ROS_BIOG.HTM
Provides short biographical sketches of Julius and Ethel Rosenberg as well as other defendants, prosecution witnesses, defense attorneys, and judges.

A-BOMB WWW MUSEUM (1945)

URL ADDRESS: http://www.csi.ad.jp/ABOMB/index.html

SITE SUMMARY: This emotionally riveting site contains scientific and historical primary sources about the dropping of atomic bombs on the Japanese cities of Hiroshima and Nagasaki in 1945. Beginning with the structure of the B-29 plane named *Enola Gay*, the site provides useful background material about the heat, radiation, and bomb blast itself. A cumulative chart of "deaths of survivors from 1952–1992" is included along with significant numbers of eyewitness accounts in sound and text. There are photographs showing the destruction caused by the bombs, medical information about the second Hiroshima and Nagasaki genera-tions, and messages from the mayors of both cities. The site also features a list of books and related materials.

DISCUSSION QUESTIONS AND ACTIVITIES

1. Select *Introduction: About the Bomb*. What were the physical effects of the A-bomb dropped on Hiroshima? How many people were imme-diately killed? How many people later died of the effects of radiation?

2. Select *Voices of A-Bomb Survivors*. From your reading of their accounts, do you think that the United States should have dropped atomic weapons on Japan?

3. Select *A Child's Experience*. Read this account and imagine that you are this child. Write an essay as an adult expressing your opinion of war.

4. Select *Things that Tell the Story*. Based on this link and other information at this site, do you think that nuclear weapons should or should not be abolished?

5. Was it easier for the United States to use the bomb against people of a different race than it would have been to use it against, for example, the Germans? Argue the pros and cons of your view.

6. Under what circumstances, if any, would you justify using a nuclear weapon against another nation?

RELATED INTERNET SITE(S)

Hiroshima and Nagasaki Exhibition
http://www.oneworld.org/gallery/hiroshima/hiroshima_top.html
Contains a gallery of photographs by Yosuke Yamahata of Hiroshima and Nagasaki at the time of the bombings.

Manhattan Project
http://www.gis.net/~carter/manhattan/
Discusses the race to build the first atomic bomb. It also includes a set of excellent related links.

THE JAPANESE SURRENDER DOCUMENTS OF WORLD WAR II (1945)

URL ADDRESS: http://www.law.ou.edu/hist/japsurr.html

SITE SUMMARY: On September 12, 1945, after numerous bloody battles and the atomic bombings of Hiroshima and Nagasaki, Emperor Hirohito of Japan, Yoshijiro Umezu, Chief of the General Staff of the Japanese Imperial Army, and Soemu Toyoda, Chief of the General Staff of the Japanese Imperial Navy, signed a formal surrender document. In it they agreed to cease all hostilities and to liberate all Allied prisoners of war and internees and transport them to places as directed. The Japanese also consented to the control of their country and to obey the orders and directives of the Supreme Commander of the Allied Powers, General Douglas MacArthur.

DISCUSSION QUESTIONS AND ACTIVITIES

1. Read the surrender documents. Summarize them in one page and create a map showing all the countries and regions of the world from which the Japanese agreed to withdraw.

2. Compare the surrender documents to the Treaty of Versailles at http://www.lib.byu.edu/~rdh/wwi/versailles.html. What are the major differences?

3. Why didn't the Allies demand more from Japan? Were there lessons that they had learned from Germany's surrender in World War I?

4. Read about the Rape of Nanking, Pearl Harbor, and the Bataan Death March. What do you think of the surrender documents in light of Japan's atrocities?

5. Imagine that you are a Japanese soldier who has learned that Emperor Hirohito has just surrendered Japan to the Allied powers. How do you think you would feel?

6. Write your own documents of surrender for Japan. Include a clause about educating future generations about the causes and consequences of Japan's involvement in World War II.

RELATED INTERNET SITE(S)

Japanese Surrender Documents
http://www.yale.edu/lawweb/avalon/wwii/jmenu.htm
Provides full-text background material about the events leading up to and including the bombings of Hiroshima and Nagasaki.

NUREMBERG WAR CRIMES TRIALS (1945–1946)

URL ADDRESS: http://www.yale.edu/lawweb/avalon/imt/imt.htm

SITE SUMMARY: Following World War II, some German leaders were tried by the International Military Tribunal for crimes against peace, crimes against humanity, and war crimes. Included in this site are the motions, orders of the tribunal, presentation of cases, testimony of witnesses, and key documents related to the proceedings. The site also contains a list of additional Internet sites related to the Holocaust and other aspects of the Nuremberg Trials. Links to volume numbers of the entire proceedings can reproduce all the documents and events that occurred during a specific time span of the trials.

DISCUSSION QUESTIONS AND ACTIVITIES

1. How should war crimes be defined? In war, can there be such a thing as a war crime?

2. What do you consider crimes against humanity to be? Which countries in the past ten years have engaged in crimes against humanity? How do you think the world should deal with crimes against humanity?

3. Select *Nuremberg Trials: Testimony of Witnesses*. Most of the witnesses keep saying that they were only obeying orders and that obeying orders was part of being a good German citizen. How would you refute this defense if you were the head prosecutor? What argument(s) would you employ?

4. Read Henry David Thoreau's essay *On Civil Disobedience*. At what point do you think a German soldier should have refused to obey an order by his superior officer?

5. In 1945 the United States dropped two atomic bombs on Japan, killing hundreds of thousands of civilians. Do you think that this should have been considered a war crime?

6. What conditions in Germany may have set the stage for the Holocaust? Do you think that only the Germans could have committed these crimes, or could they just as easily have been committed by another European nation or even the United States under similar circumstances?

RELATED INTERNET SITE(S)

Cybrary of the Holocaust
http://remember.org/
   This is the largest site for information about various concentration camps, victims, and Holocaust statistics.

Simon Wiesenthal Center
http://www.wiesenthal.com/
   Dedicated to the former hunter of Nazi criminals, this site features related Holocaust links, eyewitness testimony, and information about searching for lost property and savings accounts from this time.

CRIME, JUSTICE & RACE IN SOUTH AFRICA
(1948–Present)

URL ADDRESS: http://www.uaa.alaska.edu/just/just490/

SITE SUMMARY: South Africa's history from the period of Dutch and British colonization bears the cultural, economic, and societal scars of slavery, indenture, and unfair laws that culminated in the racist laws of apartheid under the Nationalist Government from 1948 to 1993. This site contains hundreds of papers, reports, position statements, laws, policies, and other data that tell the past and recent history of South Africa. The site is searchable from a wide variety of categories such as news, history, human rights, government and politics, criminal justice and policing, and security. A search engine supports keyword as well as Boolean queries.

DISCUSSION QUESTIONS AND ACTIVITIES

1. Select *History* and click on *South Africa: History*. Prepare a hyperlinked chronology from South Africa's beginnings to the end of the apartheid era that contains significant events, people, policies, places, and wars.

2. Select *History* and click on *Conflict on the Frontiers of Colonial Expansion*. How did the discovery of gold and diamonds in South Africa set the stage for indigenous South African tribes to lose their lands? Compare these events to the effects of the discovery of gold in the Black Hills of North Dakota on the history of the Sioux tribe.

3. Select *History* and click on *The Apartheid State*. Apartheid truly constituted the dark ages of South Africa. What was apartheid? What was its ultimate goal? What were the government's policies and laws regarding it?

4. Imagine that the United States had practiced apartheid between blue-eyed and brown-eyed people from 1948 to 1993. For forty-five years, blue-eyed people have been prohibited from voting, marrying brown-eyed people, or living or working in certain areas of the country. What do you think the legacy of this practice might be in terms of the desire for revenge, justice, reparations, and equal opportunities?

5. Describe the federal and Jim Crow laws of the United States up until the civil rights movement. What are the similarities between our past discriminatory laws and practices against African Americans and those of South Africa? Compare racial discrimination in the United States to South Africa's practice of apartheid.

6. Select *Truth and Reconciliation*. What has the new government of South

Africa done to deal with its past and to avoid the bloodshed born of previous crimes, massacres, and gross injustices committed against people of color? Imagine that you are in charge of this South African reconciliation program. What things would you do to try to unite all the peoples of South Africa into one nation?

RELATED INTERNET SITE(S)

Basic Facts About South Africa
http://www.southafrica.net/reference/facts.html
Contains information about the economy, foreign relations, religions, culture, and peoples of South Africa.

JumpStart
http://www.mg.co.za/mg/jump/jump.html
Serves as a gateway site for related links about politics, business, education, and travel in South Africa.

TIBET: TRADITION AND CHANGE (1950s)

URL ADDRESS: http://www.asianart.com/exhibitions/albuquerque/index.html

SITE SUMMARY: This Asian country, often referred to as "The Roof of the World," has always been shrouded in mystery. It is home to the world's highest mountain, Mount Everest, and has unwillingly been part of China since the 1950s. Its people are intensely religious, turning prayer wheels and reciting prayers on the streets. Their religion is a branch of Buddhism called Lamaism. This exhibit of expandable images shows various artifacts that were inspired by the Tibetan religion. The explanations, by a curator of the Albuquerque Museum, are filled with excellent background material on Tibet and Buddhism.

DISCUSSION QUESTIONS AND ACTIVITIES

1. Tibetan Buddhism is a branch of Buddhism called Lamaism. What are its general characteristics and tenets?

2. In Tibetan Buddhism the Dalai Lama is central to the spiritual and temporal life of the nation. Why would the Chinese seek to undermine the power of Tibetan monks and force their leader, the Dalai Lama, to live in exile?

3. Look at some of the images depicting various Buddhas. You are an

archaeologist who has just uncovered this cache of Tibetan antiquities. Based on the positions of the Buddhas, the theme of the compositions, and the imagery portrayed, how would you characterize the people of Tibet from these previous centuries? Do you think that they were a militaristic people? What actions are the Buddhas usually engaged in that may provide you with clues about Tibetan society?

4. Look at the mandalas, images of angry deities, that are at the site. How would you interpret them if you saw them for the first time?

5. How do the gestures, attributes, and postures of the monks depicted at this site indicate that they have achieved "Buddhahood"?

6. Argue the pros and cons that the practice of Tibetan Buddhism might pose a threat to China. Give specific examples based on Tibetan religious beliefs.

RELATED INTERNET SITE(S)

Everest '97
http://www.everest.mountainzone.com/
   This extensive interactive site about the climbing of Mount Everest also has several links devoted to the religious practices of Tibetans.

Tibet Home Page
http://www.tibet.org/
   Provides background material and current information about the political situation in Tibet.

THE UNITED STATES, CHINA, AND THE BOMB
(1950s–Present)

URL ADDRESS: http://www.seas.gwu.edu/nsarchive/NSAEBB1/NSAEBB1/nsaebb1.htm

SITE SUMMARY: The United States makes it its business to monitor the proliferation of nuclear weapons to protect its citizens. It uses the data it collects to formulate American nuclear strategies vis-à-vis other countries and in negotiating nuclear power nonproliferation treaties. At this site are documents from the 1950s that show the extent to which the United States knew of Chinese nuclear development, including weapons delivery systems and strategic planning. In addition to spying on China's nuclear program, the CIA, the State Department, and the Department of Defense were interested in China's role in facilitating nuclear weapons production in other Asian countries.

DISCUSSION QUESTIONS AND ACTIVITIES

1. Select *Document 1* "Implications of a Chinese Communist Nuclear Capability" (April 17, 1964). In sections 2a–c of this document, Robert Johnson, one of the State Department's leading China experts, recommends that the United States maintain a posture that combines an "implicit nuclear threat with a visible ability to deal conventionally with Communist aggression." How does this position statement and others like it in 2a–c make it difficult for the United States to involve China in disarmament negotiations, as Johnson recommends in section 2d?

2. Select *Document 2* "The Chances of an Imminent Communist Chinese Nuclear Explosion" (April 26, 1964). The United States was beginning to escalate its involvement in the Vietnam War under President Lyndon Johnson. Vietnam shares a border with China. Why do you think that the timing of a Chinese atomic test was a source of controversy for the United States?

3. Select *Document 3* "Memorandum for the Record, McGeorge Bundy" (September 15, 1964). At this meeting President Lyndon Johnson and his top advisors have ruled out a preemptive strike against China before its first nuclear test. What is so shocking about this report? Why is the United States considering involving the Soviet Union as a partner in a possible joint military action? Why were parts of this government document excised?

4. Select *Document 4* "China as a Nuclear Power" (October 7, 1964). This document discusses the possible need to attack Chinese nuclear weapons facilities as a counterproliferation measure. What position statements and demands were the Chinese making in regard to Taiwan, South Vietnam, Korea, and other countries that may have influenced the writing of this "worst case scenario"?

5. Select *Document 5* "State Department Telegram No. 2025 to U.S. Embassy Paris" (October 9, 1964). This document discusses the pros and cons of a military attack on China's nuclear facilities. As president of the United States, what might have been your reaction to this report?

6. What right did the United States have to consider a military strike against China because it was going to conduct its first nuclear test? How would you have resolved this problem if you had been president of the United States during that time?

RELATED INTERNET SITE(S)

China's Nuclear Weapons
http://www.enviroweb.org/enviroissues/nuketesting/hew/China/index.html

This site contains information and images of China's first nuclear explosion and subsequent ones including test number 6.

China's Nuclear Weapons and Testing Program
http://www.greenpeace.org/~comms/nukes/ctbt/read11.html
This is a rather extensive site that provides a comparative history of China's nuclear testing program and its current policy regarding various test ban treaties.

KOREAN WAR PROJECT (1950–1953)

URL ADDRESS: http://www.koreanwar.org/

SITE SUMMARY: Battle maps, first-person accounts of battle, lengthy diary entries, poems, casualty lists, and information on the missing in action are just some of the useful links at this gateway site. It also provides information about the Vietnam War and includes military assistance links to make contact with former soldiers and friends. It is dedicated to providing a service to Korean veterans, their families, researchers, and military history students. The site features an excellent search engine which users can employ to efficiently find information about specific battles, fronts, generals, and much more.

DISCUSSION QUESTIONS AND ACTIVITIES

1. Select *History-Reference* and click on *Overview of the Korean War*. Did President Truman overstep his authority by not consulting Congress in ordering American troops to help repel the North Korean invasion of South Korea? Why or why not?

2. You are a fifty-seven-year-old United States veteran of the Korean War. After you finished your service you discovered that 54,200 Americans were killed and 103,300 were wounded. Describe your feelings at that time and now toward the war. Do you see any differences between the Korean and Vietnam wars? Should the United States have fought in one, neither, or both?

3. Select *Maps*. Choose appropriate maps that show the successful offensive by United Nations and South Korean troops at Inchon and the advance north up to the Yalu River border. What mistake did General Douglas MacArthur make at this point in his military strategy? What were the results of that mistake?

4. Select *History-Reference* and click on *On the Front—Recollections*. In gen-

eral terms, how would you describe these veterans' attitudes toward their participation in the Korean War? After reading their recollections, would you have wanted to fight in Korea? Why or why not?

5. Why was public dissent over the Korean War less intense than that over the Vietnam War?

6. What do you think were the political consequences of the war? Were any lessons learned?

RELATED INTERNET SITE(S)

An Eyewitness: A Korean Remembers
http://www.kimsoft.com/korea/eyewit.htm
   This site has links to Vietnam and Korean War casualty lists, information about the history of the Korean War, and materials about veterans' groups.

SENATOR JOE MCCARTHY—A MULTIMEDIA CELEBRATION (1950–1954)

URL ADDRESS: http://webcorp.com/mccarthy/

SITE SUMMARY: Recordings are excellent primary sources because they capture the emotion behind a person's words. The way a phrase is uttered, pronounced, or lingered over can have a surprising set of effects on an audience. This site includes audio excerpts, some as long as ten minutes, of speeches and other statements by Senator Joseph McCarthy during selected years of his reign of terror over government officials, Hollywood figures, and other people who crossed his path. McCarthy's unsubstantiated charges of subversive activities and Communist Party membership ruined many careers and reputations, and sometimes even caused the death of innocent American citizens.

DISCUSSION QUESTIONS AND ACTIVITIES

1. Listen to *Joe McCarthy REAL AUDIO!* From this ten-minute excerpt of a speech, how do you think McCarthy got his power? What was the political climate in the United States at that time that allowed McCarthy to thrive?

2. What right, as a United States senator, did McCarthy have to name you as a suspected communist in a public speech? Could you have sued him for libel?

3. Compare McCarthy's Red Scare to the Salem Witch Trials. What are the similarities and dissimilarities?

4. A short video of President Richard M. Nixon with Senator Joseph McCarthy is on this site. What was Nixon's role in the McCarthy Red Scare? Why might Nixon's role in the McCarthy hearings have helped him when he decided to visit Communist China?

5. Why did it take so long to censure McCarthy? What insidious political purpose did he serve in a two-party political system?

6. What circumstances could create another Joseph McCarthy in the United States? What conditions do you think must exist for someone like this to come to power? Are there any safeguards that you think the United States should have in place to prevent this from occurring again in our legislative branch?

RELATED INTERNET SITE(S)

Red Scare
http://www.scsd.k12.ny.us/alex/coldwar/redscare.htm
Provides a two-part, content-rich overview of how and why Senator Joseph McCarthy was able to come to power.

EVEREST '97 (1953–1997)

URL ADDRESS: http://www.everest.mountainzone.com/everest.stm

SITE SUMMARY: Exploration has always made the history headlines, but ever since 1852, when Everest was found to be the highest mountain in the world, it has been a constant challenge for climbers to explore its surfaces and conquer its peak. Although the summit was finally reached in 1953 by Sir Edmund Hillary and Sherpa Tenzing Norgay, it has remained unattainable to many present-day climbers. This multimedia site features dispatches from various climbing expeditions, maps and routes, responses from individual climbers responding to online questions, and a video. It also contains a section about Sherpa culture and the story of the fatal 1996 Everest tragedy.

DISCUSSION QUESTIONS AND ACTIVITIES

1. Select *Maps & Routes*. You are on an anniversary expedition that will celebrate Sir Edmund Hillary and Tenzing Norgay's successful Ever-

est ascent. Draw a map showing the route that Hillary and Norgay took and the places they camped on the way up.

2. Select *High Altitude Phys*. You have signed up to go on an Everest expedition next year. Describe the physical challenges that you may face at such high altitudes. What drugs and methods do you plan to use to acclimatize yourself?

3. Select *Sherpa Culture*. Imagine that you are a Sherpa who has assisted on several Everest climbs. How do you feel about the people who have taken credit for climbing Everest? Could these climbers have made it without the Sherpas? Write a contract that you will require the next group of climbers to sign that includes provisions dealing with royalties for book and film productions, a life insurance policy that will take care of your family, disability payments in case you are permanently injured and cannot work again, and so forth.

4. Select *The May '96 Tragedy*. The Nepalese government has placed you in charge of investigating the May 1996 Everest tragedy when ten climbers lost their lives. You are to isolate the major factors responsible for so many deaths. Analyze the failure to descend the summit by a prearranged time, the weather conditions, the physical condition of the climbers, failure to place descension ropes in place, and other factors you consider contributed to this tragedy.

5. History was made in 1953 when Sir Edmund Hillary and Tenzing Norgay summited Mount Everest. What is to be achieved by more people endangering their lives to climb in their footsteps, doing more damage to a fragile environment? Argue that climbing Everest should be prohibited because of the threat to life and the harm to the environment it poses.

6. Why is it human nature to want to challenge Mother Nature?

RELATED INTERNET SITE(S)

The Climb
http://vitalsoft.org.org.mx/mja/everest.97/theclimb.html
   Relates the story of Andres Delgado's climb to the summit of Everest. The site also contains excellent photographs.

CIA AND ASSASSINATIONS: THE GUATEMALA 1954 DOCUMENTS (1954)

URL ADDRESS: http://www.seas.gwu.edu/nsarchive/NSAEBB/ NSAEBB4/index.html

SITE SUMMARY: Most U.S. citizens think of "covert operations" as something that their government has engaged in only recently, as in the case of the Iran-Contra affair. This site presents documents that show otherwise. Fear of the growing presence of a Russian satellite in Central America caused President Eisenhower's administration great alarm. In 1954 the administration determined that Guatemala was receiving arms shipments from Czechoslovakia. A decision was made to overthrow President Jacobo Arbenz Guzmán and to arm and organize a resistance movement to destabilize the government. The U.S. Central Intelligence Agency (CIA) was commissioned to do it. This site includes an instructional guide on assassination, proposals of assassination, and a list of people to be eliminated.

DISCUSSION QUESTIONS AND ACTIVITIES

1. How did the agrarian reform policies of newly elected President Arbenz conflict with the interests of the U.S.-based United Fruit Company, which was the largest landowner at that time in Guatemala?

2. What was the CIA attitude toward the government of Guatemala? Why were they afraid of a nationalistic government, and why did they refer to it as a "banana republic"?

3. In 1952 President Truman authorized a CIA-backed operation code-named PBFORUNE. What was its purpose? What constitutional right did the president have to undertake such a plan?

4. In 1953 President Eisenhower authorized a $2.7 million budget for "psychological warfare and political action" and a "subversion" plan to overthrow President Arbenz of Guatemala and his supporters. What do you think is the legacy of such actions by our government in Guatemala? How might the United States be viewed as a country by the Guatemalan people?

5. Select the documents related to the "CIA and Guatemalan Assassination Proposals." Do you think that the United States government did or did not follow through with their assassination plans?

6. The year is 1954. You are a reporter who has just received a packet containing copies of these materials in the mail. How would you go about verifying them? Would you be afraid to publish them? Would you publish them? How do you think your readers would react? Research the political climate of the United States in the early 1950s.

RELATED INTERNET SITE(S)

Latin American Studies
http://lanic.utexas.edu/las.html

Provides excellent background material on the government and history of Guatemala.

Political Database of the Americas
http://www.georgetown.edu/LatAmerPolitical/home.html
Includes information about the government, political parties, and international affairs of all Central American countries.

U.S. NUCLEAR HISTORY DOCUMENTATION PROJECT (1955–1982)

URL ADDRESS: http://www.seas.gwu.edu/nsarchive/nsa/NC/ nuchis.html

SITE SUMMARY: This site is a work in progress as key documents are declassified and made available through the Freedom of Information Act. The National Security Archive is putting key documents online that show U.S. nuclear policy and programs. The archive is divided into two parts. The first part includes policies, intelligence reports, and plans from 1955 to 1968, when the Pentagon added the B-52 bomber and the Polaris and Minuteman missiles to its nuclear arsenal. The second part covers 1969–1992, when new systems such as the Trident and MX were introduced, and when revived confrontation and parity building against the Soviets were the order of the day.

DISCUSSION QUESTIONS AND ACTIVITIES

1. Select *Document One*. Imagine that you are a historian who has been asked to write a short article about the buildup of the military-industrial complex in the 1950s. What does this document reveal to you about U.S. nuclear readiness at this point?

2. Select *Document Two*. Every year from the mid-1950s until 1964, the National Security Council's Best Evaluation Subcommittee (NESC) presented a report to the president and the National Security Council assessing the outcome of a U.S.-Soviet strategic nuclear war. Does this report strike you as "nuclear overkill"? Why was this type of arms race so dangerous to the United States and the rest of the world?

3. Select *Document Three*. The employment of Jupiter nuclear missiles in Italy involved a system in which both Italian and U.S. Air Force officers would turn keys. Why did arming the Jupiter and using a two-key system violate the Atomic Energy Act? What were the political

implications of this practice for President Kennedy and his involvement in the 1962 Cuban missile crisis?

4. Select *Document Four*. This brief cable from Lt. General James Walsh of the 7th Air Force, South Ruislip, England, describes one of the "occasional near misses" that have characterized the history of the nuclear weapons program. Discuss factors that could have contributed to a detonation. Are some of those factors still present even though the arms race has stopped?

5. Select *Document Five*. Chapter 27 is part of a study that reveals how vulnerable the United States was to a "surprise nuclear attack." Based on the nature of our command and control systems, how vulnerable do you think we are now to a terrorist nuclear attack?

6. Select *Document Six*. This document, which was prepared during the 1961 Berlin crisis, gave considerable freedom for the United States to fly over various foreign countries and to deploy nuclear weapons in their territory. You are a member of the Canadian National Security Council. Write a report to your government on the pros and cons of signing such an agreement.

RELATED INTERNET SITE(S)

Related Nuclear Weapons Sites
http://www.brook.edu/FP/PROJECTS/NUCWCOST/RELATED.HTM
This is an extensive site containing historical and current information about the nuclear arms race, individual weapons, and their atomic legacy.

EUROPEAN UNION (1957–Present)

URL ADDRESS: http://www.europa.eu.int/

SITE SUMMARY: The European Union promises to be one of the major trading powers of the twenty-first century. Its ultimate goal is to form a closer union among all the European nations through the use of a union flag, anthem, currency, trading practices, and universal European citizenship. The site is comprehensive, and it furnishes users with an excellent history, the full text of all pertinent treaties, an agenda for the year 2000, relevant legislation, and individual nations' statistics. It also provides online access to various publications, databases, and other documents.

DISCUSSION QUESTIONS AND ACTIVITIES

1. What is the ultimate goal of the European Union? How does the adoption of a European Union flag, anthem, currency, trading practices, and universal European citizenship foster this goal? Compare this union to others that Europe has had in the past, such as its inclusion in the Roman Empire.

2. Select *Thematic Chronologies*. Choose significant events, documents, trade agreements, and other matters related to the European Union and update this chronology through the present year.

3. The European Union at present numbers fifteen countries. In "Agenda 200" the European Union intends to consider applications from Central and Eastern European countries such as Hungary, Poland, Estonia, the Czech Republic, and Slovenia. Why isn't Russia included among these countries? What are some possible implications for inclusion and exclusion of certain countries?

4. Look at the *Citizens Rights* section of this site. What are the judicial and economic powers of the European Union if a member country is found to be violating its citizens' rights? What is your opinion of the ability of the European Union to enforce these laws?

5. What problems do you foresee with regard to citizen rights? Are there member or future member countries that presently discriminate on the basis of sex, race, ethnic origin, religion or belief, disability, age, or sexual orientation? What penalties would you institute to enforce citizen rights?

6. How might the European Union threaten the heritage of ethnic cultures and communities in a way that could result in a secession movement in the next century? What will the European Union have to do to ensure that people continue to feel some attachment to their nation while simultaneously feeling that they belong to an international community?

RELATED INTERNET SITE(S)

The European Union in the U.S.
http://www.eurunion.org/
   Provides easy-to-understand information about the European Union including an excellent FAQ section.

THE U-2 INCIDENT (1960)

URL ADDRESS: http://www.yale.edu/lawweb/avalon/u2.htm

SITE SUMMARY: In 1960, before an American spy plane flown by Francis Gary Powers was shot down by a Russian plane while taking pictures of Soviet military installations, the world had been hoping that East-West relations were about to improve. Instead, the scheduled Big Four Summit was torpedoed, the Disarmament Conference dangerously delayed, and the Cold War intensified. Seven documents provide primary sources and background material that illustrate the tension of the Cold War. The site begins with a note to the USSR on May 6, 1960, acknowledging that an "unarmed weather research plane" has been missing since May 1. It continues with various U.S. State Department statements, reports of the news conference by President Eisenhower, a Soviet note to the United States, and various telegrams and memos between the two countries.

DISCUSSION QUESTIONS AND ACTIVITIES

1. If you had been President Eisenhower, would you have stated that the downed plane was an "unarmed weather research plane"? How would you have handled the incident? Remember, you have no knowledge yet as to whether Francis Gary Powers, the pilot, is alive or dead.

2. At the time, many people argued that Francis Gary Powers was flying a spy plane and that he had an obligation to keep as much information as possible about himself and the plane a secret from his Soviet captors. They even suggested that Powers should have committed suicide rather than allowing himself to be captured. Argue the pros and cons of this view.

3. Select *148 Telegram From the Embassy in the Soviet Union to the Department of State*. Based on your reading of these messages, what would be your advice to the United States on how to handle this incident once the Soviet Union had produced the pilot, Francis Gary Powers?

4. President Eisenhower never apologized to the Soviet Union for this incident, and he continued to argue that the Soviets had known of these flights for years and had never protested. Take his point of view and write a report stating that Premier Nikita Khrushchev exploited the incident to sabotage the Big Four Summit and the Disarmament Conference.

5. The Soviet Union lost approximately 20 million people in World War

II. Premier Khrushchev had just recently given orders to demobilize many Soviet troops when the spy plane went down. Argue that Khrushchev's rage, fear, and loss of trust in the United States to negotiate honestly were genuine reactions. What would you have done, if you were President Eisenhower, to reassure him of your nonaggressive intentions?

6. On several occasions, Premier Khrushchev threatened to take military action against countries allied to the United States that had been permitting these spy flights over their air space. In light of these threats to the United States and its allies, advise President Eisenhower about America's national security. Do you recommend that the United States go on a nuclear alert, remain calm, assess our nuclear strike capabilities, or do nothing additional militarily? Why?

RELATED INTERNET SITE(S)

Foreign Relations of the United States 1958–60 Volume X May-June 1960: The U-2 Airplane Incident
http://www.yale.edu/lawweb/avalon/diplomacy/forrel/5860vxp1/vx151.htm

Provides additional memoranda and telegrams between the U.S. and USSR embassies and the meeting notes of the National Security Council relating to the incident.

Spy in the Sky
http://www.pbs.org/wgbh/pages/amex/spy/story.html

Includes excellent background material about the affair, complete with photographs of Francis Gary Powers, President Eisenhower, the U-2 plane, and much more.

THE SIXTIES PROJECT (1960–1969)

URL ADDRESS: http://lists.village.virginia.edu/sixties/

SITE SUMMARY: The sixties remain a fascinating decade of American history for students because it was a period of great change on many fronts. It was an age of civil, gay, and women's rights. It was about a controversial undeclared war in Vietnam, the landing of a man on the moon, the assassination of President John F. Kennedy, his brother Robert, and Martin Luther King, Jr. It was also a time of great sexual freedom and memorable fashion trends, from Afro hairdos to platform shoes to miniskirts. This site is a gateway to many primary sources relating to the sixties. Among other items, it includes Martin Luther King, Jr.'s "I

Have a Dream" speech, excerpts from Nixon's tapes, descriptions of Haight-Ashbury in the sixties, and remarks on his life and times by Timothy Leary, the professor from Harvard who advocated the use of LSD.

DISCUSSION QUESTIONS AND ACTIVITIES

1. Select *References, Bibliographies and Historical Documents* and click on *Primary Documents*. Choose *The San Francisco Diggers (1966–1968)*. This site contains an archive about the Haight-Ashbury group in San Francisco. Before 1967, the hippies in Haight-Ashbury had espoused ending the Vietnam War, saving the environment, and other noble causes. By 1968, however, the area was portrayed by the media as a sinkhole of degradation. What was the overall philosophy of the pre-1967 hippies of Haight-Ashbury? If the world needed more love at this time in history, how did they go about providing it?

2. Select *References, Bibliographies and Historical Documents* and click on *Primary Documents*. Choose *May 2nd Movement*. On May 2, 1964, the first major student demonstrations against the Vietnam War were held in New York City, San Francisco, Boston, and Madison, Wisconsin. Compare the rhetoric in this document to some ideas expressed in the pamphlets found at Anti-Imperialism in the United States, 1898–1935 at http://home.ican.net/~fjzwick/ail98–35.html. What are the similarities and dissimilarities?

3. Select *References, Bibliographies and Historical Documents* and click on *Primary Documents*. Choose *GIs United Against the War in Vietnam Statement of Aims*. When do you think this document was written? Why did African Americans feel especially aggrieved at having to fight in Vietnam? What was going on with draft exemptions and the Vietnam War?

4. Select *Other Sixties-Related Sites* and click on *Sixties: The Players*. This site consists of photographs of people who in one way or another had an impact in the sixties. Choose three sixties personalities and write an obituary for each one. Be sure to emphasize the part of their lives that influenced the decade of the sixties.

5. Select *Other Sixties-Related Sites* and click on *Colin Haight-Ashbury Archives*. Scroll down to *Timothy Leary Memorial*. Why did Timothy Leary's lifestyle and writings epitomize the sixties?

6. Select *Other Sixties-Related Sites* and click on *Musical Festival Page*. The sixties were a time of revolution, as people rebelled against the Vietnam War, their parents, marriage, and other societal institutions. How was this revolutionary movement reflected in either the folk or rock music of the sixties?

RELATED INTERNET SITE(S)

The Sixties
http://www.slip.net/~scmetro/sixties.htm
Contains a large collection of information about the sixties including songs from Peter, Paul and Mary, the Elvis home page, *The Andy Griffith Show*, and material on the Beatles.

DOCUMENTS FROM THE WOMEN'S LIBERATION MOVEMENT (1960s–1970s)

URL ADDRESS: http://scriptorium.lib.duke.edu/wlm/

SITE SUMMARY: The letters, plays, periodical articles, speeches, and minutes of various women's liberation groups in the late sixties and early seventies reflect the radical origins of the movement. This site includes searchable subject categories under the following topics: general and theoretical; medical and reproductive rights; music; organizations and activism; sexuality and lesbianism; feminism; social feminism; women of color; and women's work and roles. It also features a keyword search engine of the entire collection.

DISCUSSION QUESTIONS AND ACTIVITIES

1. Select *General and Theoretical* and click on *The Women's Liberation Movement: Its Origin, Structures and Ideals*. Historically the women's movement has been a movement of middle-class women seeking greater opportunities outside the home. How did this women's liberation movement differ from the one in the 1870s?

2. Select *General and Theoretical* and click on *Women's Liberation Aims to Free Men, Too*. In the section *A Black Parallel*, the author calls attention to similarities in the way society views African Americans and women. What similarities between African Americans and women does the author cite as examples? Why did African Americans achieve more in the area of civil rights than did women in the 1960s?

3. Select *General and Theoretical* and click on *The Women's Rights Movement in the U.S.: A New Year*. Part of this article discusses why the word "feminist" was considered a derogatory term. Why do you think it was considered an insult to be described as a feminist? What connotation does the word have today? Why?

4. Select *Music*. Click on several scores and lyrics. What major women's

issues are being addressed in these songs? Compare some of the songs in this notebook to those sung during the civil rights movement. What are the similarities and dissimilarities?

5. Select *Women's Work and Roles* and click on *Sexism in Fourth Grade*. If this study were attempted in one of today's fourth grade classrooms, what do you think the findings would be? Would the degree of sexism be lower, the same, or perhaps higher? Why?

6. Select *Women's Work and Roles* and click on *The Politics of Housework*. Do you think that the domestic role and responsibilities of women have changed since the 1970s? Read some of the findings from Arlie Hochschild's *The Second Shift* (1989) to help you make comparisons.

RELATED INTERNET SITE(S)

The Feminist Chronicles
http://www.feminist.org/research/chronicles/fc1953.html
Provides an excellent timeline of significant events in the women's movement from 1953 to 1993.

SCUM Manifesto
http://www.ai.mit.edu/~shivers/rants/scum.html
Although Valerie Solanas was not involved with the women's liberation movement, her SCUM (Society to Cut Up Men) manifesto, written in 1967, is typical of extreme radical feminist theory.

Women's Liberation Research Network
http://www.duke.edu/~ginnyd/wlrncoll.html
This site contains a directory of scholars, researchers, librarians, and activists who are interested in researching, teaching, and documenting the U.S. women's liberation movement.

THE BERLIN CRISIS (1961)

URL ADDRESS: http://www.tamu.edu/scom/pres/speeches/ jfkberlin.html

SITE SUMMARY: In 1961 Berlin was an island city in the Russian zone of occupied Germany. The city was governed by the USSR, France, Great Britain, and the United States within a four-power Central Commission. The Soviet Union repeatedly pressed for the incorporation of Berlin into the country of Russian-dominated East Germany to stop the flow of refugees. Between 1945 and 1961, over 2 million people had left East Germany when President John F. Kennedy met with his Russian counterpart,

Premier Nikita Khrushchev, to discuss the latter's demands. President Kennedy refused them. This site contains his speech and includes the reason for his decision. As a result of President Kennedy's refusal, the Russians built a barrier wall between the two parts of the partitioned city to prevent any more departures. It became an enduring symbol of the continuing Cold War and was not torn down until 1989.

DISCUSSION QUESTIONS AND ACTIVITIES

1. In 1956 the USSR had to use tanks to ensure continued control over Hungary and Poland. Neither the North Atlantic Treaty Alliance (NATO) nor the United States responded militarily. Discuss how this action may have sown the seeds for the USSR's attempt to incorporate Berlin into East Germany.

2. Why do you think that the United States, with the cooperation of NATO, decided to stand up to Khrushchev's demands? How was U.S. credibility at stake with our Western allies?

3. Although the Soviets did not acquire the city of Berlin in this crisis, they did erect a wall that divided the city in half. Should the United States and NATO have prevented the construction of the wall militarily? How might history have been different if they had?

4. If you were Premier Khrushchev and were listening to President Kennedy's speech, which parts may have frightened you the most? Why?

5. In light of the subsequent fall of communism and the collapse of the Soviet Union, would it have made any difference if the Soviets had taken all of Berlin?

6. Read the sections of President Kennedy's speech that relate to his intention to increase appropriations for the armed forces, add to the size of the army, and construct more weapons. How would you feel as a young man living during this period? Would you be hopeful about tomorrow? Would you join a pro-peace organization? Describe the possible societal effects of living during the Cold War.

RELATED INTERNET SITE(S)

The Berlin Crisis
http://www.seas.gwu.edu/nsarchive/nsa/publications/berlin_crisis/berlin.html

Contains a comprehensive record about the formation of United States policy toward Berlin and West Germany. It also includes an excellent overview and primary source materials.

Lesson 10 The Berlin Crisis with the Russians
http://cyberschool.4j.lane.edu/People/Faculty/JaggerA/JFK1/Lessons/
Lesson10.html

Provides lesson plans for secondary school students about the 1961
Berlin Crisis.

THE CUBAN MISSILE CRISIS: FOURTEEN DAYS IN OCTOBER (1962)

URL ADDRESS: http://library.advanced.org/11046/days/index.html

SUMMARY: Most people who lived through the Cuban missile crisis
thought that it was the closest the world has come to a nuclear war. The
discovery of Russian missiles positioned on an island only ninety miles
away from the United States presented the U.S. government with the
need for a rapid response which quickly escalated military forces in Russia and America to a high alert status. Among other sources, this site
provides an excellent introduction to the Cuban missile crisis, the full-
text correspondence between Premier Nikita Khrushchev and President
John F. Kennedy, JFK's address to the nation, a Cuban missile crisis quiz,
and a list of additional questions concerning the crisis.

DISCUSSION QUESTIONS AND ACTIVITIES

1. Create a timeline of the events that you consider the most critical to
   the development and resolution of the Cuban missile crisis.

2. Well before U.S. air reconnaissance flights revealed the presence of
   Soviet missiles on Cuban soil, relations between Cuba and the United
   States were extremely tense. What evidence from the sources at this
   site supports that statement?

3. You are an American history teacher. Imagine that it is October 23,
   1962, and you have been asked by your tenth grade students to explain what will happen in this confrontation between the Soviet Union
   and the United States. What will you tell them?

4. In his meetings with various cabinet members and staff, President
   John F. Kennedy referred to Barbara Tuchman's book *The Guns of
   August* (1962). What similarities were there between the conditions-
   described in this book about World War I and the conditions surrounding the Cuban missile crisis?

5. As a member of the Executive Committee, Secretary of Defense Robert
   McNamara initially was a forceful proponent of an air attack on Cuba.

If President Kennedy had listened to him, what might have been the sequence of events?

6. What were the immediate results of the Cuban missile crisis? What were the long-term consequences in terms of our relations with Premier Fidel Castro and Cuba?

RELATED INTERNET SITE(S)

Collective Memories of the Cuban Missile Crisis
http://www.stg.brown.edu/projects/classes/mc166k/
missile_crisis_34.html

Filled with memoirs of people who were asked to describe what they were doing or thinking at the time of the Cuban missile crisis, this site will help bring the situation alive for history students. Some of the people were officers on U.S. Navy ships or living in other parts of the world at the time.

The Cuban Missile Crisis
http://www.seas.gwu.edu/nsarchive/nsa/cuba_mis_cri/
cmcchron4.html

This site contains a neutral, extremely detailed chronology of events relating to the Cuban missile crisis from January 1959 through January 1963. It also includes many primary sources such as cable transcripts, conversations, and other excerpts and quotations about the event. Short biographical sketches of everyone involved in solving the crisis are also provided.

JOHN F. KENNEDY ASSASSINATION HOMEPAGE (1963)

URL ADDRESS: http://www.informatik.uni-rostock.de/Kennedy/index.html

SITE SUMMARY: Assassination of public figures always lays the groundwork for historical speculation. The assassination of President John F. Kennedy by Lee Harvey Oswald in 1963 is no exception. Eyewitnesses have produced conflicting details on the number of shots fired and even the number of assassins. This site presents these disparate versions by providing excerpts of eyewitness testimony that conflict. Although it poses unsubstantiated scenarios concerning the assassination, the site nevertheless supplies users with original photographs, the full text of the Warren Commission hearings and reports, and a search engine to query the database. An extensive bibliography of primary and secondary sources is also included. Students should be told to rely on the official documents rather than the site designer's links for accurate information.

DISCUSSION QUESTIONS AND ACTIVITIES

1. Why did the events surrounding the assassination of President John F. Kennedy generate so many theories of conspiracy? Discuss the major sources of evidence that might lead people to question the results of the Warren Commission Report.

2. Write a crime scene report of the John F. Kennedy assassination complete with information about the caliber of the gun used, position of the cars, the number of shots fired, and other pertinent information. You may wish to click on *The Warren Commission Hearings* to retrieve eyewitness testimony.

3. Select *The Warren Commission Hearings* and click on *Oswald, Marina*. What is your opinion of Marina Oswald's testimony? Does she appear to be telling the truth? Is she a cooperative or hostile witness? What light does Marina Oswald shed on this case?

4. Select *The Warren Commission Hearings* and click on *Ruby, Jack*. Jack Ruby killed the assassin Lee Harvey Oswald as he was on his way to the state prison. What is your opinion of Ruby? Does he seem like a credible witness to you? What do you think was his motivation for killing Lee Harvey Oswald? Write a memoir as if you were a juror listening to Ruby's testimony. Give your impressions about his veracity.

5. Select *The Warren Commission Report*. Click on *Chapter 1* and select *Recommendations*. What would you add to this list of recommendations in the light of current terrorist events? What activities should a contemporary president of the United States be prohibited from engaging in in light of this assassination?

6. How did the assassination of President Kennedy create an almost mythical view of the ideal American president? What decisions did he make during his presidency that probably would have tarnished this viewpoint had he not been assassinated? Discuss the Bay of Pigs, involvement in South Vietnam, and postponement of important civil rights legislation.

RELATED INTERNET SITE(S)

Other Assassination Pages
http://www.informatik.uni-rostock.de/Kennedy/links.html

Contains the most current set of links to additional information about the John F. Kennedy assassination.

FREE SPEECH MOVEMENT (1964)

URL ADDRESS: http://www.fsm-a.org/index.html

SITE SUMMARY: The free speech movement was born at the University of California, Berkeley campus on September 14, 1964, when the dean of students informed all student organizations that the sidewalk area traditionally used by students for fund-raising campaigns and political recruitment would no longer be available for this purpose. In October, Mario Savio, the leader of the movement, stood on the roof of a student-surrounded police car and urged students to protest the arrest of a fellow student. Eventually the university restored the area to the students, but not before a massive strike and the resignation of the chancellor. This site provides an overview of the movement and an archive of leaflets and other reports. A separate screen contains a home page dedicated to Mario Savio.

DISCUSSION QUESTIONS AND ACTIVITIES

1. Select *Mario Savio links*. What kind of man was Mario Savio? Write a short biography of him and include his role in the free speech movement.

2. What events were affecting students in the 1960s that may have influenced the subsequent protests at Kent State University, Yale, the University of Wisconsin, and other college campuses?

3. Why do you think administrators at the University of California at Berkeley made the decision to prohibit students from using the sidewalk to distribute political recruitment literature? Did the Vietnam War play a part in their decision?

4. Select *FSM Progress Report*. In it you will find a list titled *ON-CAMPUS RIGHTS*. What do you think of these rules? Design similar ones for your high school. Do you think that the administrators at your school would allow some form of student rights? If not, why?

5. Select *Looking Back*. From this memoir, what do you think was the legacy of the free speech movement? What battles for future generations of college students were won in 1964?

6. Write an editorial about the University of California dedicating steps to the memory of Mario Savio. In it you may decide to discuss the

irony of the event, the healing of old wounds, the recognition of the eternal right to free speech by Americans, or some other aspect of the movement and its connection to Mario Savio.

RELATED INTERNET SITE(S)

Ceremony Honors Naming of Savio Steps
http://www.lib.berkeley.edu/MRC/saviotranscript.html
Contains articles from the University of California at Berkeley's student newspaper, *The Daily Californian*, about Mario Savio and the free speech movement.

BLACK PANTHER PARTY INFORMATION (1966)

URL ADDRESS: http://homepage.interaccess.com/~triflin/reference.html

SITE SUMMARY: The Black Panther Party was a radical political organization founded in 1966 by African Americans Huey P. Newton and Bobby Seale. Its primary objective was to protect the black community from police actions associated with brutality. It evolved in time into a Marxist-Communist group that favored violent revolution, if necessary, to effect social changes. This site provides a thorough history of the Black Panther Party and its co-founders, Seale and Newton. It also includes the original ten-point program or manifesto of what the Panthers wanted from the U.S. government in the form of reparations for slavery. A link to the Nation of Islam home page is also included.

DISCUSSION QUESTIONS AND ACTIVITIES

1. Compare the Black Panther Party to other earlier Black nationalism or Black liberation movements including the Nation of Islam. How would you describe this party in terms of its political orientation?

2. Select *What We Believe*. What beliefs do you think that "the powers that be" probably found acceptable in this document? What ones did they think were radical and totally unacceptable? Why?

3. In *belief #3*, the Black Panthers refer to an overdue debt of "forty acres and a mule." What part of history did this debt refer to? Do you think that African Americans should or should not receive reparations from the government because their ancestors had been enslaved?

4. In *belief #6*, the Black Panthers state that they "should not be forced

to fight in the military service." What war was being waged by the United States when this document was published? Why would this statement have been seen as a threat to the government?

5. Why did police departments and the FBI react so strongly to the Black Panther Party tenets? What might they have feared from the Black Panthers?

6. If you were a member of the Black Panthers today, what ten items would you want? How many are different from the ones that were asked for in 1966? Have conditions changed much in the urban African American communities of today?

RELATED INTERNET SITE(S)

Panthers
http://www.thlang-hf.dk/fagene/engelsk/1n97_98/panthers.htm
Provides an overview of the Black Panther Party and lists their ten-point program.

Seale Talks to the Badger
http://www.badgerherald.com/content/1997/fall/news/
111197news2.html
Features an interview with Bobby Seale, co-founder of the Black Panther Party, by Evan Pondel, editor of the *Badger Herald*, published November 11, 1997.

SAYINGS OF CHAIRMAN MAO (THE LITTLE RED BOOK) (1967)

URL ADDRESS: http://www.culturalbridge.com/cnadd.htm

SITE SUMMARY: The "Little Red Book" contains the sayings of Chairman Mao Tse-tung, who ruled China from 1949 until 1976. It was waved by millions of zealous Red Guards during Mao's orchestrated "Cultural Revolution" in the mid-1960s. Historians estimate that as many as 30 million Chinese died during this terrifying time when intellectuals, doctors, and many other members of the professional classes were either disgraced publicly, imprisoned, or sent to labor camps. Mao's Little Red Book at this site contains 90 translated sayings of the 427 total. They include sayings about the Communist Party, war and peace, patriotism and internationalism, and revolutionary heroism. Other parts of the site feature a children's jumprope song from the Cultural Revolution, Mao buttons, and photographs of young people training in the Red Guards.

DISCUSSION QUESTIONS AND ACTIVITIES

1. Look at the first sentence before the contents page to the Little Red Book. How was a cult of personality or almost worship of Mao Tse-tung derived from the book?

2. Select *The Correct Handling of Contradictions Among People*. In this part of the book, Mao Tse-tung discusses the contradictions between workers and peasants and intellectuals. Who were the intellectuals? What occupations represent those usually practiced by intellectuals? Why might Mao have feared them?

3. Select *The Correct Handling of Contradictions Among People*. Mao states in this part that the settling of questions is by the democratic method *of persuasion and education*. What do you think his concept of democracy is?

4. Select *Democracy in Three Main Fields*. In the *Note* section, Mao refers to *Three Check-ups*, which meant checking on class origin, ideology, and style of work. What classes of Chinese people had the most to fear from the Red Guards? How would you have advised them to behave in order to survive the Cultural Revolution?

5. In effect, Mao Tse-tung's Little Red Book was used to accuse millions of innocent people of various political crimes. Conduct a mock trial of a famous, loyal communist intellectual. Using parts of Mao's book, convict this person of not being a faithful Party member.

6. Mao Tse-tung's book was a tool in one of the largest witch hunts the world has ever known. Compare it to similar events such as the Spanish Inquisition, the French Reign of Terror, the Salem Witch Trials, the McCarthy era, or the Holocaust. What sociopolitical conditions must be present for these types of mass persecutions to take place?

RELATED INTERNET SITE(S)

Flashbacks of the Cultural Revolution
http://www.china-net.org/ccf9623/ccf9623-1.html
Provides a first-person account by Luo Ning about the different Red Guard subgroups and their activities.

WHEN NIXON MET ELVIS (1970)

URL ADDRESS: http://www.nara.gov/exhall/nixonelvis/

SITE SUMMARY: Elvis Presley was the most popular American singer in the history of rock music. His initial fame, however, came from his flamboyant 1950s concert performances where he adopted a hoodish, anti-adult manner and a hip-gyrating movement that more than suggested sex. In December 1970, Elvis entered the true mainstream of American society when he was photographed in the White House with President Nixon. This National Archive site contains the photograph and copies of all correspondence relating to the arrangement of their meeting.

DISCUSSION QUESTIONS AND ACTIVITIES

1. Read the letter by Elvis Presley in which he asks to be made a federal agent so that he can assist the government by informing on people in "the drug culture, the hippie elements, the SDS, Black Panthers, etc." Why do you think Elvis Presley was so patriotic?

2. How much leeway do American presidents have in whom they see and how their day is structured? Why do you think President Nixon agreed to meet Elvis Presley and have his photograph taken with him?

3. Do you believe that Presley, as he claimed in the letter, had "done an in-depth study of drug abuse and Communist brainwashing techniques?" If not, why?

4. Elvis Presley's huge commercial success was somewhat built on his hoodish, anti-establishment style. Discuss the hypocrisy in Elvis Presley wanting to be a secret federal agent informant.

5. Why did President Nixon's staff go to such lengths to "see if some kind of honorary agent at large or credential of some sort can be provided for Presley"? Why did H. R. Haldeman, another staff member, scrawl on this memo, "You've got to be kidding"?

6. Would Richard M. Nixon have agreed to be photographed with Elvis Presley in the 1950s when Elvis was just beginning to shock the nation's adults with his hard-driving rock music? Discuss the hypocrisy in President Nixon's agreeing to meet with Elvis in 1970.

RELATED INTERNET SITE(S)

The Commercial Appeal
http://www.gomemphis.com
  Memphis Commercial-Appeal Tennessee's oldest newspaper, features an archive of articles and photographs about Elvis Presley, the King of Rock.

Elvis Presley's Graceland
http://www.elvis-presley.com
  This is a well-maintained commercial site that includes biographical and musical information about Elvis Presley.

THE WARS FOR VIETNAM (1970s)

URL ADDRESS: http://students.vassar.edu/~vietnam/overview.html

SITE SUMMARY: Vietnam experienced more than 900 years of independence before it came under the domination, respectively, of the governments of China, Japan, France, and the United States. Included in this site is an overview of the Vietnam War from 1954 to 1975 followed by links to documents such as the Geneva Peace Accords, the Gulf of Tonkin Resolution, and memos from Secretary of Defense Robert McNamara to President Lyndon B. Johnson. It also contains South Vietnam's peace proposal and a series of additional Vietnam links.

DISCUSSION QUESTIONS AND ACTIVITIES

1. Create a chronology of the important events, people, battles, treaties, laws, protests, and other relevant matters relating to the Vietnam War from 1954 to 1974.

2. How did the 1954 Geneva Peace Accords sow the seeds for further involvement in Vietnam by the United States?

3. Discuss the pros and cons of the position that the establishment of the Southeast Asia Treaty Organization (SEATO) was a subterfuge for supporting the unification of Vietnam under a noncommunist form of government.

4. Select *White Papers*. If you were the president of the United States and had just finished reading these papers from Dean Rusk and Robert McNamara, what would be your course of action?

5. How did President Lyndon Johnson use the Gulf of Tonkin Resolution as political cover to escalate the war?

6. What do you think was the legacy of the Vietnam War for the United States? Discuss the loss of American lives, distrust of government officials, the limits of power, economic costs of the war, and the end to domestic consensus.

RELATED INTERNET SITE(S)

Center of Military History
http://www.army.mil/cmh-pg/
When you type in *Vietnam*, you will retrieve a collection of oral exit interviews of U.S. soldiers plus information about airmobile operations in Vietnam from 1962 to 1965 and U.S. Army Special Forces operations.

Vietnam Yesterday and Today
http://server.oakton.edu/~wittman
Provides excellent bibliographies and study guides for further research about the Vietnam War.

WWW Virtual Library Socialist Republic of Vietnam
http://coombs.anu.edu.au/WWWVLPages/VietPages/WWWVL-Vietnam.html
This site is an outstanding gateway that connects users to various Internet links about the government, politics, art, history, and travel in Vietnam.

THE INDIA-PAKISTAN WAR (1971)

URL ADDRESS: http://www.subcontinent.com/1971war.html

SITE SUMMARY: Pakistan was born from the religious enmity between Hindus and Muslims living in India. In 1947 British and Hindu leaders created East and West Pakistan and left 1,000 miles of Indian territory between them. The people of East and West Pakistan were divided not only geographically but also culturally. In 1971 their differences erupted into civil war. East Pakistan declared itself an independent nation called Bangladesh. In 1971 India joined Bangladesh in a war against West Pakistan. More than 1 million people died in the fighting. The site, containing pictures, text, and maps, documents the military history of the war from an Indian perspective.

DISCUSSION QUESTIONS AND ACTIVITIES

1. Draw a map showing the geographical location of East and West Pakistan. How do you think their geographical location influenced the eventual creation of Pakistan and Bangladesh?

2. India claims that the 8 million refugees (more than half of them Hindus) who flowed into India and the massacre of Bengali citizens by the West Pakistani soldiers were their reasons for aiding East Pakistan. Discuss other possible reasons.

3. Among other reasons, India claims that repeated appeals to the international community were ignored, thus forcing them into a war with Pakistan to keep their own borders intact. Compare this appeal for mediation in 1971 to the 1998 decision by India and Pakistan to test nuclear weapons because of the inability of the international community to help them resolve their dispute concerning Kashmir.

4. Explain how India won the war but in winning it sowed the seeds for future problems with Pakistan over the state of Kashmir.

5. Why did China become an ally of Pakistan rather than India in this war?

6. How would you describe the rhetoric at this site? Imagine that you are a mediator in the India-Pakistan dispute over Kashmir. How would you go about defusing the situation and getting the parties talking to one another? What suggestions would you have for the designers of this site? Would you ask them to not have it on the Internet even though it is their right? How might it inflame relations between the two countries?

RELATED INTERNET SITE(S)

Library of Congress Country Studies
http://cweb2.loc.gov/frd/cs/cshome.html
This site contains accurate information that describes and analyzes the political, economic, social, and national security systems of ninety-one countries. Pakistan and India are among those listed.

THE PENTAGON PAPERS (1971)

URL ADDRESS: http://www.mtholyoke.edu/acad/intrel/pentagon/pent4.htm

SITE SUMMARY: In 1967 Defense Secretary Robert McNamara commissioned the writing of a top-secret forty-seven-volume history of America's involvement in Indochina. Four years later, Neil Sheehan, a reporter for the *New York Times*, wrote a series of articles based on this history. Sheehan had received the papers from a former Marine officer named Daniel Ellsberg. The articles, referred to as the Pentagon Papers (and later published in book form), revealed the extent to which the United States government had been keeping information about the Vietnam War from the public. The government sued to suppress publication of the articles, and the case of *New York Times Co. versus the United States* was the result. In essence, it pitted the compelling interest of press freedom against national security interests. This site contains Chapter 1, "Background to the Crisis, 1940–50," and it sets the stage for the suicidal involvement of France and the United States in Vietnam.

DISCUSSION QUESTIONS AND ACTIVITIES

1. In this document there is much evidence that Ho Chi Minh, the eventual leader of North Vietnam, was really a zealous nationalist rather than a communist. Use evidence from this chapter to support this statement.

2. Explain the "domino theory" and why it held such power over so many presidential administrations.

3. From October 1945, to February 1946 Ho Chi Minh made several formal requests to President Truman citing the Atlantic Charter, the U.N. Charter, and a foreign policy address made by President Truman in October 1945 that had endorsed national self-determination. Why did the United States disregard the very documents that it endorsed with reference to Vietnam?

4. Chapter 1 of *The Pentagon Papers* gives numerous examples of the military capabilities of the Viet Minh (Communist Party of Vietnam), their popularity in both North and South Vietnam, and their almost fanatical determination to achieve independence. Why do you think the United States ignored these signs to its own detriment?

5. Do you think that the release of the Pentagon Papers hastened the end of U.S. involvement in the Vietnam War?

6. You are a reporter for a weekly newsmagazine. Write an editorial expressing your view that the publication of the Pentagon Papers ultimately undermined confidence in public officials.

RELATED INTERNET SITE(S)

Perspectives: The Pentagon Papers
http://www.thehistorynet.com/Vietnam/articles/1997/10973_text.htm
Authored by retired Colonel William Wilson, this site provides an excellent overview of the Pentagon Papers and the insight they provide on executive conduct of the Vietnam War.

WATERGATE (1972)

URL ADDRESS: http://www.washingtonpost.com/wp-srv/national/longterm/watergate/front.htm

SITE SUMMARY: On June 17, 1972, five men were arrested and charged with breaking into the executive headquarters of the Democratic National Committee in the Watergate apartment complex in Washington,

D.C. Two *Washington Post* reporters, Carl Bernstein and Bob Woodward, were assigned to report the break-in story, and in the course of events uncovered a conspiracy of lying and deceit that forced the indictments of forty government officials and the resignation of President Richard M. Nixon. This site features an index of all the key players, transcripts of questions and answers with the two reporters, and excerpts of Nixon's taped conversations concerning Watergate. A search engine supports keyword querying of this extensive database.

DISCUSSION QUESTIONS AND ACTIVITIES

1. Select *Watergate Chronology*. Choose the ten most important events, people, court decisions, or revelations that you believe caused President Nixon to resign from the presidency, and tell why.

2. What do you think were the motives of "Deep Throat," the person who gave reporters Carl Bernstein and Bob Woodward the leads to follow in this complicated and politically sensitive story? His revelations led to the resignation of a United States president. Do you think that his whistle blowing was the right or the wrong thing to do for the country's long-term interests?

3. Select *Players*. Choose three people whose actions in the Watergate affair you consider to be either heroic or reprehensible, and tell why.

4. In the Search box, type in the word *tapes*. The discovery that President Nixon had been secretly taping all of his White House conversations was a major factor leading to his downfall. Examine the newspaper stories about the tapes. Write a report about how crucial they were to the investigation.

5. President Nixon claimed that he was hounded from office by his political enemies and that he did nothing that other presidents of both parties had not already done. Search the stories from the *Washington Post* that directly relate to President Nixon's violations of the law. If you were a member of an impeachment panel, would you have voted for impeachment based on the evidence you have collected?

6. Select *Online Q & A with Bradlee and Woodward*. In it Woodward states that "Watergate provides a model case study of the interaction and powers of each of the branches of government." Design a case study based on this statement.

RELATED INTERNET SITE(S)

Watergate Scandal
http://www.loucol.com/studsfm/aowens/watergate_scandal.htm

This is an outstanding site for additional resources about the Watergate affair. It also provides excellent overview and background materials.

THE CONTRAS AND COCAINE (1985–1987)

URL ADDRESS: http://history1900s.miningco.com/msub5.htm

SITE SUMMARY: Sufficient time has elapsed for historians to reflect on the Iran-Contra affair, which involved illegal gun running and narcotics trafficking associated with the Contra War in Nicaragua. The monies received from the drug sales were used to supply arms and military assistance to the Nicaraguan rebels who were fighting against the government headed by President Anastasio Somoza. The primary sources at this site consist of vast selections from the report Senate Foreign Relations Committee on Drugs, Law Enforcement and Foreign Policy (December 1988), chaired by Senator John F. Kerry. A lengthy introduction states the committee's charges and also provides a thorough outline of the issues. Responses by the executive branch and testimony of all the principals are also included. At the site homepage, click on search and type in "contras" in the search box.

DISCUSSION QUESTIONS AND ACTIVITIES

1. Read sections I–IV of this Senate report. Prepare a three-page brief that provides relevant background and overview materials concerning this affair.

2. Read through sections VI and VII. Use the evidence in this report to answer the following question. Do you think that any or all of the officials associated with this affair were aware that the companies they were using to send humanitarian aid were active drug traffickers?

3. What federal laws were violated by assisting the Contras in this way?

4. You are a newspaper reporter. Imagine that these proceedings have been conducted in secret. You have received a copy of them ten days prior to their release to the public. Write a front-page story that will grip your readers and make them demand further investigations and justice for those who violated the law.

5. You are a television reporter. You know the value of sound bites and pictures to tell a story. You have just received a copy of this report and plan to make it the lead story on the 6 o'clock news. Write a script and include pictures that you hope will alert Americans to this

dark alliance between known drug traffickers and the U.S. government.

6. How do you think this affair affected American trust in public officials and various government agencies?

RELATED INTERNET SITE(S)

CIABASE
http://history1900s.miningco.com/msub5.htm
Contains a search engine that supports keyword searching of the Iran-Contra affair.

The Contras, Cocaine and Covert Operations
http://www.seas.gwu.edu/nsarchive/NSAEBB/NSAEBB2/
nsaebb2.htm
This site is a virtual electronic briefing book of declassified documents about the Contras and Cocaine Affair. It also includes testimony from Oliver North, a National Security Council aide who was a major figure in this affair.

Psychological Operations in Guerilla Warfare
http://history1900s.miningco.com/msub5.htm
Includes a copy of the CIA illegal training manual for the Contras. The manual condones the assassinations of civilians, blackmail, and the use of professional criminals to destabilize Nicaragua.

THE CHERNOBYL DISASTER (1986)

URL ADDRESS: http://www.yahoo.com/regional/countries/ukraine/ cities/chernobyl/chernobyl_accident/

SITE SUMMARY: On April 26, 1986, reactor number four at the Chernobyl Atomic Energy Station in Kiev, Ukraine, exploded, releasing 200 times more radiation than was released from the atomic bombs dropped on Hiroshima and Nagasaki combined. Because of prevailing winds, 25 percent of the land in nearby Belorussia is uninhabitable. Hundreds of children at the epicenter of the blast have been stricken with thyroid cancer. The cause of the blast was termed "the human factor" or the failure to follow various safety and site maintenance protocols. Yahoo's gateway site includes factual material, personal recollections of a Belorussian scientist, medical effects, newspaper stories, and maps. When using this site, however, remind students to note their information sources and evaluate the information carefully.

DISCUSSION QUESTIONS AND ACTIVITIES

1. Select *Chernobyl Nuclear Accident*. This is a Russian account of the causes of the Chernobyl accident. How does it compare with the account given by Dr. Najmedin Meshkati at the University of Southern California's Institute of Safety and Systems Management?

2. Select *Chernobyl Once and Future Shock*. Why were the Russians so secretive about the Chernobyl accident? What were the consequences of that secrecy with regard to exposing the public to additional radioactive fallout?

3. Select *Soviet Archives Exhibit Chernobyl*. Write a summary report about some of the construction flaws in the Chernobyl nuclear power plant. How might they have contributed to the explosion?

4. Select *Chernobyl: An Update* and click on *Global Radiation Patterns*. Using the maps and explanations as illustrations, write a story that describes the path the radiation took and discusses the future medical and agricultural implications for people and crops in the areas still affected.

5. Many of the sites refer to the lack of a "safety culture" with regard to the Chernobyl accident. What elements does a safety culture include? Design a safety plan for the nuclear power plant nearest you that covers design, operating, and emergency features.

6. After the Chernobyl accident, Sweden announced that it would not build any more nuclear power plants. Imagine that you are a Swedish nuclear scientist. What were your reasons for recommending no further building of nuclear power plants?

RELATED INTERNET SITE(S)

Chernobyl—The Human Factor
http://www-bcf.usc.edu/meshkati/humanfactors.html
Discusses the human factor as the primary cause of the Chernobyl accident and the critical role that the United Nations should have in ensuring the safety of nuclear power plants.

Earthshots Satellite Images of Environmental Changes
http://edcwww.cr.usgs.gov/earthshots/slow/tableofcontents
Provides images that show the area around the Chernobyl nuclear plant one month and six months after the accident. The images reveal agricultural abandonment of villages and the levels of radiation contamination.

REACTIONS TO THE TIANANMEN SQUARE MASSACRE
(1989)

URL ADDRESS: http://kizuna.ins.cwru.edu/asia110/projects/Qing/qing1.html

SITE SUMMARY: Although Tiananmen Square in Beijing, China, has been the scene of many student demonstrations since 1919, not until 1989 was it the occasion for one about democracy. When a former Communist leader died on April 15, 1989, his death became the forum for demonstrations by students all over China to push for democratic reforms. As the demonstrations became more vocal and the world press focused on Tiananmen Square, the Chinese government called in military units from the provinces to quell it. On June 3, hundreds of demonstrators were killed and thousands more were arrested. This site features images of demonstrations in Shanghai and Hong Kong, selected speeches and articles in Communist newspapers calling for martial law, and meetings with student demonstrators.

DISCUSSION QUESTIONS AND ACTIVITIES

1. Select *Images*. Why did Shanghai, another extremely large Chinese city, join in the protests? What are the current economic conditions in Shanghai that provide the opportunity for interaction with foreigners and their businesses? How might these relationships foster a climate in which people become desirous of political reforms?

2. Why did the Chinese government bring soldiers in from the provinces to stop the protests? Why didn't they use local military forces within the area of Beijing? What are the possible future implications of this decision?

3. Select *Links* and click on *The Gate of Heavenly Peace*. Choose *Additional Readings and Links* and read some of the participants' accounts. How would you describe the mood of the protestors? In your opinion, were they aware of how dangerous the behavior they were engaging in was? Do you think that the crackdown by the government came as a surprise to them? Why or why not?

4. Select *Chronology* and click on the editorial of *April 26, 1989*. You are a Chinese student activist. Write an article that refutes the charges alleged in the *People's Daily*.

5. Select *Chronology* and click on the full transcript of *May 18, 1989*. Li Peng has summoned several student leaders for a televised talk at the

Great Hall of the People. It is obvious that Li Peng and Wu'er Kaixi are not going to resolve their differences. You are a neutral mediator who has been asked to help the two negotiate to resolve their differences. How would you get them to talk to one another? What issues is it paramount to solve before there is bloodshed?

6. The year is 2020. You are a Chinese historian who has been asked to write about the start of the Chinese revolution. Write a paper in which you express the opinion that it started with the events involving the Tiananmen Square Massacre.

RELATED INTERNET SITE(S)

The Gate of Heavenly Peace
http://www.nmis.org/gate/

This site should be used in conjunction with Reactions to the Tiananmen Square Massacre. It has a good collection of newspaper articles, eyewitness accounts, and secondary sources.

COMPUTER HISTORY (1990s)

URL ADDRESS: http://video.cs.vt.edu:90/history/

SITE SUMMARY: Access to all the sites in this book would not be possible without the revolution that is occurring in computers. If abaci, which can be considered a form of positional rotation, are counted as precursors, then computers have been in existence since ancient times. This site consists of a series of historical exhibits on the development of the computer from before the Christian era through the 1990s. The images tell a story of building on each age's discovery piece by piece until a universally employable model was mass manufactured in the 1990s. Users can tour chronologically, perform a keyword search, or search randomly through a gallery of images.

DISCUSSION QUESTIONS AND ACTIVITIES

1. Select *A chronological look at the past (text-only)*. Beginning with *Early Years*, choose the inventions, thought processes, people, and designs that you think were seminal markers in the development of the computer.

2. Select *A chronological look at the past (graphical)*. Complete the chronol-

ogy from 1994 to 2010 by researching future inventions and predictions about the computer. You may wish to insert appropriate illustrations from your research or from your vision of future computer descriptions.

3. Both the Agricultural Revolution and the Industrial Revolution were characterized by changes or shifts in how people worked, conducted business, raised their families, and were educated. What changes have typified the Computer Revolution? How have they affected the labor, recreation, education, and even the daily tasks of people?

4. One of the indications that a country is still developing is a lack of industrialization. This means that it cannot usually mass produce many of the basic necessities for a modern society or manufacture indigenous natural resources into saleable, exportable products on a large scale. How do you think the computer revolution will affect these countries' development? Discuss the implications of a technological apartheid.

5. Select *Perform a keyword search* and type in the word *Turing*. What were the contributions of Alan Turing to artificial intelligence and computer science?

6. How soon do you think computer scientists will develop a machine that can pass the Turing Test? When they have invented it, what questions would you ask it that will prove that it can think the way a human being can? Prepare a list of appropriate questions.

RELATED INTERNET SITE(S)

Britannica Internet Guide: Computers and the Internet
http://www.ebig.com/cgi-bin/browse.tlc?HeadingUid=942

This is an excellent gateway site to previously reviewed computer science–related Internet links.

Evolution of Computing
http://www.computer-museum.org/slides/slides.html

Presents an overview of computer history with photographs up until the time of John von Neumann.

Silicon Base
http://www.stanford.edu/group/itsp/

Includes an archive of more than 2,000 multimedia images, video clips, and photographs about computer history. It also contains a search engine for keyword queries.

THE GULF WAR (1991)

URL ADDRESS:
http://www.pbs.org/wgbh/pages/frontline/gulf/index.html

SITE SUMMARY: The Gulf War, also known as "Desert Storm," was fought in early 1991 between Iraq and a coalition of thirty-nine countries organized by the United States and the United Nations. War broke out not long after Iraq invaded Kuwait, an oil-rich country at the northern end of the Persian Gulf, and then moved quickly to position its troops directly on the border with Saudi Arabia. Almost all the industrialized coalition countries viewed this action with alarm because Kuwait and Saudi Arabia were major sources for petroleum. After a few days of successful massive coalition bombing and an extensive ground attack, Iraq surrendered. Kuwait was restored to its previous independence, but not before all of its oil wells were set afire by Iraq. Hundreds of thousands of people were killed or wounded or became refugees. This site contains a chronology, maps, oral histories, and personal accounts of battlefield soldiers and pilots. It also features audio tapes of various Iraqi and U.S. government officials trying to negotiate one last time before waging war, descriptions of air wars, and a photo archive of the weapons and technology used to fight the war.

DISCUSSION QUESTIONS AND ACTIVITIES

1. Select *Chronology*. Choose the dates that you think were the most critical to the Gulf War. Design your own chronology and accompany it with relevant maps.

2. Select *Voices in the Storm* and click on *Program One*. This account recalls the last meeting between Deputy Prime Minister Tariq Aziz of Iraq and U.S. Secretary of State James Baker on the eve of war. Based on either hearing or reading the account, answer the following questions. Was there any chance that war could have been averted in this meeting? Do you think it was a public relations pro forma event on behalf of the coalition forces before they started the bombing? Had both sides reached a point of no return? If so, at what point do you think it had been reached?

3. What did Saddam Hussein hope to gain by taking over Kuwait?

4. Why do you think Iraq shot missiles into Israel when it was waging a war against coalition forces? If the Israelis had fought back, do you think that their involvement would have changed the course of the war? How?

5. How would the Middle East and the world be different if Iraq had won the Gulf War? Write a scenario based on this outcome using maps and other research from this site.

6. Select *War Stories*. Read some of the accounts of pilots and soldiers on the battlefield. This was in many ways a "push-button war." While the Iraqis lost hundreds of thousands of people, the coalition forces lost only 370. Why is this type of war dangerous even to the nations that win it?

RELATED INTERNET SITE(S)

Gulf War Photo Gallery
http://www.hoskinson.net/gulfwar/index.html
This site contains a variety of color photographs taken during the war by Ronald A. Hoskinson and Norman Jarvis. It features pictures of military life in the desert and a night artillery attack.

YUGOSLAVIA UNIVERSITY OF MINNESOTA HUMAN RIGHTS LIBRARY (1991–Present)

URL ADDRESS: http://www1.umn.edu/humanrts/icty/icty.html

SITE SUMMARY: The political disintegration of the former Yugoslavia has its roots in centuries-old hatreds between religious and ethnic groups, mainly Muslims and Christians. This site contains basic documents relating to the International Tribunal responsible for prosecuting people accused of violating international humanitarian laws in Yugoslavia and the surrounding new countries. Copies of the 1996 Dayton Peace Accords on Bosnia and the statute permitting the International Tribunal to prosecute war criminals are included. Rules of evidence, procedure, and detention and a list of International Tribunal links are also provided.

DISCUSSION QUESTIONS AND ACTIVITIES

1. Click on *Summary of the Dayton Peace Agreement*. Who has authority to invoke penalties if the countries involved continue to engage in hostilities toward one another?

2. Select *Dayton Peace Accords* and click on *Annex 6: Agreement on Human Rights*. What do you think should be done to leaders of a country who deliberately countenance violation of these rights? How far would you

go in violating their human rights to bring them to justice and prosecute them? You may wish to refer to the kidnapping of Adolf Eichmann by the Israeli government and the kidnapping of President Manuel Noriega of Panama by the United States government as examples.

3. Select *Dayton Peace Accords on Bosnia* and click on *Annex 1A: Military Aspects of the Peace Settlement*. In this part of the agreement, the United Nations requested the adoption of a resolution to establish a multinational military Implementation Force to make sure that hostilities do not break out again. Imagine that you are a general in charge of such a force. What would be your plan for making these countries independent of your enforcement and able to govern themselves and live peaceably with their neighbors?

4. Select *Statute of the International Tribunal for the Prosecution. . . .* Notice the various articles that give the International Tribunal the authority to prosecute heads of state and other government officials. Why has no one of significance in any of the former Yugoslavian countries been prosecuted for war crimes?

5. The United States claims to be a major proponent of human rights for people living in any country of the world. If it is, then why has it not signed the 1998 United Nations' Global Ban on Land Mines Treaty that 122 other nations have signed?

6. You have been asked to draft a second Dayton Peace Accord that will have military provisions to prevent further outbreaks of hostilities. Write a list of possible military enforcement techniques that you would be willing to implement if any of the countries involved violated the agreement.

RELATED INTERNET SITE(S)

Doing Research on Yugoslavia
http://www.iberia.vassar.edu/vcl/Quick-Guides/global_village/text/choose/yugoslavia.html
   Provides a bibliography and a list of Internet sites that contain background information on the history of Yugoslavia and its subsequent civil strife.

Human Rights Archives and Data on the Genocide in Bosnia
http://www.haverford.edu/relg/sells/reports.html
   Presents a numbered and indexed listing of war crimes in the former Yugoslavia which have been submitted to the United Nations Security Council.

NAFTA (NORTH AMERICAN FREE TRADE AGREEMENT) (1994)

URL ADDRESS: http://lanic.utexas.edu/la/mexico/nafta/

SITE SUMMARY: Free trade is a relatively recent goal of U.S. foreign policy. It was inaugurated with the Reciprocal Trade Agreements Act of 1934, which authorized the president to negotiate and implement tariff-reducing trade agreements with other countries, subject to congressional review every three years. This site provides a wealth of primary source documents concerning the most important North American trade agreement of the twentieth century. The social, economic, and political effects of the agreement among the United States, Canada, and Mexico are just beginning to be formally studied. The entire agreement is available as well as a list of centers and institutes that are associated with NAFTA. A documents and publications section, a news section, and a list of NAFTA-related Internet sites are also included.

DISCUSSION QUESTIONS AND ACTIVITIES

1. What is the objective of NAFTA? How is NAFTA supposed to be a win-win agreement for the United States, Mexico, and Canada?

2. Should NAFTA be considered the equivalent of the European Union? What are the major differences?

3. Many economists have debated the impact of NAFTA on U.S. employment opportunities. Which U.S. occupations are most likely to be threatened by lower labor costs in Mexico? Which U.S. occupations are most likely to grow as a result of the new free trade zone?

4. You are a member of an environmental watchdog agency, and you have reason to believe that a United States corporation is using environmentally hazardous chemicals at one of its northern Mexico factories. What part of the NAFTA agreement could you invoke to stop this practice?

5. Does the creation of NAFTA dilute the ability of member nations to regulate the health, safety, and working conditions of multinational corporations operating in all three countries?

6. The United States and Canada are both advanced economic nations, while Mexico is still an emerging nation. Write a white paper warning of the potential problems that this disparity may cause all three nations.

RELATED INTERNET SITE(S)

Fast Track Debate
http://www.usia.gov/topical/econ/fasttrak/
This site is a compendium of all the versions, articles, and administrative position statements concerning the fast track passage of NAFTA.

Public Citizen
http://www.citizen.org/pctrade/nafta/naftapg.html
Provides an online citizens' forum that contains the latest opinions, problems, and analyses relating to NAFTA.

QUEBEC SEPARATISM (1995)

URL ADDRESS: http://www.hartford-hwp.com/archives/44/index-a.html

SITE SUMMARY: The issue of sovereignty for Quebec has not subsided despite the defeat of a referendum by Quebec citizens to secede from Canada in 1995. At this site, users will find all the major resolutions, various political parties' position statements, and the full text of the actual referendum. A second section entitled "The Issues" contains background and opinion articles about the positive and negative aspects of separatism. The third section provides articles that deal with the constitutional aspects of Quebec secession, and the final section presents information about this proposal and its impact on aboriginal peoples such as the Cree nation.

DISCUSSION QUESTIONS AND ACTIVITIES

1. The problem of Quebec secession has its roots in the 1600s, when what is now the largest Canadian province was settled by French explorers and fur trappers. As the country's population grew, the English became dominant in politics and the economy. Write an article for an English encyclopedia that discusses the early history of Quebec up until the early 1900s. Be sure to include information about earlier secession movements and the grievances that Quebec has always harbored toward English Canadians.

2. What are the current issues that brought Quebec to a referendum vote in 1995? Provide this information in the form of a background paper and include information from the early 1960s to the present day.

3. Conduct a debate. The issue is "Should Quebec vote to separate from Canada?"

4. Quebec is Canada's largest province. Find information about its trading status vis-à-vis other nations and what its gross domestic product might be expected to be. Answer the following question based on your research. Would it be to Quebec's advantage to secede from Canada?

5. What problems would the secession of Quebec pose to the interests of the United States?

6. Imagine that Los Angeles, Arizona, New Mexico, and Texas decided to secede from the United States and become a new nation called Tex-Mex. What might be some of the issues that would make them wish to secede? What would be the advantages and disadvantages? You may wish to consult the book *The Nine Nations of North America* by Joel Garreau (1981) for additional information.

RELATED INTERNET SITE(S)

Quebec
http://www.gouv.qc.ca/introa.htm
Provides background material on the politics, business, territory, education, and government of Quebec.

WIDNET—STATISTICS—AFRICA: WOMEN IN DEVELOPMENT NETWORK (1995)

URL ADDRESS: http://www.focusintl.com/statr1a.htm

SITE SUMMARY: Statistics can be used to provide support for logical conclusions about the past, present, and future history of a country or region in the world. Citing statistics from the United Nations publication "The World Women 1995—Trends and Statistics," this site gives data about population, family and households, health, education and training, labor, and power with regard to women in Africa. Under each of these sections are hundreds of tables containing additional data about fertility rates, life expectancy, child mortality rates, illiteracy, and other important factors that can either contribute to or hinder a country's progress.

DISCUSSION QUESTIONS AND ACTIVITIES

1. Select *Fertility Rate of 15–19 years old women (1990–95)*. Create a graph showing which countries comprise North and Sub-Saharan Africa, re-

spectively, and show which area of Africa has the higher fertility rate. What do you think are the possible causes of the higher rate in Sub-Saharan Africa?

2. Select *Countries where the average age of women in their first marriage is less than 20 years old*. Create a chart or table showing these countries. Refer to the statistics in #8, Percentage of 20–49 years old women who had a child before 20 years old (1986/1992), for help answering the following question. What are the possible consequences from early marriage of women for the birthrate in these countries?

3. Select *Global Fertility Rate (1970–75 & 1990–95)*. Which African countries have experienced an increase in fertility? Which African countries have experienced a decline in fertility? Select the ten African countries that have had the largest increase in fertility. Research their economic status. Are they described as Third World countries? What possible connection might exist between their fertility rates and economic self-sufficiency?Prepare appropriate charts, tables, and graphs to illustrate the points you wish to make.

4. Select *Abortion Authorized? (1994)*. Why do you think so few African countries have legalized abortion? Examine and research issues such as religion, male power, lack of education, and other possible causes.

5. Select *Percentage of married women living in polygamy (1986/1992)*. Which countries have the highest rates of polygamy? Why do you think they have the highest rates? What are the implications for the birthrates in those countries practicing polygamy?

6. You are the head of a United Nations task force whose charge is to educate African nations about the need to control their population growth. Based on statistics at this site, which African countries would you make your first priority? Why?

RELATED INTERNET SITE(S)

Afriland
http://www.focusintl.com/afriland.htm
   This is an excellent gateway site that provides contemporary background material relating to African integration, gender and development, plus African Internet guides and business connections.

AfriStat
http://www.focusintl.com/afristat.htm
   Contains additional population statistics for all African countries and provides information about basic African social services and gender and development issues.

COALITION AGAINST SLAVERY IN MAURITANIA AND SUDAN (1998–Present)

URL ADDRESS: http://members.aol.com/casmasalc/

SITE SUMMARY: The era of slavery is thought of as a dark chapter in America's and other countries' past histories, but, unfortunately, it still exists in Mauritania and Sudan. Slaves, selling for as little as ninety dollars, are being given as wedding presents, exchanged for camels, weapons, or vehicles, or simply inherited as part of an estate. This site contains exposé articles, documents, position papers, and statistics that reveal the extent of this human abuse. Additional links connect users to Amnesty International, Human Rights/Watch/Africa, and other watchdog agencies.

DISCUSSION QUESTIONS AND ACTIVITIES

1. What is the history of slavery in Mauritania and Sudan? Who are the masters and who are the slaves? What is the current estimate of the number of slaves in both countries? Prepare a report containing appropriate demographic charts and graphs.

2. How is the Islamic religion misused to legitimize the institution of slavery in Mauritania and Sudan?

3. Charles Jacobs, director of the American Anti-Slavery Group, claims that "if whites were made slaves, the media would find a way to cover it." Express your views as to why the media have given so little attention to the problem of slavery in these two countries.

4. Why has civil war led to the resurgence of slavery in Sudan?

5. Imagine that you have been appointed head of an international task force to eradicate slavery in Mauritania and Sudan. Besides enlisting the help of various UN organizations and international watchdog agencies, what other measures might work in these extremely poor developing countries?

6. Write a congressional bill that would require the United States to act punitively toward any slaving nation. Your bill might want to include the following: withdrawal of all foreign aid, imposition of a travel ban, boycott of all slaving nations' exports, and divestiture of U.S. business relationships.

RELATED INTERNET SITE(S)

The African Slave Trade: 1995
http://www.columbia.edu/~sj118/casmas/nuzltr/october/
afrslvtr.html
   Provides background information about the present-day African slave
trade.

CASMAS Newsletter
http://www.columbia.edu/~sj118/nuzltr.html
   Contains additional articles about the slave trade in African countries.

Selected Primary Source Databases

African-American Mosaic
http://www.loc.gov/exhibits/african/intro.html
Furnishes a Library of Congress research primary source guide to the study of African American history and culture.

American Civil War: Documents and Books
http://www.access.digex.net/~bdboyle/docs.html
This superb primary source database is filled with letters, electronic versions of historical texts, and diaries about the U.S. Civil War.

American History Archive
http://www.ilt.columbia.edu/k12/history/aha.html
Still under construction, this site contains digitized documents and media sources about the American Revolution and the Civil War.

American Memory
http://lcweb2.loc.gov/ammem/ammemhome.html
Sponsored by the Library of Congress, American Memory includes forty-one digitized collections filled with primary sources about various periods and events in American history.

Avalon Project at the Yale Law School
http://www.yale.edu/lawweb/avalon/avalon.htm
Features primary source documents from all over the world in law, history, and government from the eighteenth through twentieth centuries.

Chicano
http://www.pbs.org/chicano/

Provides several primary sources related to Chicano history in addition to a timeline, a bibliography, a list of related Internet sites, and ideas for stimulating class discussions.

Chronology of the United States Historical Documents
http://hamilton.law.ou.edu/hist/
Contains hundreds of primary sources about United States history from the precolonial period to the present day.

Civil War Resources on the Internet: Abolitionism to Reconstruction
http://www.libraries.rutgers.edu/rulib/socsci/hist/civwar-2.html
Provides maps, letters, first-person accounts, and other primary sources about the American Civil War.

Creating French Culture: Treasures from the Bibliotheque Nationale de France
http://lcweb.loc.gov/exhibits/bnf/bnf0001.html
Includes selected primary sources from France's National Library, ranging from sources about various French monarchs of the late eighth century to documents relating to present-day France.

Diotima
http://www.uky.edu/ArtsSciences/Classics/gender.html
This is a comprehensive site that presents materials about the study of women and gender in the ancient world.

The Documents Room
http://kuhttp.cc.ukans.edu/carrie/docs_main.html
Features a full-text electronic library of primary source documents about the Catholic Church, the United Nations, Europe, world constitutions, and much more.

Duke University Special Collections Library
http://scriptorium.lib.duke.edu/
Presents digitized collections from Duke University's Manuscript and Rare Book Departments about subjects such as papyrus, African American studies, and women's studies.

Early America
http://earlyamerica.com/
Includes primary source materials from eighteenth century America.

The Ecole Initiative
http://cedar.evansville.edu/~ecoleweb
Furnishes full-text documents about early Christian Church history.

EuroDocs: Primary Historical Documents from Western Europe
http://library.byu.edu/~rdh/eurodocs/

An extensive primary source database that focuses on key historical happenings in Western Europe from medieval times to the present. Searchable by country.

Exploring Ancient World Cultures
http://eawc.evansville.edu/chpage.htm
Accessible by country, this site includes the primary religious, military, literary, and historical texts that characterize each ancient culture's heritage.

FDR Cartoon Archive
http://www.wizvax.net/nisk_hs/fdr/index.html
Features cartoons from the presidency of Franklin D. Roosevelt from 1932 to 1943. The cartoons have been arranged within categories related to the New Deal, foreign relations, farm issues, the Supreme Court, and other areas.

Frontline: The Gulf War
http://www.pbs.org/wgbh/pages/frontline/gulf/index.html
Filled with maps, oral histories, chronologies, transcripts, and graphics, this site is an outstanding primary source database for information about the 1991 war with Iraq.

Gateway to World History
http://www.hartford-hwp.com/gateway/index.html
This is a well-organized site that lists large primary source databases within selected historical periods and topics.

The Great War: Interviews
http://www.pbs.org/greatwar/interviews
Includes comprehensive interviews with world-renowned historians about various aspects of World War I.

G-Text Primary Source Archives
http://h-net2.msu.edu/~german/gtext/index.html
Contains several German primary history sources from the nineteenth and twentieth centuries that have been translated into English.

Hanover Historical Texts Project
http://history.hanover.edu/project.htm
Provides a vast array of primary sources divided by categories such as Europe, specific centuries, and continents. This is one of the best primary source databases on the Web.

Historical Documents on the Internet
http://www.cssjournal.com/hisdoc.html
This is an extensive gateway site to primary sources in history. It is

accessible by continent and also features a list of historical sites with a major emphasis on U.S. history.

Historical Text Archive
http://www.msstate.edu/Archives/History/
Contains a banquet of primary sources that are accessible by continent, resources, and topics such as war, women, and Native Americans.

History, Archaeology, and Classics
http://www.libs.uga.edu/mainref/history.html
A must bookmark for all history teachers, this site is a gateway to primary sources ranging from the ancient world to the present day.

The History Channel
http://www.historychannel.com/
The History Channel features secondary and primary resources. Primary sources may be in the form of great speeches that changed the world, first-person accounts, or a virtual tour of an ancient city.

History Online
http://www.discovery.com/past/stories/moreunforgettable.html
This site is part of the Discovery Channel. It contains selected feature stories, which may contain primary sources that are related to specific historical periods or events.

Horus' Web Links to History Resources
http://www.ucr.edu/h-gig/welcome.html
One of the best gateway sites to primary source Web sites, this site provides links to more than one thousand history sites.

HyperHistory
http://www.hyperhistory.com/
Includes a panorama of world history within a hyperlinked, colorful chronological chart.

The Labyrinth
http://www.georgetown.edu/labyrinth
Provides full-text versions of medieval documents and literature.

The Middle East Documents
http://www.mtholyoke.edu/acad/intrel/meres.htm
Includes a smorgasbord of primary source documents relating to the history of the Middle East and especially to the creation of the state of Israel.

Mining Co. News & Issues
http://home.miningco.com/issues/

Provides an excellent collection of primary sources about every period of history.

National Security Archives
http://www.seas.gwu.edu/nsarchive/NSAEBB/
This site furnishes significant research and documents about nuclear weapons issues and their history that have been declassified or requested through the Freedom of Information Act.

Normandy Exhibit
http://normandy.eb.com/normandy/
Contains a wealth of primary sources in the form of maps, images, first-person accounts, battle plans, and documents about the D-Day invasion at Normandy, France.

On-Line Reference Book for Medieval Studies
http://orb.rhodes.edu/
ORB is an academic site that provides scholarly articles by medieval scholars as well as a database of medieval documents, images, and other primary sources.

Perseus Project
http://www.perseus.tufts.edu/
Includes a massive digital library of Greek artifacts, archaeological sites, buildings, coins, sculptures, vases, and other primary sources. A search engine facilitates access.

Personal-Experience Accounts
http://www.libertynet.org/zelson/publish/list.html
Accessible by categories such as contemporary daily life and general history, this site provides links to various personal accounts and diary excerpts.

POTUS
http://www.ipl.org/ref/POTUS/
Presents background material, election results, cabinet members, and important events about each United States president.

Primary Source Documents on the Holocaust
http://www.lib.byu.edu/~rdh/eurodocs/germany.html
Includes numerous documents related to the Holocaust such as the Wannsee Protocol, eyewitness accounts, speeches, and much more.

Rome Resources Project
http://www.dalton.org/groups/rome/
Under such hyperlinked headings as religion, politics, technology, and drama, users can access a host of primary sources pertaining to Roman civilization.

Scholarly Technology Group
http://www.stg.brown.edu/projects/html
All of Brown University's Web-based projects can be accessed from this site, including such sites as The Victorian Web and World War II.

Temperance and Prohibition
http://www.cohums.ohio-state.edu/history/projects/prohibition
Contains numerous primary sources about the temperance and prohibition movement in America during the nineteenth century.

This Day in History
http://www.historychannel.com/today/
Primary sources are not the sole focus of this site. Many, however, appear as part of the information given about particular events in history.

Treasures Digitisation Project
http://www.bl.uk/diglib/diglib_home.html
Includes a wide variety of digitized collections and exhibitions such as the Magna Carta and Beowulf from the British Library.

U-Boat War
http://uboat.net
Filled with photographs, personal accounts, and biographical information about the submariners who commanded U-boats during World War II, this site also documents war crimes committed by both the Allied and Axis powers.

United States Historical Census Data
http://fisher.lib.virginia.edu/census/
Includes census data from 1790 to 1970 that are searchable by several variables.

United States National Archives
http://www.nara.gov/exhall/
Presents digitized primary source documents and images from different periods of history that are in the National Archives collections.

University of Kansas History Resources
http://kuhttp.cc.ukans.edu/history/index.html
Contains one of the largest collections of links to all history topics. This is an excellent history gateway site.

Valley of the Shadow
http://jefferson.village.virginia.edu/vshadow2/
Provides primary source documents, images, sounds, and historical discussions about two counties that were 100 miles apart on opposite sides of the Mason-Dixon Line during the Civil War.

Vatican Exhibit
http://metalab.unc.edu/expo/vatican.exhibit/Vatican.exhibit.html
This multimedia exhibit features portions of manuscripts, books, and maps that played a significant role in the recovery of the classical heritage of Greece and Rome.

Victorian Web
http://www.stg.brown.edu/projects/hypertext/landow/victorian/victov.html
Sponsored by Brown University, this site contains Victorian electronic texts and information about Victorian history, religion, technology, society, and philosophy.

Views of the Famine
http://vassun.vassar.edu/~sttaylor/FAMINE/
Includes numerous articles about the Irish famine in the 1800s from the *Illustrated London News, Punch,* and *Pictorial Times.*

Vincent Ferraro Home Page
http://www.mtholyoke.edu/acad/intrel/feros-pg.htm
Ferraro, a professor of international politics at Mount Holyoke College, has amassed an impressive set of Web links pertaining to international relations and U.S. foreign policy.

Voice of the Shuttle History Page
http://humanitas.ucsb.edu/shuttle/history.html
Accessible by continent, country, and topic, this site is one of the best history gateways for beginning any search for primary sources in any area of history.

Wiretap Documents Server
http://wiretap.spies.com/Gopher/Gov/
Includes a collection of historical documents that are in the public domain.

World Scripture: Comparative Anthology of Sacred Texts
http://www.ettl.co.at/uc/ws/index.html
Contains essays and excerpts from all the sacred texts of the world's religions.

World-Wide Web Virtual Library: History
http://history.cc.ukans.edu/history/WWW_history_main.html
Provides a vast array of secondary and primary sources ranging from subject catalogues to electronic documents about many different periods and events in history.

Index

Abelard, Peter, 57–58
Abolitionists, 116. *See also* Slavery
Absalom, Absalom! (Faulkner), 170–171
Accidents, 87–88, 158–159, 225–226
Adams, Abigail, 107
Addiction, 116–117
Aeneas, 34
Africa: ancient civilizations, 34–35;
    fifteenth–sixteenth centuries, 74–75;
    twentieth century, 172–173, 193–
    194, 235–238
African American History, 115–116,
    128–132, 206–207
African Americans, 94–95, 109–110,
    115–116, 118–119, 128–131, 215–216
African slave trade, 237–238
Aguirre, Lope de, 83–84
Alaska, 132
Alcoholism, 138–139
Americas, discovery of, 71–73
Amherst, Lord Jeffrey, 101–102
Amistad Research Center, 96
Anarchy, 148–149
Ancient texts, 33–37, 39–40, 45–46
Anthony, Susan B., 124–125
Anti-imperialism, 149–151
Anti-Japan movement, 157–158

Anti-semitism, 145–146, 166–167, 178–
    180, 185
Anti-temperance movement, 139
Anubis, 37
Apache tribe, 137–138
Apartheid, 44, 193–194
Apedemak, 35
Apparel: Byzantine, 53; Chinese, 62–
    63, clerical wear, 82–83; England, 82–
    83; France, 82–83; military, 82;
    nobility, 82; Poland, 82; Russian, 82,
    U.S., 107
Aquinas, Thomas, 48–49
Archaeological sites, 33–34, 38–46, 49–
    51, 167–168
Archaeology: methods of study, 38,
    45–46, 167–168
Architecture: Chinese, 65–66; English,
    87–88; Mayan 39–40
Arctic, 102–103
Arnett, Benjamin, 115–116
Art: interpretation of, 23, 55, 60, 67–
    69, 96–97, 122
Art of War, The (Sun Tzu), 39–40, 99
Arthur, King (fictional character), 55–
    56
Artificial intelligence, 229

Artists, 67–69, 96–97, 106–107, 171–172
Ashley's Mine Commission, 101
Asia: ancient civilizations, 39–40, 46–47; early Christian era, 53–54; eleventh–fourteenth centuries, 62–63, 65–66; fifteenth–sixteenth centuries 74, 76–77; seventeenth–eighteenth centuries, 90–91; nineteenth century, 151–152; twentieth century, 157–158, 175–176, 181–185, 189–191, 194–197, 199–200, 216–217, 219–221, 227–228
Assassinations, 200–201, 212–214
Athens, Greece, 43
Atlantic Charter, 183–184
Atomic bomb, 188–190, 195–196, 225
Atomic Energy Act (U.S.), 202–203
Atrocities, 101–102, 166–167, 178–180, 191–193, 231–232
Augustine, Saint, 48
Australia, 105–106
Automobiles, 152–153

Babylon, 40–41
Balfour Declaration, 155
Bangladesh, 220–221
Beijing, China, 65–66
Bell, Adam Schall von, 76–77
Bentham, Jeremy, 91–92
Berlin crisis, 209–211
Bernstein, Carl, 222–223
Berry, Jean de (Duc), 67–68
Beyond the Textbook (Kobrin), 6
Biella, Italy, 61–62
Bismarck, Otto von, 160–161
Black death, 63–64
Black Panthers, 215–216
Bolsheviks, 161–162
Boniface VIII, Pope of Rome, 48
Book of Hours, 67–68
Book of the Dead (Egyptian), 36–37
Bosnia-Herzegovina, 160–161
Bradlee, Benjamin, 222–224
Brady, Mathew B., 107, 129
Brest-Litovsk, Treaty of, 163
Brown, John, 116
Bubonic plague, 63–64
Buddhism, 53–54, 194–195

Bundy, McGeorge, 196
Bunnell, Lafayette Houghton (Cpt.), 127
Bush, George W. (Pres.), 230–231
Byzantium, 52–53

Cahiers of 1789, 108–109
Cairo Conference, 183–184
Calendars, 38, 67–68
California: agriculture, 127; Dust bowl, 186–187; first-person accounts, 126–127; folk music, 168–169; Japanese internment, 181–182; San Francisco earthquake, 153–154, Yosemite Valley, 132
Camelot, 55–56
Camolim, King, 74
Canada, 102–103, 147–148, 233–235
Capital punishment, 75–76, 78, 81
Caribbean island societies, 71–72
Carnarvon, Lord, 167–168
Carter, Howard, 167–168
Carthage, 34
Cartoons, political, 160, 171–172
Casablanca Conference, 182–183
Casmas (Coalition Against Slavery in Mauritania and Sudan), 237–238
Castro, Fidel, 211–212
Catapults, 44
Catholic church. *See* Roman Catholic church
Census data (U.S.), 109–110, 129–130
Central America, 38–39, 71–72, 200–201, 224–225
Central Intelligence Agency (CIA), 195–196, 200–201
Charlemagne, 48
Charles II, King of England, 88
Chernobyl disaster, 225–226
Cherokee tribe, 93
Child labor, 100–101
Chimney sweep, 101
China: ancient period, 39–40, 46–47; eleventh–fourteenth centuries, 62–63, 65–66; sixteenth century, 76–77; twentieth century, 175–176, 194–198, 216–217, 227–228
Christianity, 46, 48–49, 53–54, 57–58,

67–68, 76–77, 79–80. *See also* Religions

Church history (early Christian), 48–49

Civil War (U.S.), 128–130, 135–136

Civilizations, decline of, 39

Class structure, 97–98, 119–120, 134–135, 140–141, 144–145

Cleopatra, 33

Cleveland, Grover (Pres.), 107

Clothing. *See* Apparel

Cocaine, 224–225

Cochise, 137

Cold War, 22, 187–188, 195–196, 198–199, 205–206, 209–210

Collectivization of property, 162–163

Colonies and territories, 83, 86, 90–91, 97–98, 104–105, 137–138, 151–152

Columbus, Christopher, 70–73

Comanche tribe, 137–138

Commerce, 46–47, 86–87, 90–91, 103, 123–124, 233–234

Communism, 91, 120–121, 157–158, 161–164, 198–199, 216–217, 221–222

Communist Party manifesto, 120–121

Comnena, Anna, 59

Computer science, 228–229

Concentration camps, 179, 181–182

Cone, Hannah, 135–136

Confederate States of America. *See* Civil War (U.S.)

Conferences: Cairo, 183–184; Casablanca, 183–184; Potsdam, 183–184; Yalta, 183–184

Confessions, 116–119

Conservation movement (U.S.), 132–133, 174

Constantine I (the Great), 48

Constantinople, 53, 59

Constitutional amendments (U.S.), 115–116, 124–125, 138–139, 221–222

Constitutional Convention (U.S. 1774–1789), 104–105

Continental Congress (U.S.), 104–105

Convicts, 104–105

Copernican theory, 85

Corn Laws, 119

Covert activities, 163–164, 195–196, 200–201, 205–206, 222–225

Cowboys, 168–169

Creationism, 133–134

Creek tribe, 93

Crime and punishment, 17, 75–76, 78, 105–106, 134–135, 142–143, 222–223

Criminals, 142–143, 149, 212–214

Critical thinking: application of results, 5–6; characteristics 3; definition 1–2; research results, 3–5

Critical Thinking: What Every Person Needs to Survive in a Rapidly Changing World (Paul), xvi

Critical thinking skills: content approach, 12–13; history, 6–7, 12; process approach, 10–11

Crow tribe, 92

Crusades, 58–59

Cuban missile crisis, 8, 211–212

Cultural revolution (China), 216–217

Dalai Lama, 194–195

Darwin, Charles, 133–134

Das Kapital (Marx), 120–121

D'Avenant, Charles, 90–91

Dawes Act, 137–138

Dayton Peace Accords, 231–232

Dead sea scrolls, 45–46

Death penalty, 36–37, 78

Democratic National Committee, 222–223

Depressions (Economic), 29, 168–171, 185–187

DeQuincey, Thomas, 116–117

Desert Storm, 230–231

Diamond Cutter Sutra, 53

Dido, 34

Disasters, natural, 50–51, 87–88; human factor, 153–154, 170–171, 199–200, 225–226

Discovery and exploration, 71–75, 83, 102–103, 199–200

Diseases, 51–52, 63–64, 101–102, 136–137, 200, 225–226

Dissent, 79–80, 85–86, 108–109, 111–112, 124–125, 145–146, 148–149, 206–207, 215–216

Domino theory, 222–223

Donner party, 127

Douglass, Frederick, 115–116
Draft riot (U.S. 1863), 116
Draft status (U.S. Vietnam War), 206–
    207
Dreyfus, Alfred, 145–146
Drugs, 116–117, 224–225
Dust bowl, 126–127, 186–187
Dynamite, use of, 154

East India company, 90–91
Economics, 112–113, 119–120
Ecuyer, Simeon (Capt.), 102
Edicts of: Milan, 49; Toleration, 49
Education requirements, xv–xvi
Education-income connection, xiv–v
Egypt, 33–34, 167–168
Eichmann, Adolf, 179–189
Eighteenth Amendment (U.S.), 138–
    139
Eisenhower, Dwight David (Pres.),
    200–201, 205–206
Elections: medieval Italy, 61–62; U.S.,
    124–125
Electronic equipment requirements,
    xviii
Elizabeth I, 80
Emancipation, 95–96
Emigration. See Immigration and
    emigration
Employment trends and computer
    dependency, xiv
Engels, Friedrich, 120–121
England. See Great Britain
Enlightenment (France), 96–97
Enola Gay, 189
Environmental movement. See
    Conservation movement
Equiano, Olaudah, 94
Eskimo (Inuit) tribe, 92
Espionage, 129–130, 163–164, 187–188,
    195–196, 205–206
Essenes, 45
Ethics and values, 36–37, 40–41, 48–
    49, 53–54, 61–62, 79–80, 83–84, 101–
    102, 111–112, 38–139, 151–152, 180–
    181, 222–225
Ethiopia, 172–173
Europe: early Christian era, 48–52, 55–
    56; eleventh-fourteenth centuries, 57–

64; fifteenth–sixteenth centuries, 67–
    84; seventeenth–eighteenth
    centuries, 85–92, 96–101, 105–106,
    108–109, 111–113; nineteenth
    century, 114, 116–121, 133–134, 142–
    143, 145–146, 151–152; twentieth
    century, 160–161, 165–167, 176–170,
    183–184, 191–192, 203–206, 209–210,
    231–232
European Union, 203–204
Evelyn, John, 88
Everest, Mount, 199–200
Evolution, 133–134
Excalibur, 55
Exodus (Bible), 41
Exploration and explorers, 71–75, 83–
    84, 102–103, 199–200

Factories and industrial plants, 100–
    101
Famine (Irish), 121–122
Feminism, 111–112, 124–125, 149–150,
    208–209
Feudalism, 108–109
Fichte, Johann Gottlieb, 114–115
Fires: London, 87–88; San Francisco,
    153–154
First Amendment (U.S.), 221–222
First Ladies. See United States First
    Ladies
Florence, Italy, 63–64
Forbidden City (China), 65–66
Ford, Henry, 152–153
Foreign Relations (U.S.), 200–201, 205–
    206, 211–212, 224–225, 234–235
Four great vows, 54
Fourteenth Amendment (U.S.), 115–
    116, 124–125
Fourth Amendment (U.S.), 181–182
France: apparel, 82; Dreyfus affair,
    145–146; enlightenment, 96–97;
    French Republic, 83; plague, 63–64;
    revolution, 82, 108–109; social life
    and customs, 88–89; Treaty of
    Versailles, 165–166; World War I,
    160–161; World War II, 183–184
Free love, 125
Free speech movement, 214–215
Freedom and human rights, 94–96,

111–112, 115–116, 124–125, 178–181, 209–210, 237–238
French and Indian War, 87, 101–102. *See also* Wars
French enlightenment, 96–97
French revolution, 23, 108–109

Galileo, Galilei, 85–86
Gama, Vasco Da, 74–75
Game laws, 132
Games, 44, 53
Gender issues, 42–43, 61–62, 70–71, 87, 92, 103, 107, 111, 124–125, 181, 208–209
Geneva Peace Accords, 219–220
Genocide, 166–167, 175–176, 178–180, 231–232
Germ warfare, 101–102
Germany: Berlin crisis, 209–210; Holocaust, 178–180; Nuremberg trials, 191–192; Treaty of ersailles, 165–166; U-boat wars, 176–177; Wolf Lewkowicz, 166–167; World War I, 160–161; World War II, 183–184
Gold Rush: California, 126–127; folk music, 168–169; Klondike, 147–148; South Africa, 193–194
Goldman, Emma, 148–149
Gone with the Wind (Mitchell), 170–171
Government, forms of, 43, 91–92, 114–115, 140, 161–162
Grapes of Wrath (Steinbeck), 170–171
Gray, Thomas, 118–119
Great Britain: early Christian era, 55–56; eleventh–fourteenth centuries, 58–60; fifteenth–sixteenth centuries, 70–71, 75–76, 78–79, 80–83; seventeenth–eighteenth centuries, 87–88, 90–92, 100–101, 111–113; nineteenth century, 116–117, 119–122, 133–135, 142–143, 151–152; twentieth century, 160–161, 183–184, 203–204
Great Plains, 141–142
Greek civilization, 34, 42–43
Greenhow, Rosie O'Neal, 129–130
Grey, Jane (Lady), 76
Guatemala, 200–201

Guilds, 61–62
Gulf of Tonkin, 219–220
Gulf War, 230–231
Guzman, Jacobo Arbenz (Pres.), 200–201

Hammurabi, King, 19–20, 40–41, 62
Harris, Elizabeth Johnson, 130–131
Hattin, Battle of, 59
Health and safety, 100–101
Hearne, Samuel, 102–103
Heloise and Abelard, 57–58
Hemingway, Ernest, 86
Herculaneum, Italy, 50
Heresy, 79, 85–86
Hernandez, Francisco, 83–84
Herzl, Theodor, 114–115
Hillary, Edmund (Sir), 119–200
Hinduism, 53–54
Hippie culture, 206–207
Hirohito, Emperor of Japan, 190–191
Hiroshima, 189–190
History of Taron (Mamikonean), 52
Hitler, Adolf, 40, 178–179
Ho Chi Minh, 221–222
Holland, 82–83
Holocaust, 166–167, 178–180, 191–192
Holy Land, 45–46, 58–59
How the Other Half Lives (Riis), 144–145
Hudson's Bay Company, 103
Huerta, Victoriano (Gen.), 156–157
Human Rights. *See* Freedom and human rights
Human sacrifice, 38
Hussein, Saddam, 230–231
Hythloday, Ralph, 46

Illuminated manuscripts, 67–68
Immigration and emigration, 104, 122, 175
Imperialism, 151
India, 90–91, 220–221
Indigenous peoples, 71–73
Industrial revolution, 100–101, 119–120, 134–135
Internet idiosyncracies, xx
Internet selection criteria, xix
Internment. *See* Concentration camps

Inventions, 68, 85–86, 124, 189–190
Iran-Contra affair, 224–225
Iraq, 150, 230–231
Ireland, 114–115, 121–122
Islam, 49, 54, 237–238. *See also* Religions
Isolationism, 149–150
Israel, 45–46, 155, 230–231
Italy, 43–44, 61–62, 64, 68–69, 173, 203–204

Jack the Ripper, 142–143
James VI (King of Scotland), 81
Japan, 175–176, 181–182, 189–191
Jesuits, 76–77
Jewish history, 155, 166–167, 178–180
Joan of Arc (St.), 49
John, Marquis of Normanby (Lord), 90–91
Johnson, Lyndon B. (Pres.), 219–220
Judaism, 49, 54. *See also* Religions
July Crisis of 1914, 161
Justinian I, Emperor, 52

Kashmir, 220–221
Kennedy, John F. (Pres.), 209–213
Kerensky, Alexander, 162
Kerry, John F. (Sen.), 224–225
KGB. *See* Soviet Secret Police
Khan, Genghis, 47
Khan, Kublai, 62–63
King, Martin Luther, Jr., 206–207
Kings. *See specific names of kings*
Kiowa tribe, 137–138
Kipling, Rudyard, 21, 151
Klondike, 147–148
Korean War, 157–158, 197–198
Kristallnacht, 178–179
Kruschev, Nikita (Premier), 206, 209–212
Kuwait, 230–231

Laconia incident, 176–177
Lamaism, 195. *See also* Religions
Latin America: ancient civilizations, 38–39; fifteenth–sixteenth centuries, 71–73, 83–84; seventeenth–eighteenth centuries, 97–98; twenti-

eth century, 156–157, 200–201, 211–212, 224–225, 233–234
Laws, 40–41, 43–44, 61–62, 78, 100–101, 104–105, 178–180
League of Nations, 173
Leary, Timothy, 206–207
Legal texts, 40–41, 43, 61–62
Legends, 55–56, 59–60
Lenin, Vladimir, 162–163
Leonardo da Vinci, 68–69
Leprosy, 51–52
Lewkowicz, Wolf, 166–167
Liberalism, 91–92
Life histories (U.S.), 174–175
Lima, Peru, 97–98
Literacy rates, 110
Literature, 78–79, 119–120, 140–141, 151–152
London: criminals, 143–144; executions, 75–76; fire, 87–88; poor 134–135
London, Jack, 140–141
Louis XIV (King of France), 88–89, 96–99
Love, Emanuel, 115
Love and romance, 55–56, 59–60
Luther, Martin, 79–80
Lynching, 115–116, 128

MacArthur, Douglas, 190–191, 197–198
Maclean, Donald, 188
Madame de Savigne, 88–89
Madison, Dolley, 107
Maimonides, 49
Malleus Maleficarum, 70
Malthus, Thomas, 91–92, 112–113
Mandalas, 195
Mandarins, 76–77
Manhattan project, 188–190
Mao Tse-tung, 40–41, 216–217
Maps, use of, 42, 72–73, 88, 93, 103, 129, 147, 177, 197, 200
Marco Polo, 62–63
Marriage, 41, 44, 48, 58, 81, 186, 235–236
Marx, Karl, 78, 113
Mary, Queen of Scots, 81
Mass of Separation, 51

Massachusetts, 68–69, 86
Maule, Frances, 124–125
Mauritania, 237–238
Mayan civilization, 38–39
Mayhew, Henry, 134–135
McCarthy, Joseph (Sen.), 22, 198–199
McNamara, Robert, 211–212, 219–222
Mein Kampf (Hitler), 178–179, 181
Merlin, 55
Metternich, Klemens von, 91–92
Mexican revolution (1910), 156–157
Mexico, 156–157, 186–187, 233
Middle Ages, 23, 51–52, 57–59, 63–64, 67–68
Middle East: ancient civilizations, 33–36, 40–41, 45–46; early Christian era, 48–49, 52–53, eleventh–fourteenth centuries, 58–59; twentieth century, 154–155, 178–179, 191–192, 230–231
Migrants, 186–187
Military tactics, 39–40, 80–81, 99, 101–102, 176–177, 230–231
Mill, John Stuart, 91–92
Missionaries, 76–77
Mona Lisa (painting), 69
Mongols, 46–47
Morris, William, 46
Muckrakers, 144–145
Muhammed, 48–49
Muir, John, 132–133
Music: dust bowl songs, 186–187; folk music, 168–169; sixties, 206–207; women's liberation, 208–209
Musical instruments, 169
Mycenaean Greece, 42

NAFTA (North American Free Trade Agreement), 233–234
Nagasaki, 189–190
Nanjing Massacre, 175–176, 191
Nat Turner's Rebellion, 118–119
National Security Archive (U.S.), 202–203
National Security Council (U.S.), 202–203
Nationalism, 114–115
Native Americans, 92–93, 102–105, 127, 133–135, 137–138, 234–235

NATO (North Atlantic Treaty Organization), 209–210
Natural selection, 133
Nazis, 178–180, 191–192
Nepal, 199–200
New Deal, 171–172
New York City, 144
New York Times, 221–222
News and news media, 170–172, 221–224
Newspapers, 86–87, 121–122, 128–129, 147–148
Nicaragua, 224–225
Nixon, Richard M. (Pres.), 199, 217–218, 222–223
Norgay, Tenzing, 199–200
North Dakota, 141–142
North Korea, 157–158
Nubia, 34–35
Nuclear accidents, 225–226
Nuclear history, 202–203, 225–226
Nuclear weapons, 195–196, 202–203, 220–221
Nuremberg trials, 191–192. *See also* Trials

Oberlin College, 116
Occupational histories, 174–175, 185–186
Ocean voyages, 71–75, 158–159
O'Connell, Daniel, 114–115
Oil production, 230–231
Opium, 116–117
Oral histories, 174–175, 185–188
Origin of Species (Darwin), 133–134
Osiris, 37
Oswald, Lee Harvey, 212–214
Ottawa tribe, 101–102
Outlaws, 59–60, 83–84

Pakistan, 220–221
Palestine, 155
Palestinian Jews, 45–46
Palmer raids, 148–149
Pamphlets, 104–105, 115–116
Pandora's box, 33
Papal authority, 79–80
Papyrus, 35–36

Pearl Harbor, 183–184
Peleus affair, 176–177
Pentagon papers, 8, 221–222
Pepys, Samuel, 88
Periodicals, 121–122, 123–124
Persecution, 49, 58, 70–71, 92–93, 154, 198–199, 217–218, 227–228
Perseus, 42–43
Peru, 83–84, 97–98
Philby, Kim, 188
Philip II, King of Spain, 83–84
Philippine-American War, 150–51
Philippines, 150–151, 187
Philosophers, 91–92
Photographs, 19, 132–133, 141–142, 152–154
Pliny the Elder, 44, 49–50
Pliny the Younger, 9, 49–50
Poland, 166–167, 184
Political cartoons, 160, 171–172
Political philosophies: Communism, 120–121; Liberalism, 91–92; Nationalism, 114–115
Political scandals, 221–225
Pompeii, 49–50
Pontiac's Rebellion, 101–102
Population theory and statistics, 109–110, 112–113, 129–130, 235–236
Portraits, 106–107, 121
Portugal, 74–75
Posters, 180–181
Potsdam Conference, 183–184
Poverty, 59–60, 100–101, 108–109, 112–113, 121–122, 134–135, 144–145, 168–169, 186–187
Powers, Francis Gary, 205–206
Presidents. See United States Presidents; and specific names
Presley, Elvis, 217–218
Primary sources: caveats, 25; definition, 15–16; document-based activities, 28–29; electronically transmitted, 24; examples, 16–17; formats and characteristics, 18–19; instructional strategies, 26–27; instructional value, 8–10; oral transmission, 22; visually transmission, 22–24, written transmission, 19–22

Prisons and prisoners, 105–106, 147–148
Progressive era, 140–141
Prohibition, 138–139, 169
Propaganda: German, 178; U.S., 180–181
Protestant Reformation, 79–80
Protests, 227–228

Quebec separatism, 234–235
Queens: Byzantium, 52; Great Britain, 80–81, 119–120. See also specific names
Qumran community, 45–46

Racial discrimination, 44, 193–194
Radiation effects, 189–190
Ram's Horn (periodical), 139
Red guards, 216–217
Red scare, 22, 198–199
Redstone arsenal, 186
Reformation, 79
Religions: Ancient civilizations, 36–38, 45–46; Buddhism, 53–54, 194–195; Christianity, 48–49, 57–58, 67–68, 76–77, 79–80; Hinduism, 53–54; Islam, 48–49, 57–58, Judaism, 48–49
Religious orders, 57, 76
Religious texts, 36–37, 39–41, 45–46, 48–49, 53–54, 79
Renaissance, 68–69
Revolutions: American, 104–105; Bolshevik, 161–162, French, 108–109

Ricardo, David, 91–92
Ricci, Matteo, 76–77
Riis, Jacob, 144–145
Robespierre, Maximilien, 109
Robin Hood, 59–60
Rogue River War, 137–138
Roman Catholic church, 48–49, 77, 79, 85–86
Roman law, 43
Roman republic and empire, 43–44, 46, 49–51
Roosevelt, Franklin D. (Pres.), 170–172, 181–184
Rosenberg, Julius and Ethel, 130, 188
Rosie the Riveter, 181

Routine-production services, and employment trends, xiv
Ruby, Jack, 212–214
Russian history, 161–164, 225–226
Russian revolution, 161–162

Sadducees, 45
Saint Simon, 88–89
Saladin, 59
Salem witch trials, 70–71
San Francisco earthquake, 153–154
San Gabriel mission, 127
San Remo conference, 155
Satire, 78
Saudi Arabia, 230–231
Savio, Mario, 214–215
Saxe, de, Hermann-Maurice (Field Marshall), 99–100
School library media centers. *See* SLMCs
Scientific American, 123–124
Scientists, 85–86, 133–134, 228–229
Scott, Robert Newton, 135–136
SCUM (Society to Cut Up Men) manifesto, 209
Seale, Bobby, 216
Secession, Quebec, 234–235; southern states, 129–131
Selassie, Haile (Emperor), 172–173
Seletz reservation, 137–138
Seminole tribe, 93
Senneca Falls convention, 126
Sexual harassment, 57
Sharia, 41
Sherpa culture, 199–200
Shipwrecks, 158–159
Sieyes, Abbe, 114–115
Silk road, 46–47
Sioux tribe, 93, 193
Sixties, 206–207
Slavery: Africa, 237–238; ancient Greece, 43; Egypt, 36; escapes and attempted escapes, 94; families and family life, 94–96; living conditions, 94–96; narratives, 94–96, 118, 130–131; rebellion, 118; United States, 94–96, 109–110, 128–132
SLMCs (School Library Media Centers): increased access in wall-less environment, xiii–xiv; instruction in an electronic environment, xiii–xv

Slums, 144–145
Smallpox, 101–102
Smoot-Hawley Tariff Act, 90–91
Social Darwinism, 105–106, 119–120, 133–135
Social life and customs: apparel, 82; automobiles, 152–153; Canada, 103; Central America, 72; China, 66; colonial Peru, 97–98; Europe, 63; France, 88–89; Great Britain, 119–120, 134–135; music, 168–169; United States, 123–124, 138–139, 144–145, 174–175
Social theories, 78, 112–113
Socialism, 140
South Africa, 44, 193–194
South America, 83–84, 97–98
Soviet secret police, 163–164, 187–188
Soviet Union, 163–164, 184, 187–188, 205–206, 209–210, 225–226
Spain, 71–72, 83–84
Spanish armada, 80–81
Speeches and statements, 48, 104, 172–173
Spies, 129–130, 163–164, 187–188, 195–196, 205–206
Stalin, Joseph, 40, 163–164, 184
Stanton, Elizabeth Cady, 124–125
Statistics, 109–110, 129–130, 235–236
Statutes, 61–62
Stuart, Gilbert, 107
Submarines, 176–177
Subversive activities and charges: CIA, 200–202; Emma Goldman, 148–149; French Revolution, 108–109; Galileo, 85–86; Lope de Aguirre, 83–84; Martin Luther, 79–80; Joseph McCarthy, 198–199; Nat Turner, 118–119; U-2 affair, 205–206; Venona project, 187–188; witchcraft, 70–71
Sudan, 237–238
Suffrage, 124–125, 149
Sun Tzu, 39–40, 99
Switzerland, 83–84
Symbolic-analytic information services, xiv

Tainos, 71–72
Tao Te Ching, 40
Technological trends and instructional role of school library media specialists (SLMSs), xiii–xiv
Technology timeline, 228–229
Temperance movement, 138–139, 169
Tenements, 144–145
Tennis court oath, 108–109
Tetzel, John, 79
Textbook approach, deficiencies of, xvi–xvii
Theodora, Empress, 52
Thirteen colonies, 104–105
Thirties, 170–173
Thompson, Sarah E., 129–130
Thoreau, Henry David, 132–133, 192
Tiananmen Square, 227–228
Tibet, 194–195
Titanic, 158–159
Titus, Emperor of Rome, 50
Tocqueville, Alexis de, 91–92
Tokyo war crimes trial, 176
Trade. *See* Commerce
Transportation, 152–153
Treason, 81, 130, 187–188
Treaties: Brest-Litovsk, 163; Native American, 92–93; Tordesillas, 75; Versailles, 165–166; Wyandot, 93
Trench warfare, 160–161
Tres Riches Heures, 23, 67–68
Trials, 83–84, 116–117, 175–176, 179–180, 191–192, 198–199. *See also names of specific trials*
Tribes, Native American, 92–93, 101–102, 137–138
Truman, Harry S. (Pres.), 157–158, 200–201, 221–222
Turing, Alan, 229
Turner, Nat, 118–119
Tutankhamun, King, 167–168
Twain, Mark, 151
Typology, 38

U-boats, 176–177
U-2 affair, 205–206
Ukraine, 225–226

Underground railroad, 116. *See also* Slavery
United Kingdom. *See* Great Britain
United Nations, 180, 235–236
United States: seventeenth–eighteenth centuries, 86–87, 92–95, 101–102, 104–105, 109–110; nineteenth century, 115–116, 118–119, 123–133, 135–142, 144–145, 148–150; twentieth century, 152–153, 156–157, 160–163, 168–171, 174–175, 176–177, 180–190, 195–198, 200–202, 205–215, 217–219, 221–224, 230–231, 233–234
United States First Ladies, 106–107
United States Presidents: George W. Bush, 230–231; Grover Cleveland, 107; Dwight D. Eisenhower, 200–201, 205–206; general profiles, 106–107; Lyndon B. Johnson, 196, 219–220; John F. Kennedy, 209; Richard M. Nixon, 199, 217–218, 222–223; Franklin D. Roosevelt, 170–172, 181–182; Harry S. Truman, 200–201, 221–222; George Washington, 86–87; University of California (Berkeley), 214
Urban II, Pope of Rome, 58
User population and SLMSs and faculty, xviii
Utopia (Moore), 78–79

Vatel, 88–89
Venice, Italy, 62–63, 71
Venona project, 187–188
Versailles, Treaty of, 165–166, 191
Vesuvius, Mount, 41–50
Victoria, Queen of England, 119–120
Victorian period, 119–120, 134–135
Vietnam War, 40, 196, 206–207, 219–222
Villa, Pancho, 156–157
Vindication of the Rights of Woman (Wollstonecraft), 111–112
Visionaries, 38–39, 68–69, 78–79, 85–86, 133–134, 194–195
Volcanoes, 49–50

Voting. *See* Women's suffrage
Voyages. *See* Ocean voyages

Wannsee protocol, 178–179
War crimes, 175–180, 184, 191–192, 231–232
War of the Classes (London), 140–141
War, rules of, 39–40, 99
Warfare: germ, 101–102; guerilla, 219–220; mustard gas, 173; submarine, 176–177; trench, 160–161
Warren Commission Report, 212–214
Wars: Cold War, 187–188, 195–196, 198–199; French and Indian War, 101–102; Gulf War, 230–231; India-Pakistan War, 220–221; Korean War, 197–198; Vietnam War, 196, 219–222; World War I, 160–161; World War II, 175–186
Washington, Booker T., 115–116
Washington, George (Pres.), 86–87
Washington Post, 222–223
Watergate, 222–224
Wealth, 51, 62–63, 66–68, 88–89, 100–101, 167–168. *See also* Poverty
Wells-Barnett, Ida B., 115–116
West, The, 92–93, 126–127, 132–133, 137–138, 141–142, 147–148, 153–154, 168–169, 215
White Man's Burden (Kipling), 21, 151
Williamson, Alice, 129–130
Wilson, Henry Lane (Amb.), 156
Witchcraft, 70–71

Wollstonecraft, Mary, 111–112
Women and the Civil War, 129–132, 135–136
Women, stereotype, 152–153, 181, 185–186
Women's liberation movement, 124–125, 208–209
Women's rights, 109, 111–112, 208–209
Women's studies, 49, 52, 70–71, 87, 107, 111–112, 124–125, 181–182, 208–209, 235–236
Women's suffrage, 124–125, 149–150
Woodhull, Victoria, 124–125
Woodward, Bob, 222–223
Work of Nations, The (Reich), xv
World War I, 150–151, 160–161, 165–166, 177
World War II, 175–186
Wren, Christopher (Sir), 88
Writers, 62–63, 78, 111–112, 133–134, 140, 144–145, 151, 170–171
Writing, ancient forms of, 34–36, 38; illuminated, 67–68
Wyandot tribe, 93

Yalta Conference, 183–184
Yosemite Valley (CA), 127, 132
Yugoslavia, 150, 160, 161, 231–232

Zen Buddhism, 53–54
Zimmerman telegram, 153, 156–157, 160
Zoroaster, 48–49

About the Author

Kathleen W. Craver is Head Librarian at the National Cathedral School in Washington, D.C. Dr. Craver is the author of *School Library Media Centers in the 21st Century* (Greenwood, 1994) and *Teaching Electronic Literacy* (Greenwood, 1997), and has published widely in library journals.